# WORLDS OF POWER

## Series in Contemporary History and World Affairs

GENERAL EDITOR
Mark Mazower
(Professor of History, Birkbeck College, University of London)

EDITORIAL ADVISORY BOARD
*Latin America* Jeremy L. Adelman
*East Asia* Jasper Becker
*Africa* Stephen Ellis
*Middle East* George Joffé
*Eurasia/World Affairs* Anatol Lieven
*Europe* Mark Mazower

The books in this series examine a particular part of the world or a particular theme, using historical analysis to illuminate contemporary problems. The series reflects growing interest in the social, political, economic and religious organisation of specific areas – peripheries as much as centres. Transnational phenomena such as globalisation, religious resurgence, crime and political violence are also scrutinised. Each volume will combine first-class empirical research with an emphasis on narrative clarity.

1. *Worlds of Power: Religious Thought and Political Practice in Africa*
(Stephen Ellis and Gerrie ter Haar)

STEPHEN ELLIS
GERRIE TER HAAR

# Worlds of Power

Religious Thought and Political
Practice in Africa

New York
OXFORD UNIVERSITY PRESS
2004

Oxford University Press

Oxford New York
Auckland Bangkok Buenos Aires Cape Town Chennai
Dar es Salaam Delhi Hong Kong Istanbul Karachi Kolkata
Kuala Lumpur Madrid Melbourne Mexico City Mumbai Nairobi
São Paulo Shanghai Taipei Tokyo Toronto

Copyright © 2004 by Oxford University Press

Published by Oxford University Press, Inc.,
198 Madison Avenue, New York, New York 10016

www.oup.com

Oxford is a registered trademark of Oxford University Press

**Library of Congress Cataloging-in-Publication Data**
Ellis, Stephen, 1953-
Worlds of power: religious thought and political practice
in Africa / by Stephen Ellis & Gerrie ter Haar.
p. cm.
Includes bibliographical references.
ISBN 0-19-522017-X (cloth)—ISBN 0-19-522016-1 (pbk.)
1. Religion and politics—Africa. I. Haar, Gerrie ter. II. Title.
BL2400.E45 2004
201'.72'096—dc22
2004000252

9 8 7 6 5 4 3 2 1

Printed in England on acid-free paper

# ACKNOWLEDGEMENTS

We extend our thanks to those who have helped directly in the production of this book. Jan Platvoet commented on drafts of chapters one and three, and Jane Guyer on chapter six. Neither of them, of course, can be held responsible for any of the opinions these chapters contain. We are also grateful to Barbara and David Taylor for reading the whole book in manuscript. Finally, we thank Berthe Schoonman for permission to use a photo taken by her on the cover.

*Amsterdam, May 2003*

S. E.
G. t H.

# CONTENTS

# INTRODUCTION

In the late twentieth century, something remarkable was happening to religion in many parts of the world. Particularly in what used to be called the third world, there was an exuberant flourishing of pentecostal and charismatic varieties of Christianity. The Middle East and North Africa witnessed the rise of a highly political form of Islam, considered by Western countries and their allies primarily as a security threat. Asian nations saw revivals of various religious ideologies including Hinduism, Buddhism and Confucianism. New religious movements were in evidence all over the world. In the United States, a new style of Christian radicalism emerged as a formidable political force. In Eastern Europe, religious movements old and new have entered the vacuum caused by the collapse of communism, with political consequences. Western Europe has also experienced a type of religious revival due to the establishment in recent years of new immigrant communities, including many from Africa.[1] The presence of new migrant groups has raised questions about the role of religion in the public sphere.[2]

The blooming of religious movements has created international networks that bind groups of people, often without reference to states. These create effective connections that criss-cross the globe. Cassettes of sermons and other religious materials produced by Muslim clerics circulate throughout the Islamic world. Immigrant communities send to their families back home video recordings of religious ceremonies such as funerals and weddings. They send remittances too, not only for the upkeep of their families, but also to build places of worship, schools and clinics. Religious activists from all over the globe communicate through the internet and by phone, and travel overseas in the conduct of their religious affairs. Christian evangelists from South Korea or Argentina tour Africa, while Muslim teachers from Senegal and Mali can be found in New York and Chicago. African traditional healers ply their trade in cities the world over, and African divination practices flourish in Europe and North America. These connections can create new opportunities for shrewd politicians. In the United States, for example, Jesse Jackson and Pat Robertson, both Christian

1

preachers with former presidential aspirations, have used their religious channels to cultivate relationships with politicians in Africa.

The flourishing of religious networks has had a particularly remarkable effect on Africa. Religious relationships now constitute perhaps the most important way in which Africans interact with the rest of the world. From this point of view Africa, far from being peripheral to world affairs as is so often claimed, is at the heart of important new developments. In Africa south of the Sahara, there are Christian revivalist movements of all sorts and clear signs of a spread of political Islam, plus an extraordinary variety of other religious movements, from revivals of African traditional religions to movements imported from other continents. There are recent arrivals such as that commonly referred to as the Unification Church, or Moonies, introduced from Korea. In Ghana alone there are religious movements from all parts of the world, including Hindu ones such as the Arcanum Nama Shivaya Mission and the International Society for Krishna Consciousness (ISKCON), the Japanese Buddhist Nichiren Shoshu Soka Gakkai, and other Asian movements, but also new Christian and Islamic movements and neo-traditional ones.[3]

Most of the new or revived religious movements share certain characteristics. These include a highly visible occupation of public space, in the form of a multiplication of places of worship such as churches and mosques; a predilection for public ceremonies and parades; and the use of electronic media for preaching and proselytisation. Many such movements are preoccupied with combatting evil, which they often do by rooting out perceived impurity. If only for this reason, the resurgence of religion acquires an important political dimension in many places.

In Africa, religious revival has taken its most obviously political form in the shape of the well-known Islamist movements in the Maghreb, northern Nigeria and Sudan. But religious renewal movements are having an effect on politics in other parts of the continent as well. Examples include the rapid growth of Muslim missionary groups in countries with little Islamic tradition, the dynamic spread of Christian charismatic congregations, and movements that aim to revive African traditional religions. Why did this growth of religion occur, or was it there all the time in less spectacular form? What relation does it have to Africa's well-known economic and political problems? We contend that it is largely through religious ideas that Africans think about the world today, and that religious ideas provide them with a means of becoming social and political actors. The study of religious thought therefore constitutes a privileged opportunity for observing political practice in Africa.

Precisely because Africa is so tightly bound into global religious networks, study of the relationship between religious thought and political practice in Africa provides a window on an aspect of world affairs that is so much in need of new understanding today. For this reason, we believe that the insights presented in this book are relevant to other parts of the world. Rather than struggling to catch up with other continents, as it is so often said to be, Africa may be in the vanguard when it comes to understanding the close inter-relationship between religion and politics.

## *Why we wrote this book*

Religion and politics are always related to some degree, yet no scholarly consensus exists on the meaning of these terms, or on the concept of religion in particular. Social scientists nowadays tend to avoid definitions, preferring to use so-called 'thick description' of specific contexts, yet definitions often advance analysis by highlighting elements that are common to many societies. Although religion has been defined in many ways, we follow the nineteenth-century anthropologist E. B. Tylor in defining religion as a belief in the existence of an invisible world, often thought to be inhabited by spirits that are believed to affect people's lives in the material world.[4] In our view, this is the most helpful way of explaining the interaction between religion and politics in Africa. There are several reasons for considering religion this way. First, many people in the world are religious inasmuch as they believe it is possible to communicate with a perceived world of spirits. Second, our definition incorporates practices often referred to as 'magic' or 'superstition' or in similarly value-laden terms, the use of which often incorrectly excludes certain forms of religious expression from qualifying as religion at all. A third, related advantage of defining religion in the way we do is that it avoids attributing a moral value to any particular type of belief. Such a definition does not imply that religion is always in pursuit of that which is noble or good. Religion, in the sense we define it, may include both constructive and destructive practices. It is hard to understand its relation to politics in Africa without appreciating this point. Finally, to comprehend the relation between religion and politics in Africa and many other parts of the world, we must move away from a common Western tendency to define religion almost exclusively in terms of a search for meaning in life.

It is when religious belief motivates people to action that its relation to politics becomes most evident. African politicians, for example, typically pay great regard to the spirit world as a source of power. This does not imply that they are other-worldly, or that they have no understanding of the material aspects of power. Such a ruthless manipulator as Mobutu Sese Seko, former president of Zaire, to quote just one example, cultivated spiritual sources of power throughout his career, yet no one suspects him of having been naive. He is by no means unique, as we will see. Every successful politician needs to have a lively appreciation of the material aspects of politics, such as how to handle the opposition, amend the law or negotiate a loan. A politician who lavishes attention on the spirit world may at the same time show a Machiavellian talent for political manoeuvre.

Some years ago, we published an article exploring some of these connections.[5] Although it was generally well received, some readers thought we were suggesting that African politics might be fixated on the spiritual world to the exclusion of material aspects. This is not at all our point of view. One author, in the course of a penetrating study of African political thought, commented:[6]

> Most middle Africans understand that 'politics' and 'religion' are parts of the same terrain: that power flows between the visible material world and the invisible spiritual world; and that the political kingdom contains a politically significant spiritual terrain. Moreover, intelligent and gifted politicians know the contours of this terrain and are comfortable traversing it in either its material or spiritual manifestations. They understand that in their culture power is unitary and cannot be divided into separate boxes.

While we agree with this observation our point is, however, that it does not preclude the perception—which we believe to be widespread in Africa—that all power has its *ultimate* origin in the spirit world. A politician, or for that matter a farmer, or a businessman, or anyone else, may spend virtually all of his time dealing with mundane matters but still believe that these are ultimately determined in the invisible world. Hence the latter requires regular attention, much as a driver knows that his car depends utterly on petrol but does not generally spend more than a few minutes taking on fuel. It is because religion and politics in Africa are distinct but connected realms of power that this book is entitled *Worlds of Power*. The sub-title is intended to emphasise that religious thought needs to be studied seriously if we are to understand politics in Africa today. It also points to the fact that political practice concerns not only the formal activities of elected representatives or ministers of state, but also informal activities. Politics are also made 'from below', by ordinary people in the things they do and say.[7]

In the European tradition that has been exported all over the world in the last couple of centuries, a solution has been proposed to the recurring problem of the rival claims to power of religion and politics by formally separating the institutional powers of church and state. This separation is accompanied by a rigid intellectual distinction drawn between a series of binary oppositions, such as church and state, and religion and science. In some respects these couples may be traced back in European thought even before the eighteenth-century Enlightenment. One familiar version of this European history represents it as a triumph of progress through reason. The conviction that Europe had developed a unique key to human progress was used as a moral and political justification for the imposition of colonial rule by a handful of states over a large swathe of the world, to the extent that by the 1930s, it has been estimated, colonies or ex-colonies covered 84.6 per cent of the land surface of the globe.[8] Even countries that were never formally colonised, like China and Japan, were highly influenced by European ideas. The forcible opening of Japan was achieved largely by the United States, which grew in importance until emerging in the late twentieth century as the new centre of gravity of the Western intellectual tradition and the world's only superpower.

The export of European political institutions by people convinced of the rightness of their ideas and of their destiny to dominate others has led to a system whereby most parts of the globe are governed by states whose formal institutions resemble those that evolved in Europe and North America. But there are distinct signs that in large parts of the world, especially former colonies and other countries that were more or less obliged to adopt Western institutions of government, there has been a decline in belief in the value of these institutions and, above all, of the ideas that underpin them. This, as we will explain below, is one of the reasons for the rise of religion as a new public force, even a political force.

The revival or resurgence of religion as a political force in so many parts of the world is a phenomenon with historical roots that extend into precolonial times. Labelling it a 'revival' or 'resurgence' in some ways conveys the misleading impression of a trend that previously existed but that had gone underground, whereas in fact many of today's most visible religious movements have long been publicly active, but have only recently become subject to academic scrutiny. It is relevant in this respect to note that tradition and modernity, often seen in colonial times as forces locked in a universal conflict that could have only one winner, are inseparable ideas, like light and dark. On the other hand, the vocabulary of revival and resurgence conveys some of the flavour of dynamic movements that are operating in a changed global context. Both Christianity and Islam have been present in parts of Africa for a thousand years or more, and so their recent growth throughout the continent, as indeed that of other religions of non-African origin, cannot be considered simply as a break with tradition. Similarly, the revival of African traditional religions is not a simple return to the past, but, rather, a reconfiguration for modern times. All such developments are closely associated with the manner in which a world order is formed or reformed, as communities adopt religious beliefs and practices that emphasise their connection to, or difference from, other groups, in ways that have to be considered in historical depth.

Religion and politics in Africa are not identical. Some Africans are determined secularists in the sense of holding that society should be governed by institutions that have no connection with any perceived spirit world. In fact recent research suggests that more Africans are indifferent to religion today than in the past.[9] But, as one expert tells us, 'even those who claim to be atheist, agnostic, or antireligion, of whom there is a growing number, often have no option but to participate in extended family activities, some of which require the invocation of supernatural powers.'[10] Since few people are professional philosophers or theologians, they may think about the spiritual aspects of familiar actions only rarely. The same applies to politicians, who spend most of their time on the usual round of political business and less on spiritual consultations. In other words, we are not suggesting that everyone is busy with religion all of the time: we wish only to convey the message that religious thought plays a key role in political life because the spirit world is commonly considered the ultimate source of power.

To understand politics in Africa, it is necessary to consider religion in the terms we have indicated. That is the main thrust of our argument. Inevitably, since this book describes some common African ideas about religion, and analyses their political consequences, it takes a partial view of politics especially. We have deliberately paid close attention to literature produced by writers living in Africa. In particular, we have been guided by the African literature in developing the subjects of individual chapters and in analysing the relationship between religious thought and political practice as we do. Since the late twentieth century there has been a growing divergence between what intellectuals living in Africa regard as the burning issues in their societies, and what is reflected in publications emanating from North America and Europe. This, we are aware, has caused us to quote only sparingly from recent publications in a range of subjects that have attracted substantial interest in Western universities. Although some of these do refer to religion and politics in Africa, they often do so in pursuit of other issues. The main aim of our study, on the other hand, is to understand the ways in which religious thought has a bearing on actual political practices in Africa today.

Moreover, there exists a substantial literature pertinent to our subject that is rarely considered in books on religion and politics in Africa at all. The distinctive feature of this literature is that it is mostly written by Africans who are clearly religious believers themselves. It is often published in Africa. The works to which we are referring may be in the form of popular tracts and pamphlets printed in cheap editions, but they may also be produced in institutions of higher learning. In addition to the standard academic literature, we have used publications of this type extensively in this book, simply because we believe that they are highly relevant to an understanding of African public life today.

## *Themes*

There is a pressing practical and intellectual need to recognise the growing relation between religion and politics, as we do in this book. In it, we discuss a number of themes that we have tried to address in a logical sequence.

Religious ideas in Africa influence people's thinking about the world and the nature of reality, and hence are central to our project. The religious dimension inherent in such a world-view has often been overlooked in recent Western scholarship, or analysed in ways we consider unsatisfactory. Our approach takes full account of the content of people's belief, rather than regarding religion primarily in terms of social structures or processes, or treating it exclusively as a point of entry for a materialist analysis. This leads us to consider at some length how best to define religion. We favour a dynamic model of religion in Africa that stresses its political importance in precolonial and contemporary times. In summary, the opening chapter is about how to approach religion and politics in Africa.

Oral sources and how to interpret them are a key theme, for we recognise the unusual importance of stories and rumours in Africa's largely oral cultures. Narratives in this form encourage certain types of belief. Studying the rumours and popular stories that abound in Africa also provides us with an outstanding means for investigating African epistemologies, in other words the theory of the methods or grounds of knowledge. Whether or not a particular rumour is true is not of immediate relevance for our purposes: we wish to demonstrate how rumours provide insights into the way in which people apprehend ideas. We show how, in Africa, perceptions of reality, mediated by the spoken word, are inseparable from religion and politics.

Ideas about politics, relations between individuals, and historical change are often expressed in what might be called a spirit idiom. Spirits—invisible beings that are widely perceived to exist and to influence the material world—are central to the thinking of many millions of people in Africa. One of the preoccupations of those who believe that a spirit world exists and affects their lives—religious believers, in other words—is to interact with this invisible world. We examine some methods of establishing contact with a spirit world as part of a wider discussion of trance techniques not only in Africa but also in the West. We also show how communication with the spirit world is a key concern of African politicians.

In many religious traditions, great spiritual knowledge is considered esoteric, the province of elite groups whose store of learning may be incomprehensible to outsiders or even deliberately hidden from the uninitiated. Throughout history, this has led in many parts of Africa to the creation of elite associations, such as secret societies, that play an important part in both religion and modern state politics. Politicians use such bodies to smoothe their relations with other elites and to access systems of patronage, to be sure, but also to search for arcane knowledge of a religious nature.

Politicians seek power. In African societies, power is widely thought to originate in the spirit world. Spiritual power is regarded as ambivalent in the sense that it can be used for either good or ill. In recent years there has been a growing sense among Africans that power is increasingly deployed for destructive purposes, leading to a widespread feeling of the omnipresence of evil. We discuss some reasons for this belief, extending back into the nineteenth century. Both religious and political leaders tend to manifest patterns of behaviour that do not sit easily with the secular character of state institutions inherited from colonial times. A politician's drive for power may draw him (only rarely her) into the arena conventionally occupied by religious specialists. Processes of democratisation in the 1990s have had a marked effect on interactions between religion and politics. In Africa today, popular religious discourse often contains a strong political content.

These processes have had an impact on economic life too. Hence we scrutinise religious and philosophical ideas about wealth and how to acquire it. The creation of wealth has been considered inherently mysterious in many philosophical traditions. Africa is no exception in this respect. Here, bargaining with the spirit world is a widespread technique for accumulating wealth. Making money and regulating material wealth generally have become particularly unpredictable activities in Africa in recent decades.

Many of Africa's political and economic problems could be described as being connected to a lack of consensus about what forms of public behaviour are acceptable and which ones should be spurned. The prescription proposed by the modern state—the law—is hardly effective in many African countries, for historical reasons. There are many circumstances in which the law, rather than expressing a broad consensus on morally correct behaviour, provides a facade behind which individuals pursue their private interests. This seems to be a key reason for the proliferation of witchcraft accusations, which often claim a strong moral content, despite the suffering that they cause. A similar concern with public morality is reflected in a wide range of popular religious publications, which are primary sources for much that we discuss in this book.

The relationship between an individual and society is governed by changes in a person's status throughout life, in other words by personal transformations. Throughout Africa's history religion has served as a means of regulating change in both individuals and collectivities, and continues to do so. We suggest a theory that explains how religion can be an effective means of regulating transformations both in individuals and in society. This elucidates why, today, religion and politics may come into conflict, especially when mediated by institutions established during the colonial period. Consideration of why religion is re-emerging as a form of governance in Africa throws light on recent social developments elsewhere, including Western Europe and North America. Such comparisons run as a thread through this book. One of our basic theses is that African societies should be considered in terms that are also applicable to other parts of the world.

Finally, we draw together some strands of the discussion by considering their implications for Africa in a global context. Africa is fully integrated into the world, and not marginal to it as is so often thought. People in different continents live at different rhythms, with markedly different ideas about their relationship to the past. Religion plays an important role in mediating such relationships. Moreover, religious ideas are part of a disputed area of knowledge that also includes such key political and moral notions as democracy and human rights. This whole field is subject to an international debate about how the world is to be governed, in the broadest sense. To call it a 'debate' may be too timid, since it may even take violent forms when individuals and groups assert claims and counter-claims concerning those ideas they think worthy of universal respect, and those regarded as having local application only.

In the first decade of the twenty-first century, religion is taking a place that was hardly foreseen even twenty-five years ago, including in Africa. Analysing the role of religion in public life in Africa tells us something about the world as a whole. Africa is habitually seen by outsiders as a 'lost' continent, in the double sense of hardly being integrated into a globalised world and as giving no cause for hope. Even in academic circles, Africa is considered marginal, being generally studied by a small group of specialists. Although Africa is going through a difficult period of its long history, there is no reason to think that Africa has ceased to matter to the rest of the world. Africa is probably where mankind began. Today, it continues to influence the world in fields of acknowledged importance, varying from exports of oil to biodiversity to the migration of people. Africa and its diasporas are playing a key role in the realignments of religion and politics that seem set to become a major challenge to everyone in the years ahead.

# 1

# IDEAS

*El Negro and other stories*

In the spring of 2001, the River Somme in northern France burst its banks after unusually heavy rain. In Abbeville, near the mouth of the river, houses were flooded and some people had to move to temporary shelter on higher ground.

Abbeville is not the most glamorous place in France. The Somme valley does not share much in the wealth from tourism, as holiday-makers from Britain and other parts of northern Europe drive down the motorways on their way to the southern sun. The north of France in general contains a number of depressed former industrial towns that have lost the knack of making money, whose people have had to face up to the decline of their neighbourhoods.

So, the people of Abbeville complained not just about the rain but also about the government, which they thought was not doing everything it could to cope with the emergency. Some said that there was more to the floods than was apparent. It was rumoured that the system of water distribution was being manipulated by people in positions of authority—*'them'*— to the benefit of more favoured areas. It was said that there was a pumping-station somewhere between Abbeville and Paris that *'they'* were operating to make sure the rich in Paris had just as much water as they needed, while the people of the Somme valley got the excess. Government denials were of no effect. This was what people in Abbeville wanted to believe. Some journalists who heard these rumours interpreted them as a way for the citizens of an insignificant provincial town to take revenge for years of official neglect by spreading stories about the government and about the capital city.[1]

Other industrialised countries also produce rumours, not all of them directed against the government. Perhaps the best known are the urban legends that most people have heard and that are sometimes surprisingly old, like the story that there are alligators living in the sewers of New York.

This rumour, which seems to strike every generation as interesting and fresh and therefore is repeated over and over, was first recorded as long ago as 1843.[2]

It could be that France, with its curious mixture of old-world conservatism and advanced technology, is peculiarly subject to rumours used by the lower classes to take revenge on the country's notoriously arrogant governing elite. One of the most famous studies of rumour in any modern society was carried out by a sociologist interested in a story that was circulating in the French town of Orléans in the 1960s.[3] It was said that some of the shops in the town selling clothes for women, particularly those aiming at younger customers, were being used by a gang that specialised in abducting attractive young women when they went into the changing-rooms, in order to sell them into prostitution. While they were trying on clothes, the female victims were allegedly drugged with an injection, kept in a basement, and then taken away at night to some other place. It was rumoured that Jews were responsible.

It turned out that no one was being kidnapped and that there was no such criminal conspiracy. But the absence of evidence did not prevent the story from being half-believed and passed on from one person to another. Nor did the lack of factual basis prevent the sociologist who studied the Orléans rumour from detecting in it various levels of meaning, in this case stemming from anxieties among the population of a conservative provincial town unnerved by the political and social changes of the 1960s, at a time when the sexual revolution in full swing in Paris was starting to affect small-town ideas. Middle-aged parents were worried about the sexuality of their daughters, who had taken to shopping in the new type of fashionable boutiques and buying such subversive items as mini-skirts. If there was a conspiracy afoot, organised by '*them*', the mysterious manipulators of society, then surely it involved the Jews: so it was reasoned in Orléans. The atmosphere made the abduction stories both alarming and believable. The fact that France, like many countries, has a tradition of conspiracy theories, meant that the habitual scapegoats of Christian Europe were obvious candidates for the role of conspirators in this case also, in spite of the absence of any evidence whatever.

Meanwhile, thousands of miles south of France, in the southern African country of Botswana, the unusual weather patterns of early 2001 also produced their share of stories. Rumours in Botswana's capital city of Gaborone are so common that people jokingly refer to them as Radio Mall, from the name of the central shopping street. Botswana is one of Africa's few prosperous countries, but it is also a dry place where people often talk about the absence of rain. So important are the annual rains, in fact, that one of the main duties of a Tswana ruler in the past was to perform rain-making ceremonies, much as kings in some other parts of the world used to be thought able to control the earth's fertility. During the later part of 2000, people were making their normal remarks about the dry weather and wondering when the rains would come. In January 2001, though, a new element entered into popular discussion of the weather as people returned from the New Year holiday after spending time in their home villages. They began telling each other that the rains were not coming because of the return to Botswana of the remains of a dead man known as El Negro. This was the name given by the press to the body of a Tswana man who had died in 1830, probably somewhere near the present-day border between Botswana and South Africa. His body had been exhumed shortly after burial by a pair of unscrupulous French taxidermists, who stuffed it like a big-game trophy, exported it to Europe and put it on display in a Paris shop. Later, the corpse found its way to an obscure provincial museum in Spain. There the body of El Negro stayed for over a century, surrounded by other grotesque colonial exhibits, until the preparations for the 1992 Barcelona Olympic Games. At that point the existence of the stuffed cadaver of a black man—now dubbed El Negro—was publicised in international media and a lobby started pressing for his return to Africa.

The eventual outcome was the transport to Botswana in October 2000 of the bones of the dead African, mysteriously stripped of his remaining flesh, hair and other soft tissue somewhere between Madrid and Botswana. These bizarre and macabre events were the subject of much discussion in Gaborone. Many people in Botswana's capital eventually came to the conclusion that the return of the body, minus its vital organs, was related to witchcraft and that this was the reason for the failure of the rains. Some thought that it was the work of politicians from the ruling Botswana Democratic Party.[4]

## *Defining religion*

These stories, from such different places as France and Botswana, are what would normally be called rumours. Although rumour is often ignored by analysts as a serious source of information, stories such as these contain meaning. They are about ideas. Rumours are particularly important in Africa, for reasons that should become clear in due course, and this book therefore pays due attention to them. The story of El Negro, for example, collected in Gaborone, amounts to an allegation that the remains of a man dead for over 170 years have been used by politicians to change the weather through the exercise of mystical power. This is essentially a religious idea, and indeed many of the rumours that circulate in Africa contain an element of religious thought, particularly when they purport to offer an explanation for some current circumstance or series of events. Religious thought provides believers with a cosmology able to provide a comprehensive explanation of the world, including theories as to why things happen the way they do. That fact alone makes religion of great political importance in any society where the overwhelming majority of people holds some sort of religious belief.

This, of course, depends on what we mean by religion.[5] In this book we will base ourselves on the notion that religion refers to a belief in the existence of an invisible world, distinct but not separate from the visible one, that is home to spiritual beings with effective powers over the material world. Such a definition goes back to the nineteenth-century anthropologist E. B. Tylor, who described religion succinctly as 'the belief in Spiritual Beings'.[6] It has the advantage of implying the belief, common to most religious traditions, that effective communication is possible between the human and the spirit worlds. Among anthropologists, especially in North America, definitions on this line have tended to be superseded by ones emanating from sociological theories. They emphasise the social aspect of religion and its ritual expression at the expense of its ideological component. Religious belief no doubt always has some social dimension, and it is therefore important to study this. However, we believe that it is essential to study in the first instance the ideas that motivate human action.[7]

The choice of a definition is not an arbitrary matter. A definition is an analytical tool, selected for its ability to help understand the processes under scrutiny. In the same way that a carpenter does not choose a chisel to saw wood, so an analyst of religion picks a tool in relation to the task at hand. For present purposes, that task is to understand the way in which religious thought influences political practice in Africa today. Our definition may thus be called an operational one. This is a provisional definition in that it can be adapted as new data become available. It can accommodate the distinctive features of religion in Africa—or in many other parts of the world, for that matter—and is therefore well suited to countering the Western-centred elements present in existing definitions of a more essentialist type.[8] Classical sociologists like Emile Durkheim and Max Weber developed theories of religion with a different object from ours in their minds. Both men lived in an age when social scientists fully believed in the possibility of enunciating universal laws governing human behaviour in a manner that few of their successors would do today.[9]

Religion, in the sense we have just defined it, colours many Africans' view of reality. In the eyes of believers, reality consists not only of what can be observed in the material world, but also includes experiences of the invisible world. A leading philosopher, Kwame Appiah, argues that because of their belief in invisible agents, many Africans cannot fully accept those scientific theories that are inconsistent with it.[10] Other African philosophers have suggested that Africans typically have a unified vision of reality that encompasses the invisible world.[11] The social arrangements in the visible world are often thought to be reflected in the invisible world. Such 'transcendental reduplication' of the material world, so common in religious belief everywhere, has been systematically eroded in Europe through the development of philosophical thought since the Middle Ages.[12] Furthermore, religious practice requires at least the perception of possible interaction between the visible and invisible worlds. This too appears to be a factor of capital importance for understanding the reconfiguration of religion and politics in the world today. For if people aspire to communicate with an invisible world, control of such communication can become a matter of the greatest political importance.

Religion thus has implications for the mundane realm of politics, famously defined as 'who gets what, when, and how'.[13] Politics could be described less picturesquely as the activity generated by conflicts of interests and values that affect all of society, and the efforts to reconcile them.[14] It is at this point that the many studies based on analysis of religious practice alone contain relevant data. They do not easily, however, advance a basic theoretical understanding, since they leave out what most needs to be explained. Recent anthropological studies of Africa tend to see religion as a symbolic expression of destabilising forces such as globalisation, hegemonistic power in postcolonial societies, and so on. This limits religion to a passive role as a 'function of signification'.[15] It ignores that religion also constitutes a field of action that believers occupy and may control. More than a reflection of external forces, religious action is a form of self-fashioning. Religious performances reconstitute people as moral agents, using techniques that have profound historical resonance. A study of people's underlying beliefs can thus develop an understanding of how they respond to their political climate.[16]

The connection between religious and political ideas is, we believe, stronger in Africa, and for that matter in many other places, than is generally admitted by commentators steeped in a tradition of political thought that goes back to the European Enlightenment. Africa, like other parts of the former colonised world, underwent the influence of the Enlightenment in an indirect manner, mediated by colonial government or missionary education. In many respects politics and religion in these postcolonies remain connected in ways that have deep historical roots. Several commentators have noted this in recent years. The political analyst Edward Luttwak, writing before 11 September 2001, noted the inadequacy of what he calls a 'materialistic determinism' that excludes religion in analysing many of the world's conflicts, and calls religion 'the missing dimension'.[17] The anthropologist Jack Goody makes a similar point, arguing that religion actually trumps ethnicity as a determinant of conflict in many cases but is ignored by too many analysts.[18] These observations can be applied to politics more generally, and not just to conflicts.

Thus, to return briefly to the El Negro story, the perception of a religious dimension to the world has a political aspect inasmuch as it imputes to politicians the ability to manipulate mystical powers. To judge from the currency of the rumours about El Negro, many people in Botswana find it quite credible that occupants of high state office possess abilities that many Europeans and North Americans would doubt to exist in reality, and which in any event would not be considered to have a place within the field of politics.

## A study of ideas

In view of these remarks, a study of how religion and politics interact needs to draw on a number of academic disciplines, no single one of which has the right tools to treat the relevant data on its own. A particular problem arises because some of the phenomena affected or produced by the interaction of religion and politics have proved elusive to study by social scientists generally. Social science has developed through an analogy with natural science, attempting to identify precise models of human behaviour that, in theory at least, will eventually have a power of predictability as great as the theory of gravity. In the mid-twentieth century, the social science that had first arisen in European and North American centres of learning (including Marxism, which was after all a European creation) was somewhere near the peak of its self-confidence, or perhaps arrogance. This was also the period when former European colonies in Africa, Asia and parts of the Americas were gaining political independence. Politicians, technocrats and academics in those days pretty much agreed on the importance of state-building and economic development, and social scientists offered models for how to modernise traditional societies. In retrospect, it is clear that modernisation and development theories failed by and large to produce the type of Africa that planners and theorists had imagined.[19] Not least, Western-trained thinkers largely failed to foresee the resurgence of religion, because they had made a series of wrong assumptions about the place of religion in regimes of modernisation.

Some leading critics accuse certain branches of social science of simply ignoring the relative failure of modernisation and development theories, at least as far as Africa is concerned, and just continuing as before. Regarding political science and development economics, the Cameroonian intellectual Achille Mbembe judges that 'these disciplines have undermined the very possibility of understanding African economic and political facts'.[20] Ignoring religion as a matter of obvious political and even economic importance, as we hope to demonstrate, is a good example of the same tendency. Political scientists and economists specialising in Africa study religion either not at all or only as far as is permitted by the conventional instruments of their disciplines, with only a few exceptions.[21] Anthropology, however, created as a formal intellectual discipline as a result of the expansion of European interests in Africa and Asia especially, has always taken a close interest in religion. Anthropologists have examined the interaction of religion and politics in Africa but have, as we will suggest in more detail, often failed to consider a central element of religious belief, namely the perception that the invisible world is real.

One critic, Robin Horton, divides the anthropologists who have written on religion in Africa into three categories: the Symbolists (those who see religion as a form of representation, comparable to poetry or music); the Fideists, 'who like to think of all religious life as the expression of an autonomous commitment to communion with Spiritual Being', and the Intellectualists, in which category Horton places himself, who understand religion in Africa as 'a system of theory and practice guided by the aims of explanation, prediction and control'.[22] Although there have been new developments in writing on religion in Africa since Horton first made these distinctions, his basic categorisation remains a viable one. Perhaps the main feature of the Intellectualist approach is its propensity to consider statements on religious matters in the first instance in the believers' own terms before attempting to translate these into a vocabulary more appropriate to other branches of learning. To borrow a word from linguistics, it is useful to describe religion in 'emic' terms, that is those derived from the believers' own point of view, before analysing it in 'etic', or more detached, terms that correspond more closely to a scientific approach based exclusively on the rational method of determining objective truth. It is most important to note that this does not imply that an analyst who adopts the emic form of analysis shares the religious beliefs of the people she or he studies; it implies only that the observer suspends judgement by allowing believers (in this case Africans) the right to express matters in the terms they think appropriate. This is the approach we follow here.

The precepts of social science are based to a large extent on data drawn from Western societies and European and North American history, and influential theories have been based on more or less idealised readings of what actually happened in those areas. Therefore, models of social and political action that aspire to be of universal application are too often 'actually part of a culture-specific, proselytizing ethic of what remains at heart western Christendom', as the Indian economist Deepak Lal expresses the problem.[23] One way forward would be to look again at key questions and concepts in the social sciences, this time in the light of data drawn from the full range of human societies. In doing this, scholars may continue to develop theories that aspire to be universally applicable, and need not cede to the idea that there are specific cultures with ideas or practices so peculiar that they can be understood only by means of disciplines equally peculiar, or only by people born into those cultures. The general debate on whether certain social and political ideas, like democracy and human rights, are universal, or whether they are proper to particular cultures or civilisations only, is one of the most important matters at issue in the world today, as we will discuss at the end of this book. We stand on the side of those who believe that the most important ideas about how people can live together are universally applicable in at least some sense, with the important proviso that they do not necessarily find the same cultural expression in every society. To be more precise, we do not believe that the study of religion and politics in Africa reveals the existence of any key concepts that are utterly unfamiliar to other societies. Far from regarding such ideas as exotic, we believe that they can be understood in terms of universal concepts. The single-word titles of our chapters are an attempt to list some of the main ideas common to both religion and politics in Africa, but which are also known in various forms in other parts of the world.

Social scientists generally rely on precise data, including statistics, of a type produced by efficient bureaucracies able to work in well-policed societies. Africa today has rather few such bureaucracies and is not well-policed, not only in the sense that few countries have effective national police forces but also in an older sense of the term, as being effectively organised through a state. Indeed, until the twentieth century the overwhelming majority of Africans lived without writing. It is useful to recall in passing that the modern ideas of 'policy' and 'police', and 'state' and 'statistics', emerged from the formation of bureaucratic states in Europe, recognisable forebears of today's massive constructions, around the seventeenth century. They seem of ever more questionable relevance to large parts of Africa and central Asia, for example. 'The most distinctively African contribution to human history', in the opinion of a leading historian, 'could be said to have been precisely the civilized art of living fairly peaceably together *not* in states'.[24] In view of this, Africa's history should be of greater interest to social scientists than is actually the case, for it provides a historical example that challenges some fundamental assumptions about how human beings live together.

But the more prosaic problem it raises for scholars is that Africa remains the continent where the least gets written down. This is to some extent compensated by the fact that ideas transmitted by word of mouth are more important in Africa than in most other parts of the world, no doubt because of its long oral tradition. In response, anthropologists and historians have developed techniques for considering how to extract usable information from spoken words. In this book we have relied greatly on expressions of popular ideas that are normally oral rather than written, but which can be accessed through pamphlet literature, the press, videos and so on.

Previous studies that explicitly examine the relation between religion and politics in Africa have tended to focus on religious institutions rather than religious ideas.[25] Several books have been published on, for example, the role of the churches in the democratisation process in Africa,[26] or on religious revival movements.[27] Our aim, rather, is to show how religious ideas—not just their institutional channels, but the ideas themselves—are an essential part of politics in Africa at every level. Many of these ideas have a long history, which we attempt to trace in a few cases. It could be said, therefore, that this book concerns how Africa's older historical patterns, often transmitted through religious ideas and religiously-inspired behaviour, are having an impact on its modern politics.

One of the main reasons why religious ideas have been rather little studied in their effect on politics in various parts of the non-Western world is an underlying supposition on the part of many academics, journalists and others that religion is likely to decline in its public role as the world develops. The institutional separation of church and state, or of its nearest local equivalent, has been considered a hallmark of a developed political system. The aspiration to separate religion and politics, originally a key achievement of Enlightenment thought, has been imparted to genera-

tions of intellectuals from the non-Western world as a part of the programme of development recommended to them. However, events in recent
years, most particularly since the Iranian revolution of 1979, have shown
how religion has been able to respond to modern politics, even if it is not
always in ways that everyone might find desirable. This reason alone
makes it important to study religious ideas, since these can clearly motivate large numbers of people to political action. African authors seem
more aware than Westerners of the continuing importance of religion as a
political force,[28] but their views have little influence outside their own continent. In Africa itself, religious ideas are often discussed by people trained
in university departments of theology and religious studies, disciplines that
in the West have declined in importance as theology has lost the central
place it once had in academic curricula.

Hence, an analysis of religion and politics that takes full account of the
work of African academics promises to open up some new theoretical
approaches of obvious utility. If the reoccupation of political space by religious ideas has been most obvious in the Middle East, a similar tendency
has been observable in Africa in recent decades in every one of the continent's main religious traditions: Christianity, Islam and indigenous religions. Western commentators trying to unravel the impact on politics of
some of the world's most dynamic religious movements often describe
them as 'fundamentalist', a word that we will try to avoid as it has become
rather misleading.[29] In regard to Christianity and Islam this has been relatively well-documented. The revitalisation of African traditional religions
has received rather less attention.[30] The relative neglect of developments
in Africa's indigenous religious traditions may be due to the fact that these,
unlike Christianity and Islam, have tended not to be discussed by scholars
as though they were 'real' religions, enshrining theological thought. This is
no doubt largely because they lack written texts to compare with the Bible
or the Qur'an. Indigenous African religions have instead been seen as social
institutions or constructions that are interesting primarily for what they tell
us about the social organisation of those who adhere to them, and hence
little attempt has been made to trace the development of religious ideas in
Africa over time.[31]

Ideas that Western scholars may regard as purely religious are actually
of great political importance if politics is seen as the debates and activities
relating to the distribution of resources in society in the largest sense, and
not just in formal and institutional terms. In the seventeenth century, one
of the first Europeans to publish a lengthy description of an African society based on extensive first-hand knowledge concluded that the people

among whom he had lived—in southern Madagascar—had no religion. This was not because the author (an official of the French Compagnie des Indes) was ignorant of Malagasy customs, but rather because he could identify no ritual, dogma or clergy that, in the opinion of a contemporary European, qualified as religion.[32] In much the same way today, observers may mistakenly conclude that many African countries have little in the way of politics, because the institutions and activities that, to outsiders, seem to constitute politics, are insubstantial there. Much of the real politics occurs elsewhere, in activities more conventionally thought of as coming within the sphere of religion, or usually considered as 'superstition'.

While the present book concentrates on certain aspects of Africans' thinking about politics today, we argue that the problems of African societies are no different from those of any other continent. For purposes of analysis, we generally take Africa to be one single arena. Some readers may object by pointing out that African countries and societies differ significantly from each other. So they do, but Africa's ethnic diversity, which is a telling factor in certain contexts, is less so when considered in terms of world-views. Just as it is conventional to discuss or write about Europe or even the West[33] on the grounds that geographically scattered countries with distinct histories have much in common due to their shared heritage of the Enlightenment, so, as we discuss below, there are grounds for assigning sub-Saharan Africa to one category for some purposes. Furthermore, we do not see Africa as a battleground between tradition and modernity. Victorian explorers tended to conceive of Africa as a continent without history and therefore without experience of change, where everything was done in a manner passed on from one generation to the next. Later, academic theories of development and modernisation were invoked to justify imposing innovations from elsewhere. But it is now evident that tradition cannot be accurately thought of in this way. Tradition certainly exists in Africa, as it does elsewhere, in the sense of patterns of behaviour and understanding that are transmitted from one generation to another, or that are attributed to earlier generations even when they are invented afresh. However, it is now abundantly clear that Africans experienced meaningful change before colonial times and that they have assimilated innovations easily throughout history. By the same token, they have abandoned some older practices without any obvious sense of loss.

## A dynamic model of religion in Africa

It is still all too commonly supposed that precolonial Africa consisted of thousands of distinct political or social units formerly called 'tribes', today known more politely, but with little change in meaning, as 'ethnic groups'. Each of these ethnic groups is supposed to have had its own 'tribal' religion: thus, there are books on Zulu religion, Yoruba religion, Ashanti religion, and so on. This conforms to the idea that old Africa was divided into thousands of micro-units, each defined by a more or less coherent set of political and cultural institutions, rather like miniature versions of the nations that Europeans have come to regard as the standard form of political organisation.

There are increasingly persuasive reasons, though, to suppose that this old-fashioned view is unsatisfactory. The British historian Terence Ranger has written an illuminating essay[34] in which he contends that twentieth-century anthropologists, reacting against the false history written by their evolution-minded nineteenth-century forebears, have often ceased to ask historical questions about religion altogether. Ranger therefore proposes a model of religion in Africa that both incorporates historical data and offers a means of analysing the current state of affairs. He notes that it is possible to identify extensive regions within Africa that existed in precolonial times, far exceeding the boundaries of any one ethnic group. Within these larger areas there were enduring patterns of interaction and exchange between individuals and communities. These extensive regions of contact—usually without fixed boundaries—constituted fields within which people travelled, including groups mobile by nature such as hunters and traders, for example, or pilgrims on their way to local shrines or other centres of spiritual power. Thus population groups that in many respects were highly localised, perhaps speaking a language proper to only a small area and engaged primarily in agriculture, were in communication with others much further afield. Such transactions involved an exchange of religious ideas and practices. Ranger points out that African religious ideas are largely about relationships. These are often conceived of as existing between the human and the spirit world, inhabited by ancestral spirits, spirits of the land, water or forest, alien spirits, and so on. This spirit idiom, which we analyse in more detail in chapter three, thus posits the existence of identifiable spirit-beings.

Each set of relationships in such a wide system of contacts and exchanges implicates people at various levels of interaction and is expressed in a religious form that changes according to circumstances. Ancestral cults for example are a historical feature of many parts of Africa, expressing the special relationship that people have with their ancestors. Historians have also identified territorial cults, related to the various relationships people have to the land, or so-called 'cults of affliction', which attract people believed to have been afflicted by the same spirit. In short, there are many cults, which may overlap, intrude upon, or compete with one another, and which have arisen, flourished and disappeared over time, to be replaced by others. Drawing attention to this aspect of life in Africa emphasises not the atomisation of the continent's people both in precolonial times and today, but the social relations that have continued to integrate various types of relationship: between kin, neighbours, migrants, nomads and travellers. The networks of relationships in the past were not only those between people, but also between humans and their natural environment, including the land they cultivated or where they hunted, and the taboo forest groves that could not be entered. Relationships of this type were important in Africa's politics in the past and they continue to be important today, nowadays entwined with the formal politics of sovereign states.

The individual spirits that are held to govern relationships between people and objects in the material world are considered by believers to be real, even though invisible. For purposes of analysis it is not necessary to share this view of reality, but it is important to take account of it. A helpful analogy is the idea suggested by the French philosopher Gilles Deleuze, who describes the imaginary as 'not the unreal, but the realm where the real and the unreal become undistinguishable from one another'.[35] Situated at this same point is another couple as difficult to disentangle as real and unreal, namely true and false.[36] The imaginary, we suggest, is where facts merge into non-facts; it is where perceptions of truth are formed. That which people imagine changes over time; but certain products of the imagination recur in societies and show continuity over many generations. Even the most determinedly materialistic societies make constant use of entities that are imaginary in this sense, such as capital, the market, and the economy.[37] But of all forms of imagination, arguably the most influential is religious belief, which has such a well-attested history the world over.

Tracing how certain products of the religious imagination change over time sheds light on perceptions of matters such as the moral character of power, the nature of good and evil, and similar ideas of obvious importance for politics and society. Included in the sets of relationships that constitute the fabric of society, and which change over time, are those between individuals and collectives, such as ethnic or national groups. The West today tends towards a near-obsession with the autonomous self,[38] a hallmark of modern industrial or post-industrial society that often distances Westerners from people who, as in Africa, tend to think of themselves and their rights and duties towards others primarily in terms of relations.

A dynamic model of the religious history of Africa thus offers insights into how people assimilate new religious ideas and practices and how new religious movements spread. It can include the diffusion of African religious traditions outside the continent from the slave trade until today. It can also encompass historical developments in Christianity and Islam, both of which have been established for centuries in some parts of Africa and have to be considered part of the range of African religious traditions. Such a model can also incorporate data concerning Africa's insertion into the world, whether in terms of traditional religions helping slaves to survive in the Americas or of conversion to 'world religions' helping Africans to enter global markets. Not least, a historical model of this sort helps to illuminate one of the main problems in interpreting Africa's political history, namely the absence in many places of any political constructions before colonial times closely resembling the modern idea of states.

Modern bureaucratic states hardly existed in Africa south of the Sahara until the nineteenth century, when they were created on the initiative of Europeans. Certainly, medieval Mali and Ghana and old Zimbabwe, to name three examples, all held sway over large areas, but they were not based on monopolies of the means of coercion held by centralised bureaucracies in quite the same way as occurred in Europe from the sixteenth or seventeenth century, with a formative influence on modern ideas of statehood worldwide. Some parts of precolonial Africa consisted of so-called 'stateless societies' in which governance was exercised through socially constituted networks like age-sets and lineages, in which initiation groups and masking societies exercised significant authority. All of Africa's many forms of government were associated with relationships between individuals and social groups, usually expressed in a spirit idiom. Authority over the spirit world thus translated into authority over people, making religion an outstanding means of instrumentalising political power by dominating webs of relations over a wide area. Hence, in 'stateless societies', in chiefdoms and in the great empires of medieval Africa alike, political power was largely exercised by people using essentially religious techniques which enabled them also to command material aspects of power such as armed force and rights of taxation or tribute. All of these older traditions of governance continue to have an effect on African politics.[39]

## Causation

While religious ideas may constitute a basis for political authority, they also provide a framework for understanding the causes of events. These two functions are related. Those Batswana who wondered in 2001 why the rains had not come on time, speculated that it might be because of the machinations of powerful people using mystical techniques. This is in effect a theory of causation based on religious belief, and supports the view that one of the functions of religion is as a system aiming at explanation, prediction and control.[40]

The story of El Negro also suggests that politicians who wish to stay powerful need to give at least the impression that they can command the vagaries of chance and climate. Politicians all over the world try to cultivate a reputation for being in full control of everything that affects public life. In the West, they do this in part with reference to scientific and technological expertise. In European and North American history, scientists have been overwhelmingly successful in explaining *how* things happen, but less successful in explaining *why* they happen. This may be one reason for the widespread existence of conspiracy theories even in societies with a high degree of scientific knowledge. The popularity of a vast range of conspiracy theories in the United States is testimony to this, including elaborate hypotheses about the assassination of John F. Kennedy and stories of abduction by aliens. In the Middle East, pervasive religious belief plus decades of undemocratic government have made even the most intelligent and best-educated people highly susceptible to conspiracy theories, such as that Princess Diana was murdered by the British secret services or that the 9/11 attacks on New York and Washington were masterminded not by Islamic militants but by Israelis or Americans, in a monstrous manipulation of public opinion. Stories about the workings of invisible forces appear to be a universal way of attributing causes to otherwise inexplicable events, even in countries where the provision of public information is dominated by powerful corporations and where institutions of learning or of commerce proffer scientifically validated explanations.

The stories of floods in Abbeville, abduction in Orléans, alligators in New York and El Negro in Gaborone all contain popular ideas. They are popular, however, in different ways. In a European country like France, subject to a rigorous separation of church and state for more than two centuries, where the secular and religious realms generally are regarded as intellectually discrete, rumours such as these are generally regarded as a popular delusion. They are considered of mainly sociological interest[41] and are rarely shared by elites. In any African country, and for that matter in other parts of the world, rumours, like certain other expressions of popular belief, tend to be shared even in elite circles. Most importantly, they are more likely to be taken seriously. To call a rumour 'popular' is not to distinguish it from some idea of 'high' culture, as sometimes occurs in Europe, but rather to imply that it is not the property of any one segment of society, such as a particular class or ethnic group.[42]

Even in highly secularised European countries, then, or ones with huge expertise in science and technology like the United States, many people find appealing rumours that purport to offer explanations for certain events. Often such rumours refer to invisible beings, such as aliens, or they may attribute inexplicable occurrences to the machinations of an invisible force that people believe to have effective power over their lives. This may refer to an existing organisation, such as the CIA, or to an alleged network such as an international Jewish conspiracy, or to a personified natural force, such as El Niño. It appears that people everywhere are inclined to seek explanations for unusual or important events, which in turn seems to imply that the more unpredictable events become, the more people are inclined to construct some theory of causation. Thus men and women all over the world may consider and accept explanations that refer to invisible beings or forces, which, we have argued, are at the heart of most religious belief. Considered this way, rumours become highly relevant to the study of religion.

In academies of learning, theories about why—not how—things happen are conventionally the domain of theology and philosophy. In Africa, however, this is a subject much discussed in streets, offices and homes, in the form of communication called *radio trottoir.*

# 2

# WORDS

One of Africa's leading novelists, the Ivorian Ahmadou Kourouma, maintains that religion and politics are inseparable in Africa.[1] His best-selling *En attendant le vote des bêtes sauvages*,[2] a literary prize-winner, concerns a man from a remote rural area who joins the army, participates in a successful coup and becomes president of his country. Along the way he has several fantastic experiences of the spirit world. Kourouma has revealed that his characters are barely-disguised descriptions of African presidents, some of whom he has known personally, and that he wrote the book in deliberate imitation of the stories told in the evenings by hunters in West African villages in the old days about 'the hunters' life, and their magical battles against the animals, themselves believed to have magical powers'. Hunting is thus 'a contest between rival magicians'.[3] Even today, youngsters may sit and listen to these stories of a world of men and animals outwitting each other by the use of cunning and magical power.

The South African theologian S. T. Kgatla makes a similar point in his studies of witchcraft accusations, which are particularly rampant where he lives, in Limpopo Province. It is in social gatherings, when people come together to tell stories by the fire, that ideas of witchcraft are acquired by children, who later come to apply them in practice. 'Most witchcraft accusations', he maintains, 'emanate from the "home" and the family, thus where people spend most of their time together as relatives, friends and kinsmen.'[4] Belief in witchcraft is just another of the spiritual beliefs that many Africans share, although one that can have tragic consequences.

The stories about El Negro transmitted by Botswana's Radio Mall—in other words, told by people chatting in taxis, bars, offices, and markets—are similar to tales told every day throughout Africa. There is one crucial difference, though, between the rumours of Abbeville and Orléans and New York, and those of Africa: in the latter case, rumours circulate in a political and social environment that endows them with far more importance than in industrial countries where information is a highly organised

27

commodity, traded by professional elites via high-technology media that reach every corner of society. Africans are statistically less likely than people in any other continent to read newspapers or to watch television and are less disposed, from necessity but also from habit, to take their opinions from those sources.[5] They are more likely than people in Europe and North America to derive their information from discussion with family, friends and colleagues.

Rumours in Africa are generated in environments where the boundaries between what is real and unreal, or true and false, are often unclear. But the essence of rumours, as we will shortly see, is that they are credible. Rumours therefore provide an important avenue for exploring commonly held ideas concerning the nature of reality, and this is why we accord them such importance in this study. We consider them together with other, more orthodox, sources of information that may shed light on the relation between religion and politics in Africa, including the press, locally-authored pamphlets and videos, opinion polls, academic studies and so on. All of these are relevant to an analysis of how religion and politics are related.

## Pavement radio

Decades ago, Africans themselves noticed the importance of rumours in the towns and cities which grew massively in every part of the continent throughout the twentieth century, sometimes going from nothing to agglomerations of several million people in just three or four generations. They gave names to this type of oral communication and news-telling, often jokingly suggesting it as an African alternative to the European types of mass media introduced mainly in colonial times. Thus, as well as Botswana's Radio Mall, in Guinea people referred to Radio Kankan, and in Côte d'Ivoire to Radio Treichville, while in North Africa they called the rumour-mill *le téléphone arabe*. South African political exiles in the 1980s sometimes referred to rumours as Radio Potato. All of these names have been used in particular places to designate rumours interesting enough to be listened to and repeated. Perhaps the nearest equivalent in English is 'bush telegraph', although that has an old-fashioned ring and is therefore not a very accurate translation. The ever-inventive citizens of Brazzaville and Kinshasa, the twin capital cities which sit back to back on opposite shores of the Congo river, coined the name *radio trottoir* ('pavement radio'), one which so nicely describes the phenomenon of modern, urban discussion of matters of public interest that it is used throughout French-speaking Africa.[6]

African politicians and journalists take the rumours emanating from *radio trottoir* very seriously indeed.[7] That malign political genius Mobutu

Sese Seko, a journalist before becoming president of Zaire, openly acknowledged the importance of *radio trottoir* in his own country.[8] Sometimes it
turns out to be an accurate source of news about tensions between rival
politicians or planned military coups that cannot be found in any formal
media. Sometimes it is the source of bizarre inventions, like the rumours
sweeping West Africa in the mid-1990s that there were evil magicians at
large so powerful that they could cause men's penises to vanish with a single look. There have been cases of people being beaten to death by angry
mobs after being mistaken for the dreaded penis-thieves.[9] In similar vein,
in southern Africa there are persistent stories of a clandestine trade in
human heads and other body-parts said to be exported from Zimbabwe to
South Africa.[10] Every part of Africa has histories of story-telling of this sort
that can be traced back over decades or centuries, like the stories about
firemen in East Africa in colonial times that suggested these public servants were in fact human vampires who would lure people into their fire-
stations in order to drain their blood,[11] or the stories in Madagascar, dating back to the slave trade but still very much in existence today, about
mysterious heart-thieves who are said to require human organs for sale
overseas.[12]

According to Léopold Sédar Senghor, a major poet and intellectual as
well as the first president of Senegal, 'of all the cultural manifestations of
black Africa, orality is one of the characteristics they hold in common'.[13]
Oral communication is particularly important in the many countries
where writing was more or less unknown until it was introduced by European missionaries and colonisers, sometimes only in the twentieth century.
Moreover, Senghor goes on to say, 'Orality is more than just languages',[14]
as it carries with it particular modes of thought. Even in societies where
writing was associated with theological learning and occasionally used for
poetry or for secular purposes, most obviously those with a significant
Muslim population, writing was still not used before the twentieth century
on anything like the scale that developed under the bureaucratic states
that emerged over time in Europe and elsewhere. Rumours have sometimes played a major role in European affairs too, even at a time when
these were supposedly coming to be dominated by more rational forms of
communication, such as during the French revolution.[15] Modern America
too is full of conspiracy theories, retailed these days by the internet especially, but these do not have the power of stories contained in the mainstream media and rarely acquire the degree of public credence that they
may be afforded in Africa or the Middle East.

*Radio trottoir*, the socially-channelled, oral discussion of current events in
Africa, is more than rumour alone. It conveys information and news but is

also used for entertainment and almost as a collective form of psychotherapy. It is perhaps comparable in this regard with talk radio as it has
emerged in the United States and is now growing in Europe. The fact that
Africa's *radio trottoir* is undeniably popular does not mean it is spurned by
elites, which make use of their own forms of *radio trottoir*. Although in
Africa discussion of this sort can be placed in a long tradition of oral cultures, these days information transmitted by word of mouth is mixed with
news gleaned from newspapers, television and radio, and even the
internet, although these media are much rarer than in industrialised countries. In 1998, only 11 newspapers were produced for every thousand people living in Africa, compared with 96 per thousand for the world as a
whole.[16] Over the period 1995–2000, on average 198 per thousand people
in sub-Saharan Africa had a radio, and 59 per thousand had a television.[17]

African politicians sometimes express their exasperation with *radio
trottoir*, which indeed carries plenty of stories that are scurrilous, fantastic,
factually incorrect, politically damaging, or all of these at once. Cameroon's President Paul Biya once stated a widespread official point of view
more revealingly than he may have realised, in a clumsy attempt to warn
people against believing anti-government rumours, when he said that
'Truth comes from above; rumour comes from below'[18]—a shameless
statement when one considers the lies and propaganda routinely dissemi-
nated by Cameroon's official media.

## *News and media*

During the first two post-independence decades, when one-party states
were in power in much of the continent, it was quite conventional for African intellectuals and international experts to talk of the need to make
every organ of state and institution of society subservient to state planning
and development. Under those circumstances, it was possible to consider
*radio trottoir*, rather like East European *samizdat*, as a form of improvisation
by people determined to speak their minds in the face of official censor-
ship. It has certainly played that role often enough. But since the early
1990s the introduction of liberal democratic constitutions throughout
Africa has created far more space for freedom of expression. Every country in Africa now has opposition or independent newspapers, and often
independently owned radio and television stations as well. Yet *radio trottoir*
is still as alive as ever. Africans, owning less gadgets and being less likely to
live in towns than people in many other parts of the world, are not saturated
to the same degree as their counterparts in rich countries with information

from mass media. Even when they do have access to reasonably accurate news media, many still pay particular attention to *radio trottoir*. Many Africans seem almost on principle to prefer news that arrives via conversation with friends and acquaintances, and consider it more reliable than news from impersonal sources because it emanates from more trustworthy sources than formal media. *Radio trottoir* is rooted in social relationships that are vital for survival. In almost every African country, the inadequacy or absence of state welfare services obliges people to rely on their social networks for security of all types, from physical protection against violence or theft to provision in sickness or old age. *Radio trottoir* is of a piece with this. It is also a source of free entertainment, making maximum use of drama and burlesque. It contains a delicious element of revenge, in the form of the slanderous or obscene stories that people gleefully recount about politicians who are normally glimpsed only through the shaded-glass windows of their limousines.[19] Not least, it is in a direct line of descent from the oral cultures of precolonial times generally referred to as oral tradition.[20]

The free media that have blossomed in Africa have not generally lived up to the expectation that they would transform the terms of debate, as some liberal reformers hoped when Africa underwent its wave of democratisation in the early 1990s. Official state and ruling party newspapers and radio stations no longer have the monopolies they once did, but many African countries still lack a respected, independently-owned, newspaper whose journalists publish only accurate, rigorously researched stories. Like newspapers and electronic media in the industrialised world, African news media are often in thrall to commercial interests. Some are owned by politicians who use them to promote their own views and attack their rivals. And some journalists shamelessly use their position for personal profit, threatening to libel people who refuse to pay them (a practice known as 'blackmail journalism', according to one African newspaperman[21]) or accepting money from those they interview.[22] By comparison with what is taught in US schools of journalism, African newspapers in general are extremely casual about establishing hard facts. They cannot be regarded as reliable sources of factual information or as journals of record other than in a few cases. African newspapers are, in fact, better considered as written forms of *radio trottoir* than as vehicles for rigorous reporting. If they are read with this caveat and considered as a privileged point of access to public debates in Africa, they can be treasure-houses of information.[23]

Perhaps one should not be too harsh in judging the quality of Africa's mass media. The number of African journalists killed in the course of their work is testimony to the courage with which many of them report what they see as the truth in the face of low salaries, a lack of computers, telephones and transport and political obstacles. The media in the industrialised countries may be more assiduous in their search for individual nuggets of information that can be classified as facts, but they are hardly paragons of objective observation. Moreover, they have changed enormously in recent years. 'Journalism is becoming less a product than a process witnessed in real time and public,' laments one senior US journalist. 'A journalism of unfiltered assertion makes separating fact from spin, argument from innuendo, more difficult, and leaves society susceptible to manipulation.'[24] The Western news media exist increasingly to entertain, and ultimately to deliver customers to corporations, and ever less to provide information about politics or major public issues dispassionately and even-handedly. Moreover even a financially and politically autonomous news medium, whose reporters painstakingly verify every fact in the pursuit of public-interest stories, can still offer only a partial view of the world. For news stories are no more and no less than short narratives constructed in set patterns that readers know and recognise. Journalists and editors therefore labour to fit information into familiar formats[25], hardly an ideal method of exploring the world in all its complexity. The best reporting in the Western tradition of journalism may be factually correct, but that alone does not make it the whole truth.

It could be argued that if news media are of high integrity, offer facts and strive to be objective, then the public forms its own opinions on the basis of the available information. According to this argument, even though no news medium can ever provide the whole truth about anything, it can at least offer readers the opportunity to make up their own minds. But this argument takes no account of the degree of selection that takes place in the presentation of all news. Editors and other news managers sift hundreds of potential stories every day before deciding which ones they will use. Factually accurate information such as the best newspapers or broadcasters aspire to provide is inevitably the view of an elite, offered to the public by media professionals who operate with a large degree of consensus about what constitutes news and truth. Even the relative openness offered by the internet has not decisively changed this state of affairs.

The provision of information by a relatively coherent professional elite is a central element of industrial or post-industrial societies. As early as 1928, one of the founders of modern public relations wrote concerning the United States:[26]

[T]he conscious and intelligent manipulation of the organized habits and opinions of the masses is an important element in democratic society…Those who manipulate this unseen mechanism of society constitute an invisible government which is the true ruling power of our country.

We are governed, our minds are molded, our tastes formed, our ideas suggested, largely by men we have never heard of.

This was written before the age of television.

Already, seventy-five years ago, in the world's leading industrialised societies it was not only opinion that was being formed overwhelmingly by coteries of professional communicators, with and without the use of facts, but also memory and emotion. Earlier still, in 1922, one of the greatest of US newspaper editors wrote that Americans were living in what he called a 'pseudo-environment', in which people derive information and even emotion from messages transmitted by mass media rather than from direct personal experience.[27] The very personalities of successive generations in industrial societies have been shaped by processess of communication between media corporations and their publics; the emergence of the internet has done no more than raise a question-mark as to whether the supply of information can be wrested from the hands of professionals. Those whose characters and ideas are moulded in such societies find it difficult to appreciate how people may view the world in other ways, and how they may think about the relations between themselves and others, in societies where information is gleaned primarily from family, friends and acquaintances who have no formal training in communication techniques, and where direct experience is the main source of emotion.

*Radio trottoir*, by contrast, is a product of the masses. It could be said to be the voice of the general public in Africa, were it not that most African countries, lacking media that reach throughout society, do not really have a single public but, instead, a 'plurality of publics'.[28] *Radio trottoir* reflects what these publics find both believable and interesting. In that sense it is a profoundly democratic medium, of the utmost political importance. Some people may think that the freedom to make up one's own mind without professional elite guidance is incompatible with the development of economically advanced modern societies—an interesting idea, but not one that need detain us further.

## Rumours and facts

Rumours have been aptly described as 'an attempt at collective conversation by people who wish to enter their sentiments into a public discourse'.[29] At the very least, listening to *radio trottoir* can tell us something of what Africans like to talk about and what opinions they hold. To analyse *radio trottoir*, we may begin by taking as an example allegations that have been made in both Ghana and Togo in fairly recent times, passed from person to person and occasionally appearing in print, that the head of state has physically attacked one of his ministers in an argument at a cabinet meeting.[30] These are fairly typical examples of *radio trottoir* stories in the sense that they are transmitted mostly by word of mouth and are deeply disrespectful of politicians. On the face of it, a story like this may or may not be true, but it is certainly physically possible. With an effort at corroboration, such as by interviewing those present at cabinet meetings, it might be possible for a researcher to verify or dismiss such a story.

However, this is far from the case with many *radio trottoir* stories. One of the medium's most striking features is the apparent unconcern with which it mixes such plausible stories with those that are impossible according to the tenets of science—for example, that a president has acquired from one of his spiritual advisors a mystical power such that it makes him invulnerable to bullets.[31] Anyone who believes that the world is governed only by forces that can be measured by science and who is imbued with a respect for empirical fact has to regard the latter story as unbelievable. Most Europeans and North Americans dismiss stories of amulets able to make people bullet-proof as sheer nonsense, and might shake their heads in wonder that there are people still ignorant enough to believe this sort of thing. But, whether or not one believes in the possibility of such mystical forces, this type of response is rather thoughtless. Above all, it is no longer viable to suppose that beliefs concerning the influence of spiritual forces on the material world—religion—are doomed to disappear over time, or at least are destined to become purely a private matter. These days, there are countries governed by elites that profess strong religious beliefs, but which also possess scientific knowledge and advanced nuclear technology. India and Pakistan are two examples; the Christian influence in the Bush White House suggests that the United States might be a third. Wars taking place today involve protagonists who have the skills to operate sophisticated weapons and the intelligence to devise stratagems of all sorts but who nevertheless believe in the effectiveness of bullet-proof amulets.[32] In short, it is no longer tenable to assume, as modernisers often did in the twentieth century, that many religious beliefs are destined to be displaced by modern, rational ways of thinking deemed necessary for economic and political development. On the contrary, a person or even a nation may have a sophisticated understanding of advanced technology while also believing as strongly as ever in the reality of an invisible world.

Hence, stories told by *radio trottoir* have to be considered other than as reservoirs of clues to possible facts. Although at some stage the assiduous inquirer has to try to separate fact from non-fact, this is probably not the best way to proceed with stories from *radio trottoir* in the first instance. Nor is it helpful to see rumours primarily as evidence of mass affliction, describing them with metaphors drawn from psychiatry as delusions or fantasies and disqualifying them from the outset as representations of reality.[33] Rumours, whether factually based or not, are repeated by people who believe them to be true in some sense. This is a crucial point, implying that the initial question to be asked about any rumour is why people find it believable. Not all rumours are attempts to explain one particular occurrence, with a factual point of departure. An example is the one from Orléans: no young women had in fact disappeared and there was no traffic in prostitutes of the sort suggested.[34] The rumour was empirically baseless, but nonetheless rich in meaning.

Many rumours, especially in African *radio trottoir* but also in Abbeville and Orléans and elsewhere, amount to an elaborate conspiracy theory, a staple of politics in many parts of the world largely because it provides a form of explanation for whatever is thought to have taken place. A conspiracy theory may function as a scapegoat mechanism by identifying a person or group of people—the mysterious '*them*'—thought to be responsible for life's misfortunes. The witchcraft accusations that abound in Africa are one example of the widespread tendency for people to attempt to identify the hidden hand behind observable reality. For other people—in the West—foreigners, extra-terrestrials, Freemasons, or the CIA fulfill this role. No doubt this is one reason why people the world over tend to blame their government for many things, even for those over which politicians may have little real control, such as bad weather and poor performances by the national football team.

Above all, people must want a rumour to be true, for otherwise they would hardly bother to repeat it, and a new story would never gain currency. Rumours reflect the prevailing mood of a society or a group within it at any particular moment, so that people may for example interpret certain events as harbingers of disaster or signs of the time. Some rumours last for only a few days, while others, like the New York alligators story, endure for decades. Rumours come from a credible source—one's friends and acquaintances. The words used in rumours can easily lose their reference to specific physical objects and come to refer more generally to mental images or representations only, such as the supposition that the white slavers rumoured to exist in Orléans in 1969 were Jews: the allegation was plausible not because there were many particularly anti-social Jews in the town, but simply because it fitted into an existing mental frame of reference.

Rumours therefore represent people's attempts to understand the world, usually by attributing causes to events. The force of a rumour 'derives from its ability to structure our perception of the world...Rumour thus constitutes a system of explanation able to organise a great number of loose facts into a coherent whole'.[35] People often seem comforted if they can designate somebody or other as responsible for situations that are otherwise inexplicable, perhaps because it helps them to feel that their world is not utterly out of control. Research into rumours in modern industrial societies confirms these general precepts, and also concludes that there is no structural difference between that which is believed and that which is imagined.[36] According to specialists various modern urban myths or rumours, including alien abductions in the United States, also contain a form of moral statement and may, with some help from the mass media, shape definitions of moral norms by highlighting perceived causes of deviance, through what is sometimes called a moral panic.[37]

An inquirer into Africa's *radio trottoir* has at least two avenues of investigation open. The first, and probably more important, is to understand how any given item reported on *radio trottoir* becomes believable in a particular context, which requires familiarity with a wide range of ideas current at the time and place where the rumour was collected. A rumour tells us a great deal about the mentality of the group in which it circulates. In that sense rumours may be analysed as types of stories, like myths or folktales, that reveal something about the societies that produce them, or even about the human condition in general, even though they may not contain a single fact in the sense of a record of an empirically verifiable event. It is useful, therefore, having encountered a rumour, to seek out various antecedents, to investigate the circumstances in which it circulates, and to consider why people may find it credible. It is only after this first stage that one can begin to separate the possible facts in a rumour from what the analyst considers to be obvious non-facts. Even here, distinguishing the one from the other may not be easy. For, if developments in social theory over recent decades have taught us anything, it is that the world is not best understood as consisting of aggregations of unalterable facts, constituting the truth, which can be neatly separated from non-facts and that form characteristic patterns in an ideal type of modern society. Demonstrating the fallacy of such a supposition has been probably the single most important trend in the social sciences and humanities in recent decades.[38]

A useful way of inquiring more precisely into any given story, with a view to identifying its possible factual content, is to look for internal contradictions or flaws of construction. Certain reports might be composed of verifiable facts but amalgamated in such a way as to tell a story we nevertheless do not find convincing. In US public life, for example, great formal respect is accorded to the notions of truth and facts, and yet there have been many examples of strings of facts being assembled into stories whose essential credibility is debatable. For decades, the fact that the Soviet Union had all the attributes of a military superpower was incorporated into a doctrine, shaping public opinion and state policy, that communism was successfully subverting the United States from within and without. Although based on facts, this view was itself a hypothesis, one that seemed more credible to some people than to others. Or we may take the Monica Lewinsky affair, which became public in 1997. This major political scandal was based on a few facts that were eventually established concerning sexual contacts between an American president and one of his office interns. What was at issue between politicians, the mass media and the public was the nature of the aggregation of known facts. Did it amount to evidence that the president was such a monster of infamy and hypocrisy that he must be removed from office at whatever political cost? Or was it more persuasively seen as evidence that he was a man who, irrespective of his political virtues or vices, sometimes had difficulty with sexual restraint, rather like millions of his fellow-countrymen, including some of his leading accusers? These views depended not so much on individual facts as on the ways in which they were put into sequence and on the meaning attributed to them. There is a comparison to be made here with *radio trottoir*. In both cases, facts are not always easy to distinguish from non-facts. The narrative into which established facts are incorporated may or may not be convincing to the bulk of the population. Whether in the United States or Africa, this is a matter of great political significance.

Although individuals may differ in the meaning they attribute to strings of facts, there are clear patterns that can be detected over time in various societies.[39] To continue with the examples from the preceding paragraph, it is notable that Americans' views both of the cold war and of the proper sexual comportment of their president have been formed by the religious history of their country. Orthodox Christian views of sexual morality, of the nature of evil, and of the ultimate expectation of a cosmic contest between the forces of light and the forces of darkness have all contributed to shaping how Americans think about public affairs. A relevant precedent is the famous occasion in 1938 when a radio play by Orson

Welles about an invasion by Martians caused many Americans to believe that a real attack had started. The fictional story was believable largely because of current speculation about a forthcoming world war (alas, all too accurate) and because of a deep-seated Christian belief in the imminence of the end of the world.[40] Traditional Christian beliefs, this time concerning morality, also played a role in the Monica Lewinsky affair. One eminent cultural historian points out that the wave of Bill Clinton jokes this inspired could be interpreted in terms of a pattern by which sexual gossip transmits views on the legitimacy of those in power, like the scandalous rumours about the sex life of the queen in *ancien régime* France.[41]

If history can have such a formative influence on the perception of truth in the United States, so too does the same apply to Africa. There are differences, though, in the way that this occurs, due to the different historical experiences of the two sub-continents. Information in Africa has always been transmitted largely by word of mouth, sometimes accompanied by forms of ritual activity that are of great effect in communicating meaning.[42] One example is the significance ascribed to oaths and curses. These are a form of words that are not mere statements, but themselves contain an action, sometimes called 'performative utterances'.[43] Oath-taking is fundamentally a religious act, with serious consequences believed to affect those who break the oath, and this is so not only in Africa. By virtue of its supposed spiritual power the content of an oath becomes a reality for those who subscribe to it. The same is true of curses.[44] This is the effective power of the word.[45] For the same reason there may exist verbal taboos, implying that certain words, or verbal references to these, are strictly forbidden. Such is the case among the Akan of Ghana, who fear that uttering certain words—including references to objects believed to be imbued with potentially destructive spirits[46]—may unleash forces of instability natural or social. Oaths are also known in Europe, where they have lost some of their potency because of a general decline of religious belief. Even in America, where religious belief remains important and where oaths are commonly used on formal occasions, such performative utterances probably have less power than in Africa because of the great reliance placed on written records throughout US history.

In many parts of Africa before the spread of writing there were accepted procedures for disseminating information that was considered important for society (such as rights to ownership of land, rights to political office, the definition of crime or transgression), but also for individual health and well-being (such as how to identify forms of sickness). In many places information of this sort was legitimised in part by incorporating it into stories about the past, including genealogies and myths. Rather as anthropologists used to consider indigenous religions, historians of Africa have tended to consider identifiable systems of remembering in precolonial Africa as 'ethnic' oral traditions, such as the great epic poems. They have been rather less inclined to consider how these oral performances were flexible enough to incorporate changing social and political relationships.[47] *Radio trottoir* can usefully be considered in the light of the older modes of speaking and remembering known as oral tradition. Although colonisation and intensive development have certainly had a major effect on systems of remembering the past, *radio trottoir* continues to display features that show continuity with older forms of oral communication in Africa. Today, alongside the traditional story-tellers and troubadors or *griots*, certain other categories of people have a privileged place in the transmission of stories through *radio trottoir*, such as long-distance taxi- and truck-drivers, hairdressers, and drivers for the rich and powerful. Information broadcast on *radio trottoir* is authenticated by appealing to personal relationships, such as a person who tells a story of some elite manipulation that he then authenticates by claiming he heard it from a cousin—generally unnamed—who works in a minister's office. Locations for diffusion include especially bars, markets and taxis, all of which offer the right combination of public space and a feeling of uninhibitedness and intimacy. These have tended to replace the king's court or the chief's compound as the place where the most influential oral performances take place.

*Radio trottoir* properly consists of stories recounted in public, such that anyone present can question the accuracy of what is said or add embellishments of their own to correct or complement the story. *Radio trottoir* is a feature of societies in which many people do not earn salaries and can count on no bureaucratic form of social welfare, and where even policing and punishment are often not undertaken by organised bureaucracies. Anyone who has seen the ghastly spectacle of a mob attacking a pickpocket in an African market will appreciate the frightful power of such self-policing. In such circumstances a person's reputation is all-important, and, as in early modern Europe, life is to a considerable extent 'a public performance, in which through "self-fashioning" an individual could, within limits, manipulate the way one appeared to the wider world', including through masquerades and carnivals.[48]

## Rumour and religion

Taking *radio trottoir* seriously is essential for an analysis of how African publics think about the world. Making sense of what *radio trottoir* is about—

that is, what information can be gleaned from it, and not only considering its formal properties—becomes much easier if one uses operational definitions of both religion and politics, of the sort discussed in the previous chapter. If, for example, many people believe that their president really is invulnerable to bullets, as *radio trottoir* quite often reports, this indicates that their perceptions of reality are rooted in ideas about the nature of interaction between the visible and invisible worlds. The political implications of such a story are also clear, as it implies that a president protected against bullets cannot be overthrown in a conventional military coup. Underlying many *radio trottoir* stories are historically rooted religious ideas and perceptions of politics that extend far beyond the formal sphere of the state.

Some of the changes over time in the pervasive oral culture called *radio trottoir* may be documented, for example by reference to the literature circulating in the southern Nigerian city of Onitsha, West Africa's largest market-town. Around the time of Nigeria's independence, market-stalls in Onitsha began selling cheap, locally-produced publications of the type that used to be known in England as chap-books. These Nigerian works were first discussed in the 1960s by scholars who noted the extent to which they contained stories that were intended to entertain but that also carried moral messages, sometimes drawn from English literature or other foreign sources, while still bearing a close relationship to folktales as told in Nigerian villages.[49] More recently, Onitsha's markets have also been noted for their thriving trade in videos,[50] a form of communication immensely popular all over Africa today. Modern Onitsha videos, although often recognisably similar to the chap-books of an earlier generation, are far more ostentatiously religious, and often feature people possessed by spirits or attacked by witches. These are themes popular in videos in many parts of the continent. It is interesting that interaction with the spirit world is also a pervasive theme of a more self-consciously literary form of 'high' literature by internationally acclaimed authors such as Amos Tutuola, Ben Okri and Ahmadou Kourouma.[51] As with many lesser-known productions, this oeuvre is characterised by the lack of a clear dividing line between the material and spiritual world, where the constraints placed on ordinary people do not apply. This is perhaps related to a quality observable in African philosophy in the form of a tendency to assimilate phenomena into an overarching framework rather than to proceed in the form of rigorously dualist distinctions of the type either/or and true/false.[52]

In addition to works of fiction that contain many references to religion, there is also a thriving trade in religious literature of a more conventional type. Books relating to the Bible or the Qur'an are sold in many towns in

Africa, by the few formal bookshops and the far more numerous market-stalls and itinerant hawkers. Another common sub-category of religious literature is testimonies of personal religious experiences. Much of this literature hardly makes its way outside Africa and is only rarely to be found in even the finest Western academic libraries.[53] Probably the most puzzling genre is that of the numerous accounts of witchcraft and other forms of perceived evil, sometimes in the form of a description of a personal journey into a world of spirits. While many pious works on Christianity to be found in Africa are authored by American evangelicals and published in the United States, popular books and pamphlets on witchcraft and mystical voyages are almost invariably written by Africans and published locally. Similar material is circulated through charismatic churches, often in the form of video recordings. This is also true of African-initiated churches founded among diaspora communities on other continents.

The ubiquity of publications and videos dealing with religious matters in the broadest sense, from popular theology to novels featuring magical transformations, suggests that interest in such matters is widespread. Not only do pamphlets describing mystical journeys appear to circulate in large numbers,[54] but such accounts can clearly be situated within a long tradition of stories about witchcraft and journeys into the underworld. If stories of this type are popular, it is to some extent because they bear a resemblance to many people's perceptions of what is happening around them. Studies of almost any part of Africa indicate that subjective experiences of the spirit world are fairly common, and have been for as long as it is possible to trace. Such evidence may be drawn not just from studies of the pentecostal churches that have attracted so much scholarly interest of late,[55] but also of many other churches, including African independent congregations, as well as of Muslim communities and African traditional religions. Thus, the popular literature written by those who claim to have experienced spiritual journeys or to have expert knowledge of witchcraft, and the fictional videos depicting similar experiences, are not an ephemeral genre but rather represent a modern form of an important tradition of mysticism.

Taking the history of such literary productions into account, it is striking that they are increasingly concerned with the presence of evil. Many recent publications can be read as expressions of deep concern about the moral confusion that arises when people feel themselves threatened by physical and metaphysical danger at every juncture, or where they are no longer able to distinguish easily between that which is right and proper and its opposite. This is less evident in the popular literature produced three or four decades ago. If one were to ask why evil should be perceived as increasingly prevalent today, it would not be difficult to find material causes such as the existence of war in some areas, the spread of AIDS, and so on. Many reports peddled by *radio trottoir*, and many texts of the type we will discuss further, suggest not only that people consider such threats to be related to activity in the invisible world, but that those who feel themselves threatened in this way aim to restore the moral balance of their environment. It is in this respect that religious activity may be considered as an expression of a political will, in the sense of politics 'from below', that begins with a reconstitution of the self as a moral subject. As others have noted, this is so 'to the extent that a wish for political, economic and social change translates itself into the establishment of a new ethical and spiritual existence, or in other words by a change in the self'.[56]

These reflections allow us to draw some provisional conclusions from the long-term study of rumours and pamphlets. One such inference is that the many popular texts with some religious content—in terms of our definition, those that treat of interaction with an invisible world—can be seen as an attempted remedy for adversity by a reordering of power. This is notably so in the considerable number of African countries where formal political institutions have largely broken down. To this extent, many popular religious texts reflect the preoccupation of Africans with how power is exercised in their societies, which is often in ways that tend to fall outside the scope of orthodox models of politics and economics. This we will consider in more detail in due course.[57] Since the texts to which we refer[58] are concerned with power in African societies, or to be more exact with the dangers which may arise when it is not properly regulated, they can be considered a commentary on a world in which power is often seen as an instrument of evil people, who conspire to use it to destroy peace and harmony. To that extent, they are also an oblique criticism of government or of misgovernment. This is not to say that religion in Africa today is concerned solely with combatting evil. But it is undeniable that there is a growing concern with a perceived presence of evil, to judge from the best available measures of popular opinion.

Apart from their growing concern with evil, popular stories and rumours in Africa also frequently report another type of interaction with an invisible world. There are many accounts, written and oral, of physically impossible events, said to have become feasible through the use of metaphysical power. Belief in such occurrences provides further evidence for the strength of popular religious views. Miracle-stories, for example, are abundant, and sometimes make their way into African newspapers. Charismatic churches are especially noted for their alleged healing miracles. The Virgin Mary, who is said to have appeared, most famously, at Lourdes in France in the nineteenth century and at Fatima in Portugal and Medjugorje in former Yugoslavia in the twentieth, has in recent decades been reported to have appeared in Rwanda, Cameroon, Kenya and elsewhere in Africa.[59] Islamic miracles often take the form of a mysterious apparition of the name of Allah. It is interesting to note the tone of press reports of such purported miracles. When newspapers in the industrialised world write about such events they adopt a sceptical tone. The African media are generally more sympathetic, with journalists and editors often seeming to take such events as empirical facts, or in any event assuming that this is what their readers will think. So, whereas a classic Catholic miracle, such as Italy's weeping statues, is likely to be covered in the Western press as an oddball story, in a humorous or mocking tone, the reported appearance of Jesus Christ in Nairobi on 11 June 1988 was treated by leading Kenyan newspapers very seriously. Senior journalists interviewed eye-witnesses who claimed that they had seen Jesus himself, real and alive. To supplement their reports, the press published a photograph showing a tall, slim man, described as swarthy and intense-looking, dressed in white robes and with a turban, whom bystanders recognised as the Son of God. 'I am convinced this was a miracle', said Job Mutungi, the editor of the Swahili edition of the *Kenya Times*, a respectable newspaper. 'I saw a bright star in daytime thrice. This person appeared mysteriously in the crowd, and he had a light around his head and sparks from his bare feet'. Mutungi went on to describe how Jesus had blessed the crowd in Swahili, promising them 'a bucketful of blessings', after which he left in a car driven by one Gurnam Singh. On reaching the bus terminus the purported Jesus told Singh to stop the car as he wanted to return to Heaven. Then, wrote the reporter, 'he simply vanished into thin air'.[60]

This is an interesting example of a modern Christian miracle. Whatever exactly happened, it took place among people who had gathered for a prayer-meeting in Kawangware, one of the slums of Nairobi, where they were addressed by Mary Akatsa, a well-known preacher and healer, who herself claims to have died and been resurrected. It is quite common among religious leaders in Africa to claim to have died after serious illness and to have miraculously returned to life, charged by God with a special task. In this logic, a spiritual death is considered to be 'real'. The content of the message Akatsa claims to have brought with her from the invisible world shows similarities with other incidents, concerning as it does a moral mission to heal the sick and cast out devils. Mary Akatsa has reportedly carried out many acts of healing that she ascribes to the work of God, sometimes performed simply by touching people with the Bible.[61] She was famous enough to earn visits from her country's then president, Daniel arap Moi. She is not the only prophet to have been sought out by politicians who consider it in their interest to associate with powerful spiritual leaders. In societies where religion and politics are more closely related than in Europe, politicians may routinely act in this way. Examples include Nelson Mandela who, although not known for his religious leanings, has several times visited the Rain-Queen, an esteemed religious specialist, in South Africa's Limpopo Province.[62]

Miracle-stories are similar to many other accounts related both by word of mouth and by the mass media in Africa in that they accept the possibility of an event occuring outside the rules deemed to govern the material world. Miracles are so often described by *radio trottoir*, and sometimes written down, that people who are exposed to such accounts from their infancy may easily believe in their empirical reality, or at least may be unable to say whether they are true or not. 'I was socialised into this belief and interpretation of most incidents in witchcraft/*juju*/marabout terms', writes a Ghanaian journalist who now lives in Canada, mixing three words of different provenance in an attempt to designate mysticism in general. 'As a resident of Kumasi and now of Ottawa, I can see the difference of not…constantly hearing people complaining and accusing witches for their misfortune and other incidents'.[63]

The popularity of miracle stories or other explanations that suppose the existence of extraordinary powers, such as witchcraft tales, whatever their lack of factual basis in the visible world, attests to their credibility and to the interest they generate, as with pervasive rumours elsewhere. In analysing miracle or witchcraft stories it becomes difficult to distinguish between those elements that have at least some clear empirical basis in the material world and those that do not, or the mixture of fact and hypothesis that is always the work of imagination. The conditions of life in Africa over recent decades have been so volatile that even the most extraordinary or unlikely things can actually come true. Nelson Mandela really was elected president of South Africa in 1994, after twenty-seven years in prison during most of which he seemed to have no hope of release. This part of his career displays fascinating similarities with that of Simon Kimbangu, a prophet who, in March 1921, began to heal people in public, creating a popular movement in the Belgian Congo. Kimbangu was arrested by the Belgian colonial authorities just five months later and sentenced to death, later commuted to life imprisonment. He died in prison in 1951 after thirty years of incarceration, during which his reputation as a healer and divinely-inspired prophet only increased.[64] Today the church founded by his followers has many millions of adherents and is a member of the World Council of Churches. Almost as astonishing is the story of Laurent-Désiré Kabila, a small-time bandit chief and smuggler who played a minor role in the Congolese civil war of the 1960s and then dropped almost entirely from international view, before emerging from nowhere, as it were, to become president of Congo in 1997. More generally, Nigeria in the 1970s and 1980s saw a number of people, many of them virtually unknown and with no kind of traditional title to privilege or high office, grow unimaginably rich almost overnight on the wealth of the country's oil exports, as their fellow-countrymen could not fail to notice.[65] When such rags-to-riches stories are well-attested, it is small wonder if people believe that the most amazing changes of fortune are possible. Africans live in an environment that is volatile in the extreme.

People may make connections between categories of fact that to others might appear unusual, unlikely, or definitely mistaken. For example, whereas in the West scientists may debate whether AIDS is an old disease among animals that was transferred to humans, or whether it stems from another source, possibly even a misguided medical experiment,[66] in Africa it is quite often discussed in other ways. The disease may be seen as connected to various forms of wicked or wrong behaviour not on the part of the person who contracts it, but of others. In Zaire, for example, AIDS was rumoured to have been spread from centres of political power where people are accustomed to enriching themselves at the expense of others, both through plain corruption and by the manipulation of spiritual forces. Thus, AIDS was said actually to have originated in certain state organisations including the national bank.[67] AIDS is also seen, in Zambia for example, as caused by witchcraft.[68] In many parts of the continent the disease is thought to have been spread to Africa from the West, allegedly in order to depopulate Africa, and people hold all sorts of further beliefs related to this basic conviction. There are youths in Bamako, Mali, for instance, who claim 'to have heard on the radio that condoms...are actually infected with the AIDS virus and are being donated by agencies as part of a conspiracy by the West to control the Malian population'.[69]

In some parts of Africa where the AIDS virus is rampant, and where there is also a widespread (and not unjustified) perception that many of Africa's problems are manipulated by people outside the continent, funds given by charities to construct AIDS hospices or to help people smitten with the disease are interpreted as being intended to encourage Africans to die. After all—so the reasoning goes—if certain rich countries once colonised Africa in order to dispose of its resources as they wished, and if they continue to have great financial and political control, then is it not logical that Westerners should want to kill off Africans altogether?[70]

The primacy of oral communication in a continent with hundreds of languages has resulted in a high and widespread degree of linguistic accomplishment. Many Africans can speak several languages fluently, sometimes as many as seven or eight. People develop an extraordinary dexterity, often expressed in word-plays. Making puns out of sets of bureaucratic initials is a favourite pastime, used for amusement but also to puncture the pretensions of governments and international organisations. When AIDS was first publicised in the 1980s, often by international health agencies who coupled it with warnings about safe sex and birth control, many Africans refused to see it as a serious threat, considering that if the disease existed at all, its deadliness was being exaggerated by outside agencies and Western governments concerned to limit the number of Africans. A common joke was that AIDS stood for American Invention to Discourage Sex, or the French name for the disease, SIDA, as *Syndrome imaginaire pour décourager les amoureux*.

Alas, AIDS has been revealed to be every bit as deadly as the greatest pessimists foresaw. What has remained is a conviction, even among the well-educated, that it is in some sense part of a Western conspiracy to depopulate Africa. In Malawi and elsewhere, many Africans not only think that AIDS is somehow being spread from the West, but also make an association between the word 'AIDS' and the almost identical word 'aid', which also comes from the most developed countries.[71] This is an easy connection to make in any largely oral society, where *radio trottoir* is a prime source of information and where words are generally heard rather than read. This is more than a simple linguistic mistake: it reflects a profound ambiguity in the ideas people have about the true nature of the power that emanates from the West.

People all over the world worry about AIDS and may wonder how the pandemic started. The interest of *radio trottoir* stories from all over Africa is to show the different idioms in which people think about the causes of AIDS. Westerners are more likely to seek a medical or biological explanation, and Africans one that is spiritual or politically related. The latter view is not simply a reflection of ignorance about how AIDS is spread, which is now widely known throughout Africa, but rather is due to a different theory of causation. In other words, rumours that the AIDS epidemic is the result of a conspiracy by Western scientists and politicians reflect a debate not about how, but about *why*, AIDS appeared in the continent in the late twentieth century.

To suggest that the biomedical and what might be termed 'biospiritual' modes of explanation are credible in different societies is not to imply that both are equally valid in medical terms. Although some social scientists and cultural theorists claim that theories even in natural sciences such as biology or physics are simply ideological constructs,[72] we do not hold such a point of view, preferring to believe that there are such things as facts and that some scientific theories are of universal validity.[73] There are two corollaries to this, however. The first is that the precise manner in which established facts are compiled and evaluated is a subjective process, which in advanced industrial countries, far more than in Africa, is entrusted to experts whose opinions carry great authority with the general public. These days, in North Atlantic countries especially, the experts whose job is to pronounce on what is scientifically true or false are unlikely to couch their explanations in a religious idiom. The second corollary is that, in Africa, certain facts of universal application may actually be known to rather few people, leaving the rest of the population to manufacture their own theories from the limited stock of facts at their disposal. This was the case, certainly until quite recently, in those African countries whose governments at first did so little to inform their publics of the causes of AIDS, leaving people with only a few elements from which to form usable theories as to the cause of the disease.

Notwithstanding these differences, interesting similarities between scientific and non-scientific forms of explanation remain. Even in countries where medical discourse is dominated by a technical language of cause and effect concerning viruses or other micro-organisms, there is a detectable popular tendency to connect certain forms of illness with morality, as though they were a punishment. AIDS is an obvious example, since it is spread largely through sexual contact, and is therefore easily equated with certain styles of sexual behaviour.

Furthermore, powerful metaphors drawn from disease may be transferred to other sectors. One American media analyst cites the example of how the notion of a newly-identified virus able to destroy human flesh was taken up by journalists as a striking image and then applied to the ebola virus when it emerged in central Africa. Since then, the epithet 'flesh-eating' has become a favourite of the US media, applied for example to computer viruses.[74]

The way in which information is fitted into culturally known patterns, authenticated and propagated is a central element of governance in any society. The information in circulation is always related not only to what-ever philosophical or theological views are generally accepted within a society, but also to the opinions and interests of the relevant authorities and the institutional forms these assume. These change over time. Most Africans daily hear, sometimes read, and often repeat stories that are reli-gious inasmuch as they concern supposed interactions with an invisible world. These might feature powerful amulets, the use of mystical forces for material purposes, miracles and witchcraft. People keep an open mind about such stories, but since they overwhelmingly believe that the invisible world exists and affects their lives, they are also prepared to believe that communication with it is possible. Moreover, stories of interactions between humans and spirits circulate in a context in which it is often impossible to say for sure whether a particular item of information is true or false. One has to take this pervasive atmosphere into account as a prelude to a study of more particular aspects of religious belief and the political implications thereof, as the next chapter does by looking at the nature of the spirit world in Africa.

We have already described how many aspects of social and political life in Africa have historically been expressed in a spirit idiom. In such a world-view, life-enhancing relationships depend on effective communica-tion with invisible beings with names and individual personalities, just like living people. The relationship between a woman and her children, a man and his ancestors, a farmer and the soil, are all deemed to be governed by such spirits. So much of what people do, everywhere in the world, is based on products of the mind that are themselves invisible but in which they believe. They are all mental constructs.[75]

# 3

# SPIRITS

*Evangelist Mukendi's visit to the underworld*

One of the many popular pamphlets that circulate widely in Africa is a memoir by Evangelist Mukendi, a born-again preacher from the former Zaire, today the Democratic Republic of Congo. According to his own account, Mukendi was weaned by a mermaid and pledged to Satan by his father, a witch.[1]

*Snatched from Satan's Claws*[2] is the title of a short book in which Mukendi relates the story of his visits to the place where witches are believed to live, which, he writes, is reached by going under water. In this underworld, he claims, there are institutions created and used by witches, including universities and an international airport directly underneath the city of Kinshasa, the capital of Congo. This is not exceptional because, he maintains, 'every town or village in the world has some hidden activities under the water nearby'. It is in these underwater locations that the spirits of people who in life were controlled by fallen angels congregate and communicate with the 'witch doctors, sorcerers, and magicians' who still live on earth. In their underwater dwellings, these agents of the devil feast on human flesh. They promote 'sorcerers, magicians and witch doctors' to high positions in the towns above ground, in the visible world. Underground, they manufacture diabolic objects including 'cars, clothes, perfumes, money, radios and television sets' which they peddle on earth to try to 'distort and destroy the lives of those who purchase such items'. There are even underground scientists employed by the fallen angels. Mukendi claims to know all this on the basis of personal experience. The ultimate purpose of all this underground activity is 'to steal, kill and destroy'.

According to Mukendi, some major underground cities are located in Congo, one near the Inga dam and another near Matadi. (The Inga dam is an enormous dam in the Congo river, notorious as a failed 'white elephant' development project; Matadi is the country's seaport, located at the mouth of the river.) Here, there are diabolical underground conference centres 'where many decisions affecting the countries and continent of Africa are effected'. Mukendi claims that these places are close to an underground highway to other parts of Congo and to the other side of the Atlantic Ocean in America. There is even a 'very busy international airport for all sorts of sorcerers and magicians, flying in and out'. Some of the travellers there are described as 'magicians', being witches who transform themselves into white people:

> These false white persons will then get out of their 'planes' and enter into bigger ones awaiting at Mukamba Lake [the international sorcerers' airport] destined to Europe, America or any other countries of the world. Their purpose is to acquire jobs in those countries posing as specialists or expatriates, to earn big salaries to be used for the international organization of sorcerers of the world.[3]

Mukendi claims to have taken part in such trips while he was still a witch. To judge from his personal account, Mukendi is convinced that the visible world is intimately connected to an underground domain of evil which contains the same features as the material world, but in malign forms that are inversions or perversions of their visible representations.

Mukendi's book is just one example of an abundant African popular genre on human involvement in the spirit world. Many readers of such an account may conclude that these are bizarre and puzzling tales that hardly merit serious attention, even if the authors of such texts believe that they are recounting 'true' stories or discussing 'real' occurrences. In our book, we take these authors' personal experiences and the beliefs on which they appear to be based as the starting point for our inquiry. Religious ideologies, after all, deserve to be examined just as much as secular ideologies, since both represent ways in which people view the world.

The need to study the specific content of religious beliefs was long ago noted by Clifford Geertz, the doyen of American anthropologists. The 'anthropological study of religion', he wrote nearly forty years ago, is 'a two-stage operation: first, an analysis of the system of meanings embodied in the symbols which make up the religion proper, and, second, the relating of these systems to social-structural and psychological processes.' Geertz went on to express his 'dissatisfaction with so much of contemporary social anthropological work in religion' at the time he was writing, not because it concerned itself with the second of these two stages, but because 'it neglects the first, and in so doing takes for granted what most needs to be elucidated'.[4] Accordingly, unlikely as texts such as Mukendi's may seem, they should be considered first in the terms that their authors apparently intend them to be understood: as a true story, written to be believed. It takes us back to the vital question discussed earlier, namely the nature of reality as considered in Africa and other areas of the globe where people's material and spiritual worlds merge.

Mukendi clearly does not regard the spirit world as a metaphor for the 'real' or visible world, but as an integral part of reality, in fact its most important part, since this is where the vital decisions are taken that affect people's lives. No wonder, then, that it is of great importance to individuals to try to influence the decision-making process through interaction with the spirit world. Relations with the latter are an extension of the social fabric into the realm of the invisible. Many Africans today who continue to hold beliefs derived from their traditional cosmologies apply these to everyday life even when they live in cities and work in the civil service or business sector.[5] Religious world-views do not necessarily diminish with formal education.

Thus, religious belief, although not universal in Africa inasmuch as the continent has its own share of professed atheists and other non-believers, operates at every level of society. Popular priests and prophets work in areas where the poor live, while the rich may have their own spiritual advisors. Some religious specialists minister to both the rich and the poor. Plural religious allegiance is common, with individuals frequenting several religious communities at once or practising rituals regarded in the West as belonging to different or competing systems of belief, such as Christianity and Islam, or Christianity and 'traditional' religion. If, as many Africans believe, both human suffering and human prosperity have their origins in relations with the spirit world, cultivating that relationship assumes great importance. At times this may become a costly and time-consuming business since, as with all social relations, one has to invest in the maintainance of spiritual connections if they are to remain sound.

## The spirit world

The invisible world that most Africans believe to exist may be inhabited by all kinds of invisible beings, but spirits of various sorts undoubtedly hold a prominent place in it. As described by Mukendi in his account but also more generally, the spirit world resembles the visible world, and is deemed to have many of its characteristics. According to him it has universities, scientists, an airport, and all the other features of a modern city, and the underworld's inhabitants can even infiltrate international organisations. The invisible world is described by Mukendi as peopled with 'witches', who have their own government, organised as in the visible world, except that those in charge are women. In this and many other respects, the invisible world is a mirror of the visible one, an accurate reflection except that everything is the wrong way round. Since Mukendi's story is a treatise on evil, the striking prominence of women in the world beneath the waters suggests that they are considered potential agents of the devil, a reminder of the connection often made between women and witchcraft. This is a subject to which we will return.[6]

That access to the underworld is via water is one of several features of Mukendi's account that has a clear resemblance to older traditions, recorded over a long period throughout the area of central Africa inhabited by the Bakongo people who live in parts of the modern republics of Congo-Kinshasa, Congo-Brazzaville and Angola.[7] The figure of the mermaid or female water-spirit is a very familar one that is itself a subject of popular literature and, increasingly, of academic study too. In fact, the idea that waters contain the entrance to the spirit world is widespread throughout coastal areas of West and central Africa and into southern Africa, transcending ethnic groups.[8] It is a good example of one of those African religious traditions current over very large areas that were mentioned in chapter one. In this respect Mukendi's story is of a type well-known to many people and resonates with a variety of ideas in wider circulation.

One of the most remarkable religious developments in the continent today is that of Christian revivalist movements, often referred to as neo-pentecostal or charismatic movements, whose most notable feature is a belief in the active presence of the Holy Spirit. Such movements can be situated in the long tradition of African independent churches that has proved so vital over the years.[9] Nor is such a spirit-oriented world-view exclusive to independent churches. It is also reflected in the growing influence of charismatic movements within the former mission churches,[10] and is present in the Sufi tradition of Islam that is long-established in Africa. In short, many of the numerous religious movements and organisations flourishing in Africa show the same propensity towards a belief in the existence of distinct spirits, conceived of as entitites that are invisible yet real. In African religious traditions, the representation of spirits as real beings emphasises the personal rather than the metaphorical aspect of relationships between the visible and the invisible worlds. In light of this widespread tendency to consider spirits as individual beings with a personal identity, spirituality is not an abstraction, of interest only to theologians and philosophers, but becomes a power within the reach of all. Similar ideas are current in many other parts of the world. In the West, too, people sometimes personalise invisible forces by giving names to, and talking about, them as if they were people with personalities, such as when they discuss recent climate changes with reference to an invisible force called El Niño, or when they give personal names to hurricanes. The personalisation of whatever invisible powers people believe to exist is characteristic of a spirit idiom.

Perhaps the best way to begin an exploration of the spirit world is through the opinions of one of the most articulate African experts on the matter—Emmanuel Milingo, former Catholic Archbishop of Lusaka and later a highly controversial Vatican official. In Africa he is most famous as a Christian healer.[11] Milingo's formal religious education consisted of sixteen years of orthodox Catholic training in church schools and seminaries, originally in Africa and later in Europe, almost exclusively at the hands of white missionaries. His interest in popular views of the spirit world arose only after he had been appointed archbishop of one of Africa's major cities, Zambia's capital, when he came into close contact with parishioners who consulted him about various forms of sickness that they ascribed to evil spirits. These were problems for which his training had not prepared him. So, after a period of reflection, Milingo decided to familiarise himself with the spiritual beliefs of his fellow-Zambians. Since then he has written numerous books and pamphlets that reflect not only his extensive study of the subject, but above all his intense interaction with people who believe themselves to be possessed by spirits. As an orthodox Catholic, Milingo was intent on finding a way to reconcile this new knowledge with conventional Catholic dogma. This led him to contextualise some of the theological insights of the Catholic Church, notably concerning the Holy Spirit, not for academic purposes but in order to help people who believed themselves to be affected by evil spirits. He concluded that the Church, intent on spreading a Western view of Christianity via its missionaries, had made no effort to understand the spiritual beliefs and needs of Africans, and in particular the growing tendency to ascribe sickness and other problems to the presence of evil spirits. For many Zambians, Milingo realised, the spirit idiom serves as a framework of explanation for illness, adversity and other forms of misfortune, experienced as a rupture in the relationship between the human and the spirit worlds. Traditionally, in order to restore balance, a healer must identify which spirit is causing the disturbance and needs to be propitiated. Milingo decided that he could invoke the power of the Holy Spirit to cure his patients by liberating them from evil spirits. It was this which made him wildly popular as a healer in Zambia, from where his fame spread throughout Africa and other parts of the world.

Although African traditional religions have always taken account of the presence of troublesome spirits, older techniques for dealing with these by exorcising or neutralising them have generally ceased to be effective for reasons connected with changes in the nature of religion in Africa generally. As we saw in chapter one, African traditional religions are oral in origin and in character and have no written doctrine. In the past, they ascribed to the spiritual powers of the invisible world a morally neutral character, instead of considering them intrinsically good or evil. Rather, the moral nature of spirits traditionally depends on the nature of the relationship between human beings and the spirit world with which they interact.[12] People may seek good offices from a spirit, such as to protect themselves, or malevolent services, in order to harm others. For a stable life, they need a good relationship with the spirit world, which requires regular attention, as do all social relations. If the relationship is well maintained the spirits will be content and placid; if not, they will attract attention to themselves by fomenting trouble.[13]

Hence, whereas people once considered spirits to be morally neutral forces that could be used for particular purposes in a form of negotiation between the spirit and the person interacting with it, many have come to see traditional spirits as being harmful by nature. As a result, traditional techniques for dealing with spirits have become less effective. This was a gap that Archbishop Milingo proposed to fill. For him, as for the thousands of people who seek his help, it is self-evident that the spirit world really exists, and this forms the basis for all his healing activities. But the healing ministry Milingo developed in Africa brought him into trouble with his superiors in Rome, creating a controversy that has never been resolved. In the view of his superiors in the Catholic hierarchy, Milingo is confusing two worlds—Christian and traditional—that are fundamentally different and should be kept apart. They consider African ideas about the spirit world to be a form of superstition out of tune with modern times, a view no doubt related to the fact that many Vatican officials are themselves Europeans and North Americans.

Milingo has set out his ideas in a series of writings that incorporate insights from the traditional spirit world of Zambians. According to him, the cosmos consists of essentially three parts.[14] These are the earth, the dwelling-place of human beings, which is the visible world; the world in-between, as Milingo consistently calls the spirit world, where both good and evil spirits abide; and the heavens or 'final world' where God resides. Although the cosmos is divided into three distinct parts, it remains an integral whole where the different categories of beings live in constant communion. Vital to Milingo's representation of the cosmos is the ability of humans to communicate with the spirit world, which they do through the world in-between, the meeting-place for the two other spheres that brings the world 'below' and the world 'above' together. Milingo calls it a 'world of transformation',[15] somewhere between heaven and earth, where the people from heaven can sample the atmosphere of the earth and vice versa. It is in this world in-between that the final decisions are taken governing the fate of individual people.

It is interesting to note that Milingo's view of the cosmos, heavily influenced by Catholic theology as well as by the views of his Zambian informants, shows some similarities to that contained in the story told by Evangelist Mukendi, quoted above. Both contain the idea that decisions affecting life on earth are made outside the visible sphere of the cosmos, reflecting the relative importance that many Africans attribute to the spirit world. From this it also follows that it is of the greatest importance for people to have some form of effective communication with this invisible world, since it is believed to be the place where the key life-affecting decisions are made. It is also useful to consider the parallel between the idea of a tripartite cosmos and the philosophical insight that the realm of the imagination may be considered as the meeting-place of the 'real' and the 'unreal'. As we have noted, products of the imagination are not necessarily untrue or unreal.[16] Thus, one way of rendering the resemblance between these statements, couched in religious and philosophical terms respectively, is to say that in much African religious thought, the real and the unreal merge in a product of the imagination known as the spirit world.

Ideas about the spirit world similar to those put forward by Milingo and Mukendi are widely shared in all parts of the continent, as is clear from the writings of various African intellectuals, including novelists as well as academics.[17] The same is also apparent from the widespread belief in divination and other techniques for influencing decisions that are believed to be made in the spirit world. Many of Nigeria's 120 million people, for example, at every level of society, believe that their 'real' destination in life is known in the spirit world. Underlying this idea is a notion that each person has his or her origin in the spirit world, but loses any memory of it at birth in the material world. The direction of one's life therefore has to be literally dis-covered if it is to stay on course. This is commonly done through divination or other techniques that, in the hands of an expert, are thought to reveal what the spirits hold in store.[18] Divination is not a passive consultation to discover what the spirits have decided about an individual fate, but is a process of active intervention, intended to shape the course of life through communication between the human and the spirit worlds. Just as ordinary people think it necessary to keep their lives on course, so too do rich and powerful ones, for whom it is important to keep the good fortune that is theirs. Many politicians, in constant need of power, consult spiritual experts regularly. Requiring more than usual power, they seek spiritual advice from experts with more than ordinary abilities.

Many societies throughout the world accord some degree of recognition to seers or other persons believed to have an ability to communicate effectively with the spirit world and thus to discover the proper path of an individual life. While purported seers also exist in modern Western countries (and, famously, President Ronald Reagan allowed his meetings schedule to be influenced by astrology[19]), their nearest functional equivalent in the West is probably in the profession of psychiatry. The British psychoanalyst Donald Winnicott maintained that 'no human being is free from the strain of relating inner and outer reality', and that relief is provided by an intermediate area of experience, in which both art and religion have their roots.[20] This is a description that could equally be applied to aspects of spiritual communication common in Africa.

## Communication with the spirit world

People who believe in a spirit world, logically enough, may communicate with it. This they may do through prayer or divination and other forms of ritual, but also through dreams and visions or spirit possession. Religious behaviour aiming at interaction with a spirit world can easily acquire political significance, as many studies have shown. Spirit possession, considered, with shamanism, to be one of 'the two grand anthropological categories for human-spiritual relations',[21] is a particularly important characteristic of religious experience in Africa, notably in traditional religions. It is worth studying in some detail since it reveals many of the characteristics of the spirits that religious believers perceive to exist, and shows how communication with the spirit world may take place. It may be helpful to state at the outset that in many parts of the world spirit possession is not regarded as intrinsically harmful or shameful, as we shall discuss below. Modern research has demonstrated that possession trance can be used as a positive force, similar in some respects to psychotherapy.[22]

Spirit possession, then, is a religious term expressing the belief that a person who shows certain symptoms has been taken possession of by an invisible being deemed to have effective powers.[23] This may be explained by recourse to a helpful analogy suggested by the anthropologist Felicitas

Goodman, who refers to it as the 'soul theory'.[24] A human being may be
likened to a car with a driver. In the analogy, the human body is the car
and the driver the soul. The soul activates the body just as the driver puts
the car into motion. On occasion, the owner may give the keys to someone else, who owns no car and may drive her friend's car for a while. So,
in spirit possession, the soul that normally dwells in a given human body is
temporarily displaced by a spirit that comes in from outside and directs it
for a while, like an unfamiliar driver taking over the controls. This may be
the spirit of an ancestor, a deity, or even an animal.

Spirit possession may be—and often is, in fact—displayed in quite spectacular behaviour marked by dissociation and attended by rather vehe-
ment and uncontrolled movements of the body. Such behaviour can be
described as a form of possession trance. To be more precise, it is characteristic of hyperkinetic trance, to be distinguished from the hypokinetic or
still type of trance known in mysticism. Both are universal human potentialities, because people all over the world share the same neurobiological
constitution. Altered states of consciousness—to use the scientific term—
can be produced by a wide variety of techniques and may appear in almost
any type of setting. There is an optimal range of so-called 'exteroceptive
stimulation' (that is, the absorption of external stimuli) necessary to maintain normal waking consciousness. Levels above and below this range are
conducive to the production of altered states of consciousness.[25] Whether
or not these human potentialities will be used, in what way and to what
degree, depends largely on the cultural mechanisms at work. In a culture
or society where possession trance is a normal and accepted phenomenon,
and where possession behaviour is part of a social role, trance may easily
be induced. People expect it to happen, and so it does.[26]

In African traditional religions, where the more spectacular form of
hyperkinetic trance is quite common, spirit possession is an important process that opens up a field of communication with a world beyond ordinary
human experience, believed to be inhabited by invisible beings that can
influence the lives of their human counterparts for good or ill. In other
words, spirit possession is a religious concept with an ambivalent content
in African traditional religions in the sense that the possessing spirit may
be thought of as both good and evil by nature. Traditionally, constructive
types of possession are channelled by spirit mediums, who thereby acquire
prestige. When mediums become vehicles for a possessing spirit, they are
no longer considered to be their real selves. In such cases, in the view of
believers, during possession, the possessed person *becomes* the spirit; or, to
put it the other way round, the spirit assumes human form. Thus, we may

make yet further useful distinctions, such as between possession cases in which people aim at the permanent expulsion of an undesirable spirit through some form of exorcism, and those in which they aim to establish a lasting relationship with the possessing spirit by accommodating it. In the second of these two cases, a person may become a recognized spirit medium, able to communicate between the spirit and the human world. Both types of possession are known in Africa: that is, possession by a desirable spirit accommodated through mediumship, and possession by spirits that cause harm and have to be expelled by exorcism.

Belief in spirit possession is widespread. One study in the 1970s found that in a sample of 488 societies in all parts of the world, 437, or 90 per cent, had some form of institutionalised, culturally patterned form of altered states of consciousness.[27] The author of this study used these statistics to argue that altered states of consciousness are a major aspect of human behaviour based on a universal neurobiological capacity, and that they have a significant impact on the functioning of societies. It appeared that 251, or 52 per cent, of the sample of 488 societies associated altered states of consciousness with possession by spirits[28] or, in other words, that just over half of the sample interpreted the experience in religious terms. In sub-Saharan Africa spirit possession was identified in 66 per cent of the sample societies. Unlike in most Western societies, in Africa there is normally no negative connotation attached to spirit possession, unless it is by evil spirits. It is notable that belief in possession by evil spirits is increasing rapidly in Africa, for reasons we will examine in due course. In other cases, possession is seen as desirable and may even be intentionally induced.

Westerners who travel to Africa and who witness spirit possession at first hand often feel disturbed by a phenomenon they find difficult to understand and that they are inclined to see as one more obstacle on the road to economic progress and development. Quite apart from the idea of possession, the entire concept of a spirit world hardly fits into the secular frame of mind of most Western expatriates in Africa, whether they are business people, development workers, academics, or even religious practitioners themselves. They sometimes assume that possessed individuals are suffering from mental illness, despite the lack of consensus among psychiatrists about what exactly that may be.[29] This viewpoint has long been adopted by many Western churches, which tend to qualify manifestations of spirit possession as a form of hysteria. However, spirit-oriented belief and behaviour are increasing worldwide, including in the Western world. The clearest evidence of this is the striking growth all over the world of pentecostalism and other charismatic movements.[30]

Since the Enlightenment, cultural mechanisms operating in most Western countries have led over the centuries to the rigorous suppression of these human potentialities. Yet there are signs of a resurgence in the West of trance experiences, both in the religious sphere but also, most especially, in a secular setting. In the 1970s, there was a clear growth in interest in Western universities in altered states of consciousness, which has resulted in some valuable studies. No doubt this academic interest was sparked partly by the alternative approach that was fashionable at the time to understanding reality other than in terms of Western rationality. Since then, interest in the subject may have declined in university departments, but there is every sign that it has been spreading in various forms more broadly throughout Western societies.[31] Churches in Europe and North America have witnessed a significant degree of charismatic renewal,[32] while outside the Christian context there has been a rise in the popularity of New Age spirit beliefs and forms of spiritual healing. Far more striking, though, is the upsurge of trance behaviour in Western countries that is not of a religious nature. A good example is the rave parties that are now massively popular with young people, all-night parties in which hours of dancing to rhythmic music, often accompanied by light-shows and the consumption of drugs, bring dancers into a state of trance and euphoria in which hunger and fatigue disappear. It is not for nothing that the most popular rave drug is called Ecstasy. The main difference between the type of trance achieved by an African believer and a European raver is in the attribution of the state of mind to spiritual beings by the first and not by the second.

Altered states of consciousness may serve different functions, both adaptive and maladaptive. 'Adaptive' altered states of consciousness refer to conditions that enable the individual to acquire new knowledge or experience, to express psychic tensions or relieve conflict without danger to himself or herself or others, and to function more adequately and constructively in society. This constructive type of possession can have important functions both for individuals and for societies. Adaptive altered states of consciousness have played a major role in various healing arts and practices throughout history and have been employed for almost every conceivable aspect of therapy. They are also used to acquire new knowledge, inspiration or experience. Prophetic states, mystical and transcendental experiences, and divination are all examples. Such states are often believed to impart a type of knowledge that can not be gained during waking consciousness.[33] 'Maladaptive' states may be regarded as mental conditions that serve no constructive purpose and that may endanger the individual or hamper his functioning in society. There are many such maladaptive expressions or uses of altered states of consciousness. One potentially dangerous use involves their calculated production for eliciting confessions, changing attitudes, brainwashing, and controlling behaviour.[34]

## The politics of possession

The preceding categorisation may also be applied to the use of memory, which is closely linked to the concept of spirit possession in several ways. Cases where a person is believed to be possessed by an ancestor spirit— whose memory is thus publicly recalled—can assume considerable political importance, for example when someone claims possession by the spirit of a deceased king from a dynasty rivalling the one currently in power. People so possessed may have no conscious memory of their performance while in trance, since it is not they who are thought to have spoken but the spirit, for whom they have simply acted as the vehicle. This form of amnesia absolves spirit mediums from blame for their pronouncements, which are attributed to the possessing spirit. This gives spirit possession obvious value as a political strategem, and there is a rich literature showing how possession trance may thus acquire importance as a form of political contestation.[35]

Spirit possession has been analysed in many ways, most recently by scholars who emphasise its aesthetic dimension as part of a cultural performance. It is 'a profound religious drama', which is regarded by those who experience it as 'real'.[36] For present purposes, however, we are most interested in the political aspect of spirit possession. A helpful model for understanding the politics of possession has been suggested by the British anthropologist I. M. Lewis,[37] whose most important work on this was originally published in 1971 and updated in a new edition in 1989.[38] Recent studies have refined some of Lewis's ideas concerning the motivation of possessed women,[39] while other anthropologists have conveyed the importance of spirit possession in specific locations, without, however, proposing any new general theory of possession.[40] Lewis's model thus remains the most useful guide to understanding the politics of spirit possession in broad terms.

Lewis's main inquiry concerns the relationship between the dominant type of possession and the type of society in which it occurs. He focuses on the way in which spirit possession can be used as an instrument of power by looking at why people become possessed. He argues that people 'use' spirit possession as a means either to consolidate power and the relationships through which it is articulated, or to try to alter these relations. In the former, where spirit possession legitimises existing power, we may speak of 'central possession', in which the possessing spirits hold a central position in a belief system and serve to uphold and sustain the prevailing public morality. They do so through their chosen instruments, the spirit mediums or other religious specialists who represent divine authority among ordinary people. Obviously, there cannot be very many such mediums because of the claims to power that go with the job. Lewis contrasts central possession with 'peripheral' possession, by which he means cases where spirit possession is used by subaltern or marginalised people to try to change existing power relations for their own benefit. It differs from central possession because peripheral possession provides, in principle, a way that is open to everybody, and not just to a few selected mediums. It is usually marginal or alien spirits that in such cases are believed to take possession of a person—spirits that play no immediate part in the upholding of public morality. In terms of power, peripheral possession may be seen as an attempt to improve one's lot within the margins of a social system. The effect may be a temporary relief from feelings of oppression or a modest rise in status.[41]

Central possession, then, is a way to power, but so too is peripheral spirit possession, although it concerns a different group of people, employing different tactics. Whereas central possession is generally used by men who perform their role in the centre of society, peripheral possession is often a women's affair that takes place on the margins. Lewis speaks in this connection of the 'sex-war',[42] in which women resort, so to speak, to a peripheral type of possession in an attempt to change the balance of power. Hence, peripheral possession cults, too, constitute a way to more power and higher status. But it is a path that comes to a dead end long before, or far away from, the centre of power. As in central possession cults, the way usually begins in misery and suffering, often in the form of illness, believed to be caused by the possessing spirit. The characteristics ascribed to such a spirit are in fact similar to the social characteristics of the possessed. Both are marginal beings, in the spirit and the human worlds respectively. However, the possessed is able to 'use' her suffering as a means to improve her situation. As a vehicle for the spirit, she is allowed to act in ways, and to make demands, that would not normally be admitted.

It is in ways like these that political relationships can be affected by the spirit world. A good example of the political dynamics of spirit possession is found among the traditional practice of the Zezuru Shona of Zimbabwe, where a remarkable shift has taken place in the possession pattern, with central possession becoming peripheral and vice versa.[43] It is a shift that has happened among the Zezuru on more than one occasion, from precolonial days, through colonial times, to the period of white settler government after the Unilateral Declaration of Independence (UDI) in 1965. In precolonial times Zezuru central mediumship was almost exclusively a male affair, but during the colonial period many mediums left the profession in order to become teachers and evangelists and affirmed their social and political positions through these new avenues. As a result their former roles were now taken by women. The social changes taking place in the colonial period affected the traditional religious structure in such a way that the originally central possession cult became increasingly peripheral. That is, the *makombwe* ancestors (those whose sphere of influence and authority goes beyond that of the family ancestors) began to lose their central position as upholders of public morality and increasingly were seen as peripheral spirits that cause illness or other misery for no particular reason. At the time of UDI this trend radically changed again, although not for long. The Rhodesian whites' rejection of black majority rule and the reaction against this led to a revaluation of precolonial practices, including in traditional culture and religion, and to a widespread repudiation of many European ideas and practices, particularly in Christianity. As a result, traditional religion and mediumship became popular again and the number of male mediums increased dramatically. Interestingly, they included many evangelists.

The terms 'central' and 'peripheral' possession, then, have been chosen on account of the relative position of the possessed in a total network of social relations. The sociological functions of spirit possession, although by no means the only important aspects, provide a particularly useful angle for the analysis of the political role of possession cults today. Another scholar, Erika Bourguignon, supports this line of argument by introducing the concepts of 'micro-change' and 'macro-change' with regard to spirit possession. These terms refer respectively to types of change at the individual and the collective levels, or in the personal and structural spheres, and indicate the connection between the dominant type of possession and the type of society in which it occurs.[44] Her conclusion is that possession trance leads to a modification in the social position of the afflicted individual ('micro-change'), but not to a restructuring of society ('macro-change'). In this respect Bourguignon's concept of possession trance conforms to Lewis's concept of peripheral possession. In both cases, spirit possession is seen as an indirect strategy that may bring relief to the individual but is yet a device within the existing social pattern and, therefore, may be considered conservative by nature.

Trance behaviour is to a considerable degree learned behaviour. It is a type of expression that takes place in a social setting where those present channel the trance into the direction they desire through their reactions. Individual behaviour evolves in social settings, and the one has an effect on the other. By the same token, the general absence of possession trance in modern Western societies led to its effective disappearance for most of the twentieth century. We noted in an earlier chapter the observation by a prominent American journalist in 1922 that his countrymen were living in what he called a 'pseudo-environment', in which they received information about the world indirectly, via mass media.[45] This made certain forms of direct experience unusual, undesirable and even literally unthinkable. However, the place of trance experiences in mainstream Western societies has to be reassessed as a result of the introduction of hallucinogenic drugs that open the possibility of undergoing trance simply by ingesting a pill or administering an injection. This was experienced as a liberation by Aldous Huxley,[46] who had himself injected with LSD as he lay on his death-bed. The use of consciousness-altering drugs has now become a popular social activity among many young Europeans and Americans, in what may be interpreted as a rejection of a long tradition of suppressing certain forms of direct experience.

This short summary of spirit possession helps in understanding the account of a trip to the underworld that opened this chapter. In it, Mukendi describes himself as the son of traditional religious practitioners, and he seems to have learned from them techniques for entering into trance and experiencing a world outside everyday perception. In societies where spirit possession and possession trance are valued, they take on distinct cultural forms and are subject to standard forms of description. Mukendi's story is presented in a form instantly recognisable to many people in Africa, who are familiar with representations of the spirit world as an underworld, today often considered as a lair of evil by born-again Christians especially. At some stage, perhaps at a time of illness or through an experience of having travelled far into the spirit world, Mukendi underwent a crisis of conscience. This he experienced as a conversion to the Christian God through the power of the Holy Spirit. Indeed, in the West too it is not unknown for people who have been close to clinical death to describe their out-of-body sensations, rather like an astronaut who has been to outer space and returned to tell the tale. Experiences of this sort often lead to religious belief. In Mukendi's case, he came to the conclusion that, in retrospect, during his earlier life he had been acting as an agent of Satan. All the features of the spirit-world that he had learned from his childhood he now saw as thoroughly evil by nature.

## The pathology of the spirit world

As the cases of Mukendi and Milingo demonstrate, a great range of physical, psychological and spiritual ailments may be attributed by Africans to the presence of evil spirits. There are sharply differing views on how to react to evil spirits, with a new generation of neo-pentecostal Christians regarding traditional forms of propitiation as absolutely unacceptable. Hence the great interest today in the practice of exorcism in many of the new churches. This is a subject on which more will be said in due course.[47]

Much of the recent literature on religion in Africa suggests that belief in evil spirits has become so common as to lead to a general preoccupation with evil in the broadest sense. Evidence of this can be inferred from the tracts sold all over Africa, in markets and on street-corners, describing experiences of evil like Mukendi's descent into the underworld, or recommending methods of self-protection. People ascribe to evil spirits such typically modern problems as unemployment, lack of money, marital strife, and so on.[48] They realise well enough that the immediate cause of losing a job may be a new management or a downturn in the economy, but these are not regarded as sufficient explanations. Why these misfortunes should occur at a particular juncture, creating a sense of despair felt as a force within, is often explained as the consequence of an evil spirit dwelling inside a person.

The personification of evil as an identifiable being is not unique to Africa. Winston Churchill used to refer to a mood of despair that came upon him from time to time, almost immobilising him, as 'Black Dog'. A similar attribution of misfortune to a living being, perceived as having a personality of its own, can be found in the history of most religions. In the West, however, under the modern influences of rationalism, individuality and consciousness of the self, combined with a general increase in the comfort and predictability of life for the wealthiest part of the world's people, the concept of evil has become increasingly less tangible and has been reduced to little more than a metaphor. It is interesting to see, however, how it may be revived under certain conditions. An illuminating example is the murder in May 2002 of the Dutch politician Pim Fortuyn, which, according to press and public in the Netherlands, was the result of his 'demonisation', meaning his representation as the living epitome of evil. In this case the final responsibility for his death was attributed to those rival politicians and other critics who are held to have created a climate in which it became conceivable that society had to be freed of the 'demon' named Fortuyn, if necessary by killing his spirit. A study of a moral panic concerning satanic rituals of child abuse in 1980s Britain also suggests how, even in societies that are highly secular in many respects, potent mechanisms may still exist for identifying certain people as agents of an evil force with an individual name and personality.[49] The point of interest in these comparisons is the underlying belief in a wide range of societies in evil forces that may become personalised if and when a social need arises. From such a perspective the personification of evil apparently meets the need of a great variety of people to come to grips with the 'enemy', to actually locate and expel him. Rather more common practices, such as the burning of effigies during public demonstrations, are similar manifestations of this belief.

With Africa today being such a troubled continent in so many respects, people often understand their difficulties as the result of a general presence of evil reflected at every level, from the problems of daily life to a cosmic force that can affect the whole of society. This pervasive concern seems one important reason for the attractiveness of Islamic and Christian revival movements that have recently become an object of Western academic scrutiny, and for the popularity of exorcism as a religious practice. The exclusive monotheism of orthodox Christianity and Islam has had an important effect on people's perceptions of the moral qualities of traditional spirits, including some that have been identified and addressed by specific names for many generations but whose original characteristics have been radically altered. As is well known, the core doctrines of orthodox Christianity and Islam have been recorded in sacred books that are considered by believers to be the product of divine revelation and to have binding authority. This gives both these religions a tendency towards exclusiveness in the sense that those who do not adhere to the doctrine recorded in the sacred texts are beyond the pale, at least by implication. One of the effects of the spread of Christianity and Islam with their dualistic world-views has been to demonise the traditional spirit world, all the more so as modern mass media have brought in new theological views from the United States and the Middle East. This tendency towards exclusion, intrinsic to monotheistic religions based on sacred scripture, has been reinforced in the last couple of centuries in Africa by reform movements aiming to win new adherents or to impose a stricter code of worship on those who already profess. Christian missionaries from Europe and other continents have been very active in Africa, while some Muslim areas have undergone waves of reform inspired by ideas from the Arab world over roughly the same period. Today, continuing efforts at renewal in Christianity and Islam are led by both Africans and non-Africans, frequently leading to the emergence of revivalist movements that are often referred to as fundamentalist. Successive waves of conversion, reform and revivalism that aim to promote more exclusive forms of belief and worship have also had a number of important by-products that have not often been noticed. For example, they have caused some adherents of traditional religions to conceive of their own belief in a more exclusive manner and to identify a doctrine where none previously existed, such as in the Mungiki movement among Kenya's Gikuyu people.[50] The introduction of literacy, often through religious education, has enabled adherents of traditional religions to create quasi-sacred texts of their own.

Hence, in all of Africa's major religious traditions—traditional, Muslim and Christian—there has been a change in the nature of the relationship between the human and the spirit worlds, with a tendency for certain spirits to become regarded as inherently evil. As a result, they can no longer be accommodated. What was previously dependent on the nature of the relationship between person and spirit, and therefore the responsibility of the human agent, has evolved into a view of the intrinsic nature of a particular spirit.

## Spirits and politicians

Where communication with a spirit world is common, it easily becomes subject to control by individuals or institutions whose prestige derives from the authority they are thought to have over access to the invisible world. While control of this interaction is likely to be the task of religious specialists, it is also a political resource inasmuch as it may give such experts a degree of influence over aspects of material life. This was generally the case in Africa before colonial times.

Thus, because they concern the invisible world that is thought to underpin the visible one, the story of Evangelist Mukendi's trips to the spirit world and many other descriptions of the same type are at least implicitly political in nature. This does not mean that stories like Mukendi's are conscious attempts to broadcast a political message in the sense of commenting on state politics or government policy in the form of an allegory. In the spirit idiom, easily understood by African readers or listeners, popular pamphlets like Mukendi's articulate a critique of the morality and organisation of power both locally and internationally. Discourses of this sort are not limited to those African countries where religious institutions can be regarded as alternatives to secular ones due to the decline or even the collapse of the state, such as in Somalia and the Democratic Republic of Congo, where the conventional apparatus of the state hardly functions. They are also found in places where the state cannot be regarded as having collapsed, such as South Africa or Botswana. Religious discourse has implications for most, if not all, countries in Africa, even those that cannot be described as weakly governed or in crisis. All over the continent, even in places with relatively efficient states, deeply rooted concepts of power tend to merge the religious and the political.

In these circumstances, religious and political leaders more easily become rivals than in situations where a separation of religion and politics has been institutionalised over a very long period. It is not surprising, therefore, to learn that politicians in Africa may, and often do, use all sorts of methods to derive advantage from the religious authority of others, including through co-opting them into patronage systems and consulting and paying religious specialists. Evidence of this may be found in all parts of Africa. A classic of anthropological research describes how, during Zimbabwe's liberation war in the 1970s, Marxist guerrillas systematically sought out spirit mediums—people thought to be possessed by the spirits of deceased chiefs and ancestors—as a way of getting support from the population.[51] Quite often heads of state publicly declare their religious sympathies or allegiances and even require these to be government policy. Former President Frederick Chiluba of Zambia, for example, having become a born-again Christian, declared his country to be a Christian nation. Mozambique's President Joaquim Chissano, once the intelligence chief of a Marxist-oriented liberation movement, discovered Transcendental Meditation, the teaching of the Beatles' guru Maharaishi Mahesh Yogi, in 1992. 'First I started the practice of Transcendendental Meditation myself', he is quoted as saying, 'then introduced the practice to my close family, my Cabinet of ministers, my government officers and my military'.[52] He is also reported to have stated that this has contributed to peace in his country. Since 1994, his government has required members of the police and armed forces to meditate for twenty minutes twice per day. Transcendental Meditation was placed on the syllabus at the national military academy.

Political elites all over the continent use religious communities for the purposes of mobilising voters, creating clienteles or organising constituencies. Sometimes they use such mundane means as appointing religious leaders to public committees and awarding them marks of honour, like the pre-genocide government of Rwanda that appointed the Catholic Archbishop of Kigali, Mgr. Vincent Nsengiyumva, to the central committee of the ruling party.[53] In Senegal, both Catholic and Muslim politicians have cultivated the spiritual leaders of the main Muslim brotherhoods, and notably the Mourides. The influence of marabouts or Islamic holy men belonging to the main Sufi brotherhoods has been recognised as a key source of political influence in Senegal for decades.[54] In South Africa, politicians of all parties and backgrounds have competed to court religious support. In 1985, much to the indignation of anti-apartheid opinion abroad, the then President P. W. Botha addressed the Easter gathering of the Zion Christian Church (ZCC), the annual assembly of hundreds of thousands of members of the largest independent church in South Africa. Clearly, this was an attempt to win black support, which provoked much criticism of the ZCC in South Africa and beyond.[55] Almost a decade later, in 1994, when the political situation had changed dramatically and general elections were approaching, the same annual gathering was attended for the same reason by State President F. W. de Klerk, Nelson Mandela and Chief M. G. Buthelezi, all competing for political support.[56]

There is nothing unique to Africa about politicians seeking to make political capital out of displays of religious allegiance or respect. Politicians in almost every part of the world visit places of worship during election campaigns for the purpose of winning votes, without necessarily being believers themselves. It can be just another stop on the campaign trail. For many African politicians, however, the cultivation of religious experts does not happen only at election time. Many of them consult spiritual leaders in private without seeking publicity, which seems to suggest that they may believe that the most effective spiritual leaders have esoteric techniques for gaining access to great power. Some of the best documented cases of politicians cultivating spiritual power have been recorded in the Republic of Congo, better known as Congo-Brazzaville to distinguish it from its giant neighbour on the other side of the Congo river. Throughout the history of Congolese nationalism, just about every political leader of substance has cultivated a reputation as a master of esoteric forces and has created a personality cult based partly on traditional religious beliefs.[57] The first president after independence, Abbé Fulbert Youlou, was a Catholic priest, who also visited traditional shrines, while a more recent leader, the former mayor of Brazzaville, Bernard Kolélas, is often represented as a reincarnation of the biblical Moses.[58] It should be noted that Congo-Brazzaville occupies a portion of the territory of the ancient kingdom of Kongo, whose kings converted to Christianity in the sixteenth century and were treated in those days as fellow-Christian monarchs by the kings of Portugal as well as by popes. This rich religious history has contributed to a formidable tradition of political messianism that shows no sign of exhaustion.

All over the continent, in private and in public, politicians cultivate religious specialists whom they, as well as the general public, believe to have the power to mediate between the visible and invisible worlds. This, though, does not prevent them from spending most of their time in much the same way as politicians the world over, studying documents, managing information, and attending meetings in an effort to control the allocation of resources in the visible world. The pursuit of power in the spirit world is not their most time-consuming or most highly-publicised activity, but it may rank as the most basic, since all power, material and otherwise, is perceived by their constituents as originating in the invisible world. Politicians in Africa, perhaps even more than in other places, need to be enormously adaptable, and skilled at speaking a variety of political languages at once. A minister may one day be locked in negotiation with officials of the World Bank, grappling with the details of financial reform, and consulting a diviner, a bishop or an imam the next day, switching easily between what would conventionally be regarded by political scientists as virtually incompatible spheres of governance.

# 4

# SECRETS

Kenneth David Kaunda, president of Zambia from the country's independence in 1964 until his defeat in democratic elections in 1991, was often seen by international journalists as a rather sympathetic head of state. The son of one of central Africa's first home-bred missionaries, Kaunda was a devout Christian. Even after his elevation to the presidency, KK, as he was known, would occasionally sing hymns in public, accompanying himself on a guitar. He sometimes wept at press conferences when describing the suffering inflicted in southern Africa by apartheid, wiping his eyes with the big white handkerchief he always carried. He seems to have struck most foreign visitors as reasonable, progressive and sincere. Kaunda steered a careful choice between East and West throughout the cold war, claiming to have invented his own brand of socialism known as Zambian humanism, but at the same time having many friends in church circles in England. He charmed Margaret Thatcher when she came to power in 1979, helping her to her first international triumph—the independence of Zimbabwe—and was photographed dancing with her at a Commonwealth summit. He enjoyed playing golf with visiting celebrities. Only towards the end of his presidency was he considered by diplomats to have lost his way among the thickets of national politics and the ruthlessness of liberation wars.

Kaunda, a skillful politician, paid careful attention to religious matters from the very first days of independence from colonial rule, when the mishandling of a movement led by a popular prophetess, Alice Lenshina, precipitated a political crisis in which hundreds of people were killed by the police and army.[1] After that, his policy had generally been to attempt to co-opt religious movements of any importance into the ambit of his ruling party. It was only vaguely known during his years in power that Kaunda had a close personal relationship to two Indian mystics who had a key position in his entourage. The few diplomats or foreign journalists who knew about his spiritual advisors generally thought that they were of no real importance. *Radio trottoir* was more accurate and, typically, showed a lively interest in the president's relation to the two Indians.

'In 1976, I heard rumours about the presence of two Indians at State House', recalls Kaunda's press secretary of the time. 'They were the President's Gurus'. The young press aide 'was warned by fellow workers that the presence of the two Indians was a guarded secret and told to keep my mouth shut or I would be booted out of State House'. The two men, M. A. Ranganathan and Mulshanker Hirji Bapuji Vyas, were both on the state payroll, with the former being allowed to transfer his salary tax free to an account in Britain.[2] According to Ranganathan, who describes himself as a philosopher, scientist and holistic health consultant,[3] he had had a series of trance experiences from his childhood. After coming from India to Zambia as a teacher in 1974, he was introduced to Kaunda by chance and established an immediate rapport with the president by telling him that he recognised Kaunda from his shamanistic travels in the spirit world.[4] Ranganathan was often rumoured by *radio trottoir* to have been introduced to Kaunda by Prime Minister Indira Gandhi after the Zambian president had asked her for help in the spiritual sector for which India is famous, but there is no evidence to support this allegation.

Only after Kaunda had lost the presidency did further information about this side of his spiritual life emerge as his closest advisors began to speak more openly about the past. It was revealed that with Kaunda's approval Ranganathan had set up a shrine known as the David Universal Temple (David is Kaunda's middle name), located in a house at 40 Ng'umbo Road, just 300 metres from State House in the Zambian capital, Lusaka. In 1990 a more expensive temple was built opposite the Lusaka Golf Club.[5] Through Ranganathan's influence senior officials including the chief justice, the inspector-general of police and others became members of the David Universal Temple, while one of Kaunda's prime ministers became the director of the cult. 'Dr Ranganathan', the president's press secretary recalls, 'became very powerful in Zambia. In private circles, he was regarded as an invisible President, and he boasted that he could recommend anyone to the President for dismissal'.[6]

There was nothing inherently scandalous about the David Universal Temple other than the degree of political influence wielded by the unelected foreign guru who inspired it. But no doubt many experts on southern African affairs would have been perplexed if they had had full information about it in earlier years, when Kaunda was generally seen as a Christian gentleman and a moderate socialist. If so, he would not be the only example of an African head of state who in private devotes considerable attention to spiritual matters at odds with his more public pronouncements on secular affairs. A leading African theologian mocks those foreign writers and activists who during the cold war used to enthuse about Africa's apparently most progressive leaders, ignoring the fact that 'many of the revolutionaries who make such ringing declarations, and many of the intellectuals who are so taken with rationalism and Cartesianism, at the same time are in thrall to all sorts of traditionalists, marabouts, fetish-priests and diviners. Some of these leaders even practise ritual human sacrifices to retain their power…'[7] This is an apparent reference to Ahmed Sékou Touré, president of Guinea from 1960 to 1984, regarded by some important sources as having performed such acts.[8]

Kaunda's Indian advisors were not the only foreigners whom he kept on his payroll. In the non-spiritual area, for example, he had bodyguards trained by British mercenaries[9] and intelligence officers trained by Israel's Mossad. Kaunda hired a couple of American technical advisors, including a nephew of former President Dwight Eisenhower, to install an elaborate electronic communication system at State House, keeping him in discreet contact with top officials throughout the country. These two Americans tried to persuade KK also to set up sophisticated—and expensive—anti-aircraft defences to guard against an aerial assault or assassination attempt.[10] This, too, was known only to an inner circle of advisors.

Anti-aircraft guns, spiritual protection, communication gadgets, were all of a piece: they were the technical devices operated by foreign experts at the behest of an African head of state who needed every means available, spiritual and material, to stay in power. To judge from the rumours peddled by *radio trottoir*, the Zambian public, like Kaunda himself, regarded it as normal that a head of state should seek both spiritual and material protection from the best available sources. If the best intelligence trainers were from Israel and the best bodyguards, weapons and communication equipment from the West, then by the same token some of the most reputed spiritual technology was from India. The discretion surrounding intimate spiritual beliefs and practices is no more than one aspect of the secrecy that attends many aspects of the lives of African leaders, which some of them cultivate assiduously.

## Secrecy in politics

Politicians the world over routinely describe themselves as democrats these days. Democracy expressed by way of elections has become the universally accepted standard of political legitimacy.

Nowhere is this truer than in Africa. Since the early 1990s just about every country in the continent has acquired a formal system of multi-party democracy. Arrangements of this sort have almost without exception replaced the single-party systems that were created in many places, including Zambia, after the flowering of independence in the 1960s. The function of elections in these one-party states, before they were swept away by the tide of change in the 1990s, was not so much to regulate political competition as to demonstrate by symbolic means that the state was based on popular sovereignty. Political power at independence was built on a nationalist myth that the country's leaders represented the will of the people, united in rejection of colonial rule and in the aspiration to development.

But if politics everywhere makes some show of democracy nowadays, everywhere too it contains an element of secrecy. Even the most demo-cratic of politicians thinks that there are certain subjects that it is not proper to share with the mass of voters, and there are major areas of state activity that are conventionally shielded from public view. This is so not just in Africa, but all over the world. Even the world's longest-established parliamentary democracies have secret services, while civil servants han-dling business in government ministries routinely regard certain types of information as confidential. Heads of state and senior politicians are sur-rounded by aides and bodyguards whose job is to keep them well-informed and safe, but who also endow them with an air of importance and mystique.

In addition to the conventional bureaucratic forms of secrecy, a partic-ular atmosphere of exclusiveness that has more than just a security ratio-nale surrounds senior politicians and heads of state in various parts of the world, like the Chinese Communist Party leadership that still cultivates some of the old traditions that once led emperors to build a Forbidden City where ordinary people are denied access. Many African presidents too cultivate a personal mystique. Some, like the late Sani Abacha of Nigeria, are reported by the local press rarely to meet their own cabinet ministers face to face. They retain personal control over a wide range of policy matters. At the same time, there are many African heads of state who will sing in public, like Kaunda, or join in collective dances on formal occasions, including such enthusiastic dancers as Zimbabwe's Robert Mugabe, Hastings Banda of Malawi, and Samora Machel of Mozam-bique. This gives them an interesting and unusual allure of being both untouchable and yet in contact with the people. Some African commenta-tors have detected in the relation between the continent's rulers and ruled a carnivalesque element of parody and excess in the extremes of luxury and consumption for which some heads of state have been notorious.[11]

Many presidents have good reason to keep their distance even from their own ministers, as Africa's history of coups and palace intrigues shows. But the cult of the presidency encourages secrecy for more than functional reasons only. It is also the reflection of an idea that high politics is, and should be, a field reserved for the head of state and his aides alone, conducted through personal relations between presidents and crowned heads and their emissaries, and quite often sealed by marriage pacts as in old Europe. This is rather like the view in *ancien régime* France that politics was 'the king's secret', the personal domain of the monarch.

In any political system, even the most democratic, gaining access to sensitive information and acquiring control of how and to whom it may be communicated are of critical importance. Modern politicians employ batteries of press secretaries and spin-doctors whose job is to ensure that the information entering the public domain is in the form that best suits their political masters. In the leading industrialised countries spin-doctoring has in a few decades gone from being secondary to the formulation and implementation of policy by means of a public administration, to become itself something close to the substance of political action, as politicians and their staffs strive to impose their own interpretation of facts on journalists and media editors, or simply to promote the slogans or photo and film images they prefer. Political journalists, these days often employed by massive corporations with a wide range of interests spanning the media and commerce, often aim to outwit the spin-doctors more than they aspire to assemble in a coherent order and in a spirit of high-minded reflection the most significant facts pertaining to a particular subject or story. In Europe and North America, there is precious little that is democratic about this process of interaction between political media manipulators and their editorial counterparts. The idea that political journalism is primarily about presenting an objective view of the facts has become naïve.[12]

Some people believe that the growth of the internet and of talk radio is providing a new popular input into public debate. In America, the political scandals surrounding President Clinton's sex life were sometimes fuelled by information and editorial comment from outside the magic circle of national media commentators, forcing media heavyweights and political spinners to struggle to assert their own control of the process of forming public opinion. Similar contests occur between corporate players and politicians in Africa, but with the difference that the influence of mass media on society there is less profound. Far more than in the industrialised world, Africans depend on information they have received from their friends and neighbours via *radio trottoir*, as we have seen.[13]

As a general rule, access to confidential or privileged information considered to be of some importance is connected to political influence and social standing all over the world. No doubt this has some bearing on the tendency for people who regularly receive particular types of specialised knowledge to form exclusive clubs, groups, societies and guilds in a great variety of situations. It is both a way of meeting peers and people with similar interests and a way of keeping others out. This too seems a very widespread tendency. Every capital city has bars, restaurants, private salons or other watering-holes where political insiders meet to gossip and do business informally. Africa is no different.

## Secret societies

One of the founders of sociology noted that 'the secret offers, so to speak, the possibility of a second world alongside the manifest world' and considered secrecy to be 'one of man's greatest achievements'.[14] If this is so, we may observe, then secrecy is a natural relative of the spirit world, which also posits the existence of a parallel universe. Throughout Africa's history, the formation of elite political groups of various types, keeping information within a small circle, has often included a spiritual aspect. It is remarkable how many African heads of state are members of closed or even secret organisations with a spiritual flavour. Some of these groups are of European origin, such as the Freemasons and the Rosicrucians, while others are indigenous.

Freemasonry, as is well known, is an international movement that arose in Europe in early modern times and that has historically been associated with various strands of philosophy and political thought. These days it includes several distinct 'rites', as the various traditions are known. Many leading thinkers of the eighteenth-century Enlightenment were Freemasons, and the symbols of masonry are to be found in productions of the period ranging from US banknotes to the operas of Mozart. Freemasons in Europe and North America nowadays generally regard themselves as members of a social movement that promotes charitable work and self-help and propagates a form of civic morality. Membership of the masonic craft is accompanied by rituals that in theory may not be made known to outsiders, an aspect that in some ways qualifies Freemasonry as a secret society and that has at times inspired all manner of conspiracy theories among non-masons.[15] In the United Kingdom and the United States

Freemasonry has a vaguely conservative political flavour. Yet it is associated in popular opinion more with particular trades or professions than with any specific political ideology. The reputation of Freemasonry, though, is different in some European countries where masonic traditions have been associated with particular political parties or traditions, especially in France and Italy where it was linked in the past with anti-clerical opposition to the Catholic Church. In one extraordinary case in Italy, an elite masonic lodge known as P-2 was shown to have been at the heart of high-level political intrigue and corruption throughout the 1960s and 70s.[16]

Rosicrucianism is rather less well-known to the general public. It arose in Europe in the seventeenth century, at roughly the same time as masonry, although both claim to incorporate older wisdom handed down in a hermetic tradition. Even more than Freemasonry, which claims an association with the wisdom of ancient Egypt, Rosicrucians cultivate arcane or esoteric spiritual knowledge, said to have been transmitted since ancient times in an unbroken chain from generation to generation, and to have been kept intact in the knowledge transmitted to initiates. All the current Rosicrucian organisations in the world, however, are relatively recent creations, including the most influential of them, the Antique and Mystical Order of the Rosae Crucis (AMORC), founded in the United States in the early twentieth century.

AMORC was introduced to France after the Second World War, and it is from there that it seems to have travelled to Africa,[17] where it has become very successful. The Rosicrucians' assertion that most of the great intellectuals and mystics of history were secretly members of the cult has helped it gain a reputation throughout the sub-continent as an appropriate group for elites, attracting 'a great number of intellectuals, politicians and businessmen'.[18] Among African heads of state who have been Freemasons or Rosicrucians, or both, are the current or recent presidents of Madagascar, Cameroon, Gabon, Togo and others in the French-speaking world, influenced by the connections between masonry and the factions of French politics. One eminent English-speaking Rosicrucian was Bola Ige, Nigeria's minister of justice, who was assassinated in mysterious circumstances in December 2001. When his allegiance became known after his death, it caused some scandal in the Anglican Church of which he had been a member, with the bishop of Lagos calling on church members to either renounce their position in what he called 'cults' or else resign from the church.[19] In response, the president of the Rosicrucian order in Nigeria, Chief Dr Kenneth U. Idiodi, wrote a rather cheeky letter to the primate of the Anglican Church in Nigeria offering free membership of the order to clerics of the church, alleging that AMORC had been propagating its 'mystical, philosophical and scientific teachings' for 3,354 years.[20]

Cameroon's President Paul Biya is particularly interested in esoteric cults of this nature, including some which have become internationally notorious. Judicial investigations into the Temple Solaire, an obscure cult associated with a mass suicide and murders in Canada, Switzerland and France in 1994–5, suggested that President Biya might have been involved in substantial financial transactions with the cult's leading officials.[21] Between 1992 and 1998, over 11 million French francs were transferred from Cameroon's national oil company to the personal bank account of Raymond Bernard, a leading French Rosicrucian suspected by French magistrates of a connection with the Temple Solaire. Bernard claimed that the money was payment for various services performed for the Cameroonian president. He also claimed that he had been appointed as an aide to President Biya, although a spokesperson for the presidency denied this and said that the two were simply friends. Other esoteric organisations received even larger sums from Biya. However, there is no evidence that Biya was a member of the Temple Solaire, although he is certainly an enthusiastic Rosicrucian. The press and French magistrates may have made an incorrect assumption about Biya's relationship to the Temple Solaire due to the complexities of the affairs of President Biya's friend Raymond Bernard.[22] The presidents of Gabon, Togo and Côte d'Ivoire too had all accepted offices in organisations run by Bernard.[23]

Probably Africa's champion joiner of secret societies is also the continent's longest-serving head of state. This is Omar Bongo, president of Gabon since 1967. He is a leading member of Ndjobi, a traditional-style religious society for men that was founded in the 1940s, and also of Bwiti, an initiation society from another region of his country. Secret societies like Bwiti exist in many parts of central and western Africa. In precolonial times they were generally conclaves where senior men could meet to govern community affairs and to interact with the spirit world. Under colonial rule, Bwiti itself spread dramatically and became connected with nationalist political intrigue.[24] Bongo is also said to be a Rosicrucian and is the grand master of his own masonic lodge, known as 'Dialogue',[25] the first African grand lodge to receive recognition from world masonry. Throughout his career he has been a leading player in the formidable complexities of Franco-African politics, developing considerable influence in the French secret services, French clandestine organisations and dubious political financing, as well as with the secretive Elf oil company.[26] His name has been quoted in connection with private banking scandals in hearings by the US Senate.[27] Having been originally educated as a Roman Catholic, Bongo officially converted to Islam and adopted the title El Hadj after a pilgrimage to Mecca.

Secret societies of European origin have been easily assimilated by African elites, particularly in former French colonies that are heirs to French traditions of masonry.[28] These sit easily with indigenous traditions of closed associations. The latter are typically sodalities or groups that require elaborate initiation rites whose details may not be divulged to outsiders, which is where the element of secrecy arises. They are widespread throughout the forest regions particularly, and may be very old. Some so-called 'secret societies',[29] such as Poro (for men) and Sande (for women), which are widespread throughout modern Sierra Leone, Liberia and Guinea, traditionally incorporate every adult in the areas where they exist, so that initiation into them is also a form of initiation into adulthood. In these areas everyone knows of the existence of these two societies, although members will not divulge details of their initiation to others. Nevertheless, the ubiquity of Sande and Poro has made it possible for scholars to study them in some detail.[30] At the other end of the scale are far more exclusive societies, whose existence might not be generally known, whose membership is restricted, and whose spiritual knowledge is regarded as being of the most esoteric sort. Some, such as the leopard societies in West and central Africa, have been associated with spiritual practices including possession by the spirits of wild animals and forms of ritual killing. In many parts of Africa, the activities of secret societies have been associated with the use of masks, suggesting that power is hidden and is never quite what it seems; it is by nature mysterious. Both of these are ideas that remain current today.

Colonial rulers sometimes outlawed indigenous initiation societies and sometimes adopted policies intended to depoliticise them by encouraging them to develop into rather harmless folklore associations, like the traditional dancers that perform at luxury hotels for tourists. In many cases, however, colonial rule did not actually disempower initiation societies, which have generally proved to be highly resilient. Under colonial systems of indirect rule, chiefs, clerks and other African agents of the administration sometimes continued to make use of traditional initiation societies for their own purposes, or established new groups that could not be called traditional but that used many ideas and methods drawn from older repertoires, assimilating some of these into the emerging style of nationalist politics. More recently, both politicians and others have encouraged the emergence of neo-traditional societies that are often used as the basis for private militias. Only rarely have we seen traditional structures of this sort disappear without trace. More often, their practices and ideas have emerged in new institutional forms that are inextricably linked with modern state politics.[31]

In those areas of West and central Africa that generally had no bureaucratic form of government before colonial times, secret societies often played an important part in politics and governance in the broadest sense. In many cases, the establishment of Christianity and bureaucratic government in colonial times has not led to these secret societies fading into insignificance but rather to their incorporation into modern systems of rule. We have already noted the ease with which African traditional religions can incorporate concepts and institutions of foreign origin.[32] In Nigeria, early British missionaries themselves joined secret societies in the conviction that it was 'the only way of wielding any influence'.[33] There has been an imbrication of Christianity and secret societies ever since that period. As with President Bongo's patronage of the Bwiti and Ndjobi societies in Gabon, successive presidents of Liberia have had themselves proclaimed leaders of the influential Poro male initiation society. William Tolbert, president of Liberia from 1971 to 1980, was both supreme *zo* of the Poro society and president of the World Baptist Alliance. A later head of state, Charles Taylor, formed an association of officials of traditional secret societies and proclaimed himself the supreme officer of the new society.[34] According to a Nigerian intelligence report,[35] he required all his cabinet members to be initiated. One of Taylor's closest colleagues has alleged that the former president also established a more personal secret society still, known as the Top Twenty, with a sinister reputation.[36] Taylor shared with the late Sierra Leonean warlord Foday Sankoh the services of a *juju* man, Alhaji Kuyateh, according to the official Sierra Leonean news agency. Kuyateh is said to have worked with various commanders of Sankoh's movement, the Revolutionary United Front, and married the mother of the most notorious of them, Sam 'Moskita' Bockarie.[37] At the same time Taylor claims to be a born-again Christian. He prayed together with former US president Jimmy Carter and regularly welcomed American preachers to Monrovia. Denis Sassou N'Guesso, twice president of Congo-Brazzaville, a French-trained army officer as well as formerly a leading Marxist, mentions his own initiation into a traditional secret society in his autobiography.[38] In 2002, he issued a personal invitation to a French cult leader named Raël, formerly a journalist and racing driver called Claude Vorilhon. In late 2002, the 55,000-strong Raëlian movement, which aims to preserve life after death by cloning, featured in the world's headlines after claiming to have cloned a human being. Of particular interest to African politicians is that the Raëlians favour the payment of compensation by leading Western governments to the victims of the slave trade.[39] President Eyadéma of Togo is one of several heads of state to have in effect created his own religious cult. In his case, this bears a close resemblance to a traditional Vodun cult. Its centre is at a spot in the north of his country where he claims to have been miraculously saved from a plane crash.[40]

The late President Félix Houphouët-Boigny of Côte d'Ivoire, widely considered one of the most successful and enlightened African heads of state and known as a staunch Catholic, was nevertheless privately devoted to secretive traditional religious practices throughout his career.[41] One leading African political scientist suggests that he may have carried out ritual killings, and that his death in 1993 was followed by mortuary slayings designed to send servants with him to the next world.[42] Only in his last years, when he devoted enormous resources to the construction of the great Catholic basilica in his home town of Yamoussoukro—an extraordinary copy of St Peter's basilica in the Vatican—did his spiritual preoccupations become fully public.[43] His great rival President Sékou Touré of Guinea, a leading Marxist in his day, was alleged by one of his cabinet ministers to have had seventy people killed in one night on the advice of one of his marabouts, who told the president that this sacrifice would put a magical spell on the detested Houphouët-Boigny. 'The seers', the minister wrote in a memoir of his own time in government, 'had convinced Sékou Touré that by sacrificing as many party and state functionaries as [Houphouët-Boigny]'s years of age, on his birthday, it would bring about his inevitable downfall.'[44] Some heads of state in both West and central Africa have been alleged by former colleagues, in press interviews, to be part of a group that meets to drink or wash in human blood.[45] Similar allegations were made in the 1970s about the notorious Emperor Bokassa of Central Africa and Idi Amin of Uganda.

Whether or not such stories appear to observers to be empirically true is perhaps not the point in most urgent need of investigation, if we are to follow the method of analysis discussed above.[46] What matters is that such stories are credible to the people who tell them and who constitute their immediate audience. Rumours drawing on the idea that great power is exclusive, and that initiation into elite networks requires ritual action that may involve blood sacrifice, lead people in many countries to associate national elections, when power is open to competition, with the abduction of children. From Guinea to southern Africa, there are frequent rumours that children are being killed in order to use parts of their bodies in rituals designed to capture spiritual power for an election candidate.[47] Even when there are no elections pending, *radio trottoir* and the local press often report such killings and attribute them to politicians. Indeed, it is said that human body-parts are bought and sold for use in rituals, and it is even rumoured that they can be procured openly in certain places.[48] In May 2002, South Africa's national television station broadcast a documentary showing how undercover reporters were able to buy human body-parts.[49] South African newspapers often carry stories about what are generally referred to as 'ritual killings', although in this case these seem to be associated with the search for money or good luck by ordinary citizens, and are not usually attributed to national politicians.

The novelist Ahmadou Kourouma has written a treatise on the esoteric practices of various heads of state, their names thinly disguised, in his book *En attendant le vote des bêtes sauvages*. 'I write the truth, as I perceive it, without prejudice. I describe things as they are,' the 72-year old Kourouma maintains, adding that the book is the fruit of a lifetime of experience and reflection that has included an acquaintance with several heads of state. 'The behaviour of African dictators is such that people don't believe it, they think it's fiction.' He assures us that 'a number of facts and events that I have described are true, but they are so unthinkable that readers consider them as fiction. It's terrible.' He continues: 'In Africa, there is not a single head of state who doesn't have his magician or his marabout; magic and political power are virtually one and the same thing.'[50]

Secret rituals are a feature of initiation into societies that are considered repositories of esoteric knowledge and power and that are often regarded as mainstays of morality and social order. Formal initiation is not confined to elite societies, for in many parts of Africa it is customary for boys and girls to undergo an initiation ritual when they reach puberty. This typically involves a period of seclusion and instruction, perhaps including a physical ordeal such as circumcision or the infliction of scars or tattoos. In some places initiates are classified as part of a particular generation or age-set, binding members of a same cohort throughout their lives. This tradition throws light on the widespread existence of secretive student societies in Nigerian universities, for example. These began in the 1950s partly as political organisations, and partly in the spirit of European student-clubs. Over the years, however, they have gained a reputation for violence and become widely regarded as sinister cults.[51] In July 1999, at Obafemi Awolowo University, five people were killed and others injured by members of one such student cult, following which the federal government of Nigeria issued a general order to the management of all tertiary institutions to rid their campuses of secret cults or risk losing their jobs.[52] In Namibia too, student secret societies, growing in number, have gained a reputation for anti-social behaviour, and are sometimes even considered satanic. In both countries, billboards are posted on campuses, and even along main roads, warning students against joining such groups.

It is not only in countries with histories of powerful precolonial initiation societies that secret societies have flourished in African politics. Another example, all the more interesting for being the product of an ethnic group of European extraction, is the South African Afrikaner Broederbond. This secret society, ethnically exclusive until recently, with several thousand members at any one time, has for most of its existence been officially dedicated to the advancement of male protestant Afrikaners. It was for more than forty years closely associated with the apartheid government of South Africa, to the extent that membership of the Broederbond was almost essential for preferment in the National Party until it lost power in 1994. In practice, however, there were always some Afrikaner nationalists who were sceptical of the Broederbond's claim to represent the entire Afrikaner *volk*, since it left no room for dissenting views.[53] Sceptics have tended to see it as an association dedicated to nothing so much as the promotion of its individual members, and there is indeed evidence that some business transactions involving Broederbond members have been associated with fraud and financial manipulation.[54] The Broederbond has a curious parallel in another political secret society active in apartheid's heyday, the South African Communist Party. Since the Party was illegal in South Africa from its inception in 1953,[55] SACP membership was secret. But the cult of inner-party secrecy went far beyond what was required to protect its cadres from arrest, since ordinary party members, including those living in exile, for years were forbidden to know the identity of those on their own central committee.[56] A degree of openness was introduced only after 1990. A similar secrecy surrounds to this day the Marxist-Leninist League of Tigray, an organisation known to be at the heart of the ruling group in Ethiopia, which was engaged in a long guerrilla war before it assumed power in 1991.[57] In neighbouring Eritrea, another victorious liberation movement was also later revealed to have a clandestine party at its core, whose existence was revealed only in 1994.[58]

Groups like the SACP and the Marxist-Leninist League of Tigray are explicitly secular in their doctrine and owe their secrecy to the structures perfected by international communist parties. As with Freemasons and Rosicrucians, there is nothing distinctively African about their mode of operation. However, when groups such as these take root in African societies that have their own traditions regarding exclusiveness of information and organisation, they take on a particular flavour. Just as membership of an indigenous society like Bwiti or Poro gives access to local networks of great interest to a politician, by the same token, a person who joins a secret society or other select body that has an international orientation automatically gains access to wider networks of influence, power and ideas. Membership of a communist party, in the time of the Soviet Union, is one such example. In francophone Africa, Freemasonry can give access to prominent figures in French business and politics, such as the late President François Mitterrand's secretary for African affairs, Guy Penne, who was a leading Freemason. Membership of elite international networks and societies enables African leaders to link with global elites in a discretion they find congenial. Even an ostensibly non-political body such as the World Wildlife Fund (now renamed the World-Wide Fund for Nature) can give access to elite connections of this type, as witnessed by President Mobutu's membership of its 1001 Club, an association where European royalty rubs shoulders with leading industrialists but also with some distinctly dubious figures from the worlds of grand corruption and secret intelligence.[59] A key attraction of secret societies is that membership provides opportunities for doing political deals unobserved by the mass of the population and for forming bonds of solidarity that go beyond the ordinary. Secrecy binds people together. It is worth noting that the type of society or organisation to which we refer often constitutes an all-male network of power. Although, as we shall see in the next chapter, women may also form their own networks of spiritual power, female initiation societies are related to political power only indirectly, if at all. State politics has generally been seen by men in Africa as a domain where women do not properly belong.[60]

It is striking that neither the African politicians who join secret societies or clubs or give themselves to esoteric cults with such enthusiasm, nor their colleagues, nor the people who vote for them, appear to see anything inconsistent, absurd or intrinsically untrustworthy in such an association. Since African believers in general do not see any contradiction in combining aspects of different religious traditions, it is at least consistent that few of them seem to consider multiple allegiances on the part of their leaders with great surprise. The existence of secret societies is often rumoured by *radio trottoir*, but if the activities of politicians in such elite groups are discussed with a fair degree of cynicism, this is no more than a reflection of a more general opinion about politicians and what they get up to.

*Arcane power and political intelligence*

Membership of secret societies and the cooptation of religion for political purposes generally are more than purely functional matters. There is every reason to believe that joining a religious group of any sort imparts a powerful sense of belonging. The more exclusive the group is, the more potent this sense may be. Secret societies both indigenous and imported impress on members during their initiation that they are gaining access to forms of knowledge that go beyond the mundane, incorporating the aco-lyte into a transcendental world of power. One might add that all power is more effectively exercised in secret than in public, as Max Weber pointed out in comments based largely on his studies of Europe.[61] The concept of secrecy implies exclusive control over types of knowledge that are not to be shared with all and sundry. Power is always related to the control and restriction of information.

All over Africa, the belief that really effective power is exercised in se-cret is particularly strong. This is a matter of frequent comment by *radio trottoir* and the press, which often attribute to politicians the manipulation of various types of secrecy and arcane power in ways that straddle the fea-sible and the fantastic. For example, Ghana's redoubtable intelligence chief in the 1980s, Kojo Tsikata, was a British-trained army officer and an orthodox Marxist who was popularly believed to have special powers that enabled him to turn himself into an owl.[62] The owl, we may note, is in many parts of Africa considered a harbinger of sinister power, being a carnivorous animal that flies at night, attacking its prey silently and unob-served. In Ghana's 2000 general elections, numerous parliamentary can-didates were alleged to be using *juju*, a word widely used in West Africa to designate any sort of mystical religious activity of indigenous origin, in an effort to secure election.[63] Liberia's former president, Samuel Doe, was another believed to be able to change himself into different forms and var-ious animals, and to be able to fly. This is a quality attributed not only to powerful politicians but also to alleged witches, which says something about popular perceptions of political power and the use to which it is put by politicians. Doe, throughout his career, avidly consulted priests, proph-ets and diviners of every type and attended both churches and mosques. When he was eventually captured by his enemies, he was finally killed for fear that he might try to transform himself into a bird and escape.[64]

Some people believe not just that powerful individuals are capable of extraordinary transformations, but that the essence of their power is by definition mysterious. In Zaire, it was rumoured that President Mobutu's main palace contained a secret room that even his wife was forbidden to enter. When she did pluck up courage to look in there, it is said, what she found was a living statue of the president. In other words, the Mobutu who appeared in public was only a simulacrum: the real, living power that propelled him resided in a secret place.[65] This conforms to some of the ideas we discuss, suggesting that real power resides in an invisible place, and that visible representations of it have no autonomous force, as is also the case with masks and amulets used in traditional rituals. Some people are thought to be not what they appear, but to be controlled by somebody else. This is true of zombies but may also be the case with powerful people, such as Mobutu, regarded as masters of dissimulation.

Politicians are constantly rumoured to be members of conspiracies, real or imagined, involving just about every imaginable abuse of power, ranging from straightforward corruption to sexual practices perceived as unusual or perverse and behaviour of the most extreme kind. Some heads of state are rumoured by *radio trottoir* to systematically demand sexual rights over the wives of their male cabinet ministers. In Nigeria, when a group of army officers attempted a coup in April 1990, they used the time-honoured technique of a radio broadcast to announce their takeover. The putschists publicly called the existing military government 'drug baronish', and alleged that people in its upper reaches practised homosexuality in a cultic manner.[66] When the country's later president, Sani Abacha, died mysteriously in 1999 while in the company of at least two women servicing his legendary appetite, allegedly having also consumed a quantity of Viagra, it merely confirmed Nigerians' views concerning elite sexual practices. Abacha's death was promptly dubbed by *radio trottoir* 'the coup from heaven', despite the suspicion that it was engineered on earth by members of his inner circle.[67] Occasionally politicians themselves publicly lend weight to the idea that elite politics is riven by conspiracies in which political intrigue is mixed with the most malign forms of spiritual activity. 'We don't know what is hitting us', said Emerson Mnangagwa, speaker of the Zimbabwean parliament, after the deaths of three of his close colleagues in 2001. 'It's not natural. We fear the hand of Lucifer is at work'.[68]

Stories like these indicate the astonishing power, often of a mystical or superhuman nature, that people frequently ascribe to their political leaders, notably heads of state and chiefs of secret services. Ordinary citizens understand well enough the role played by religion in elite struggles since many use similar techniques as their leaders to solve the problems of their daily lives by consulting healers, spirit mediums, priests, prophets, diviners and marabouts, by seeking the blessing of the ancestors or by attending religious gatherings of every variety.

Many African heads of state, the evidence suggests, tend to believe in the power of the invisible world just as their subjects do, seeking forms of power commensurate with the importance of the positions they seek to defend and of the burdens they have to discharge. Political leaders themselves actively cultivate their reputations in this regard, perhaps because they share the same beliefs as the public, and perhaps also out of a wish to impress.

One of the most instructive careers in matters of secrecy both worldly and spiritual is that of President Mathieu Kérékou of Benin, who began his career as a military intelligence officer before coming to power in 1972 in a coup favoured by the French secret services. He subsequently became a Marxist and promoted a socialist philosophy known to local wits, with the corrosive humour typical of *radio trottoir*, as Marxism-Beninism. At the same time Kérékou made use of techniques which his countrymen recognised as belonging to the repertoire of Vodun, the traditional religion of this part of the West African coast. It was while Kérékou was still in his Marxist, pro-Libyan, pro-North Korean, Vodun-influenced phase that he retained the services of a Malian spiritual expert or marabout, Mohamed Amadou Cissé, known as 'Djine' ('Devil'). Cissé had publicly announced in his native Mali that he had undergone a Faustus-like ceremony binding himself to the devil in a search for esoteric knowledge.[69] He was soon recruited to work for heads of state including Presidents Mobutu of Zaire and Bongo of Gabon through whom, it is said, he was introduced to Kérékou. The Beninese president appointed Cissé as a minister of state in his government, with responsibility for the secret services. This made Cissé truly formidable, for as well as being presumed to have a special relationship with the devil, he also controlled the secret services and torture chambers of a government known for its repression. More prosaically, Cissé gained access to bank accounts and diplomatic bags. In 1990 he was arrested in Paris on charges of heroin-smuggling and money-laundering. Extradited to Benin after the fall of his political master, he was tried and imprisoned. He was eventually convicted of fraud in a major trial.[70] A further twist to this story occurred after the replacement of President Kérékou in 1991 by a technocrat previously employed by the World Bank, Nicéphore Soglo. After his years in Washington, Soglo claimed to be sceptical of spiritual power, but he soon fell seriously ill as a result of which, he claimed in a television interview, he had come to respect the power of African spirituality, while also hinting that he might have been poisoned.[71] It should be noted in this context that a further characteristic of people advanced in spiritual knowledge is that many are reputed to have extensive knowledge of pharmacology, which again makes their access to the inner circles of power a formidable weapon indeed. In 1996, Kérékou made an astonishing comeback to the presidency, this time advertising himself as a born-again Christian.[72] It is no surprise to learn that Kérékou's totem is the chameleon.

Cissé's career makes clear the relationship between esoteric spiritual knowledge, these days often considered of an evil nature, and such worldly political skills as intelligence-gathering and illicit financing. A consequence of the frequency with which members of the elite seek advice about their most intimate spiritual problems is that some marabouts and other spiritual experts themselves become repositories of highly confidential information, since the politicians who resort to their services will divulge their most secret ambitions in a bid to attain the power they crave. In this way a leading marabout like Cissé may acquire inside knowledge of planned coups and other secrets of his elite clients. Another marabout, Amadou Oumarou 'Bonkano', also the chief of a national intelligence service, himself attempted a coup against his patron and employer, President Seyni Kountché of Niger.[73] There are doubtless many other marabouts who, sought out by an ambitious soldier who wants to know the most auspicious day to launch his military coup or by a politician planning his next manoeuvre, may choose to leak the information to another client so as to boost their own standing and reputation. In this way, a marabout, diviner, confessor or other spiritual counsellor of the mighty becomes a repository of secrets, very similar to the head of a Western intelligence service who, even after retirement, remains a fund of secret knowledge and a power-broker. Thus a ruler who takes such a person into his service acquires a valuable source of worldly information as well as special access to invisible power. By the same token a ruler who refuses to frequent such people deprives himself not only of a perceived medium of spiritual power, but also of a vital source of information.

## Governing spiritual power

If the spiritual experts who frequent the palaces of the elite acquire worldly power through their activities, so in a different way do those popular religious leaders who acquire mass followings. Leading priests and prophets become important people in a political sense simply by reason of the number of their followers. To be sure, religious leaders are not the only personalities from what is fashionably called civil society who may become influential by heading a non-governmental association, such as a professional body or a trade union. However, the influence wielded by a popular religious leader in Africa is different in many respects from that exercised by any other leader emerging from the non-state sector. A trade unionist, for example, may articulate demands for higher wages or more jobs that a government can deal with by the conventional techniques of modern politics. A religious leader, on the other hand, not only commands some degree of secular influence but is also perceived as being endowed with power stemming directly from the spirit world. Whereas the leader of a secular organisation may be placated with gifts of patronage or intimidated with the threat of exclusion or violence, a head of state finds it more difficult to identify techniques for dealing with, say, an epidemic of possession by spirits.

Temporal rulers attempting to govern populations who believe that their daily life is affected by spiritual powers lack institutional means of control. Spiritual leaders who develop a mass following, even when they have no political ambitions at all, are particularly difficult for governments to deal with by formal means. This is so because the institutions of African states, inherited from colonial times, reflect norms of government based on the classical Western separation of religion and politics into distinct systems of thought and action. Even in the heyday of one-party states, when heads of state controlled virtually every organ of associational life, the spirit world was always elusive. The quasi-religious personality cults established by the likes of Presidents Mobutu of Zaire or Eyadéma of Togo had only limited or short-lived success. For while secular government and politics may be managed with appropriate doses of patronage and coercion, the spirit world is less easy to govern, particularly in a continent where access to spiritual power is believed to be within the reach of all. In principle anyone can communicate with the spirit world and derive power from that source. Spirit mediums, prophets and priests, or other people with potent instruments of religious communication, all have access to power in a form which may pay little respect to official structures. This poses a constant threat to the ideological order and thus to political stability. This is not a peculiarity of recent decades, but was also the case in colonial times, as many examples testify.[74]

In the West, where religion and politics have been subject to such a long history of separation, politics does not normally have a spiritual aspect. Nevertheless, it is interesting to note that even resolutely secular Western governments may find that religious organisations can become suspect, such as in the case of the Scientology Church, which has been subject to official restriction in both France and Germany. In both these countries this church has been accused of criminal offences, but this is undoubtedly accompanied by an element of political suspicion. In China, where power is held by a communist party that officially proclaims itself atheist, the state regards with suspicion Falun Gong, a modern spiritual and healing movement with considerable popular support and some international backing. In the first instance, its very existence flagrantly contradicts the Marxist affirmation that religion will gradually disappear as economic development gathers pace, causing outmoded social structures to erode. But it surely reflects a far deeper spiritual malaise that is profoundly threatening to a Chinese government whose power still reposes in part on an ancient perception that those who rule the country should enjoy the mandate of heaven. In effect, China has a long history, going back at least eighteen centuries, of religious movements against established power.[75] In the past, these sometimes announced the imminent end of the world and its replacement in a new cosmic cycle. Spiritual movements in China have often incorporated in their religious thought forms of healing, including through breathing exercises and meditation. Such movements have at times been assimilated by a communist government wishing to promote 'authentically' Chinese (as well as inexpensive) forms of health care, but policies of cooptation can cease to be effective if a regime is regarded as spiritually void.

The purpose of this brief allusion to China is to argue that some of the most difficult problems facing governments in Africa also exist elsewhere. In many places political power has long had a spiritual component, where Enlightenment ideas concerning the separation of religion and politics, or spirit and reason, have not been internalised in the same way as in Europe. But almost all the world's states have institutions that reflect a Western view of government, a relic of European colonial rule. These institutions are poorly adapted to withstand spiritual challenge, particularly when the circumstances of life have robbed promises of Western-style modernisation and development of much of their appeal.

African politicians are similar to their counterparts in other continents in the sense that they may fear spiritual power falling under the control of groups or individuals that escape their own influence. In Africa, perhaps even more than in other erstwhile colonies or countries that adopted European-style institutions, the mechanisms for governing spiritual power are difficult for politicians to grasp. Many therefore resort to cooptation, joining religious groups themselves or otherwise trying to exert influence over them. African politicians, like their counterparts elsewhere, are concerned with power, whatever its source.

# 5

# POWER

The first president of Ghana, Kwame Nkrumah, was an apostle of pan-African liberation from colonial rule. Internationally famous in his day as one of a new brand of leaders in what was then called the third world, college-educated in the United States but Marxist in his sympathies, he originated a tortuous political philosophy known as 'consciencism'. Ghana was the first colony in sub-Saharan Africa to gain independence, under his leadership, in 1957. He hailed the country as the Black Star of Africa, one that would show the way to others.

Nkrumah was outraged to learn that there were rumours in circulation in Ghana linking him to certain arcane religious practices that would have shocked his foreign friends, who included a range of internationalist revolutionaries as well as the queen of England. It was said among Ghanaians that the biggest of all his grandiose construction projects, a dam on the Volta river, had been inaugurated with a human sacrifice, designed to make the project a success by securing an extra input of spiritual power. One of the president's top press aides recorded the efforts the government made to scotch this allegation.[1]

The rumour that the president of Ghana was responsible for killings supposedly meant to acquire spiritual power was not so much a sign of popular opposition as an acknowledgement of his authority. The modern republic of Ghana occupies an area that largely corresponds to one of the most powerful of precolonial African political constructions, the Ashanti kingdom. Ashanti kings and potentates, like those of many other polities in West and central Africa, could order people to be killed on key occasions, such as when an important chief died and some of his wives and servants had to accompany him to the next world where he would continue to need their services.[2] Mortuary slayings of this type were one of a range of practices regarded as legitimate in much of West Africa little more than a century ago, but which were disapproved of by Christian missionaries and outlawed by colonial governments. Some people privately continued to regard similar practices as a necessary accessory of power throughout colonial times.[3] Hence, the fact that many Ghanaians thought Nkrumah had ordered humans to be killed in order to ensure the successful completion of a prestigious construction project was based on an assumption that he wielded the same sort of influence as a precolonial Ashanti king, in addition to the bureaucratic powers that he had inherited from British governors in the form of an army, a police force, an intelligence service and all the other trappings of colonial rule, supplemented with services provided by his Chinese and Eastern European advisors. Nkrumah encouraged people to think this way by adopting one of the titles of an Ashanti chief, Osagyefo ('Redeemer'). He became officially known as President Osagyefo Dr Kwame Nkrumah, or simply Osagyefo. He even encouraged a personality cult in which he assumed the role of Christ.[4]

This formidable corpus of power was not enough to save Nkrumah from being overthrown in 1966 in a military coup widely supposed to have been encouraged by the CIA. The victorious coup-plotters were well aware of the popular view that powerful politicians make use of arcane spiritual techniques, and fed the press with news that a special room had been found in Nkrumah's presidential residence containing objects associated with bloody rituals. Nkrumah, they said, had been addicted to the advice of traditional priests who advised him to make human sacrifices. According to the Accra *Evening News* of 12 April 1966, he kept a mummified body, considered to be a repository of spiritual power, in his presidential *juju* room.[5]

Rumours of extravagant spiritual connections have continued to be attached to Ghanaian governments since then. When in 1979 a radical young air force officer, J. J. Rawlings, took power with a promise to clean the country of corruption, he soon became known as 'Junior Jesus'. Like Nkrumah, he aspired to be the saviour of his country. Later, some time after his second coup in 1981, the JJ prefix was changed in popular speech into 'Junior Judas' because of Rawlings's failure to deliver on his promises. When the urbane lawyer John Kufuor was elected to succeed Rawlings as president in 2000, he did not occupy the Castle, the formal seat of government, on the grounds that it was in need of repair. The general public, however, suspected that the real reason was that the Castle needed to be cleansed of the evil spirits believed to lurk there. This was widely discussed in radio phone-in programmes in Ghana.[6]

These accounts suggest that Ghanaians readily assume that their politicians are in communication with the spirit world, and that the connection may be sinister. Political power, like spiritual power, is regarded as ambivalent since it can be used to do good or to inflict harm. Hence, successful politicians are both admired and feared. By the same token, religious specialists who can effect spiritual cures are also presumed to have the power to harm. The ambivalence of power reflects the ambivalence of the spirit world itself.

### Spirits and the ambivalence of power

It is a commonplace to observe that Africans today are confronted with a formidable range of problems, from economics to epidemics. To judge from the popular literature sold on the streets of African cities, stories on the radio and in the newspapers, sermons preached in the astonishing variety of churches, and rumours swapped through *radio trottoir*, many people consider these matters in a spirit idiom. Although people are well aware of the material reasons for many of their difficulties, many also think about problems from AIDS to food shortages to corruption as having their deepest explanation in the actions of powerful figures who manipulate the spirit world. This is not in the first instance because of a lack of technical information, as most people seem well aware of the ways in which AIDS is transmitted or the techniques by which public monies are embezzled. But public education campaigns about safe sex do not necessarily change popular ideas about the origins of AIDS, and nor do campaigns for good governance always prevent corruption.

We have mentioned previously the rumour in Zaire that AIDS has actually been spread by officials of the central bank.[7] That public functionaries should be thought capable of doing such a wicked thing is compatible with the general view that President Mobutu was in close contact with the most evil forces of the spirit world and that his government was nothing but a gang of witches. In a documentary film, Mobutu's former propaganda chief is recorded alleging that Mobutu drank the blood of people he had had killed for ritual purposes.[8] The same former minister has also alleged that Mobutu dumped tons of 'mystical products' into the River Congo at its source to cast a spell over the entire population, and banned the sale of imported beer so that people would be obliged to drink a brew made with local water.[9] If only in its scale, this manipulation recalls the suggestion of the Zairean Evangelist Mukendi that underground witches have taken on the human form of white people and infiltrated international organisations, implying that the World Bank and other key organisations have been subverted by forces of evil.[10] In neighbouring

Brazzaville too, people refer to the governing elite as *lisanga ya ba ndoki*, a clique of witches.[11]

Throughout West, central and southern Africa, there are frequent rumours of people being killed by politicians and businessmen especially who believe that they can acquire powerful medicines with parts taken from a human body, and that these will help them to achieve material success. Although such alleged killings are rumoured far more often than they are proven beyond reasonable doubt, there are occasional court cases in which evidence is produced sufficient to secure conviction. One of the most interesting cases—since it concerned senior politicians—was that of Allen Yancy and six others in Liberia in 1979. Yancy was from one of the country's leading political families, being the son of a former vice-president of the republic and himself a former chief of police for Maryland County. He was a member of the legislature at the time of his arrest. Among his co-accused was the eldest son of the president of the then ruling party. The accused pleaded guilty to the charges of murder[12] and, although the legal process against them was flawed and politically manipulated, admitted their guilt in private also. Few Liberians have any doubts that leading politicians use a range of bloody rituals to stay in power, including a later head of state, Samuel Doe, who was rumoured to practise rituals including 'drinking the blood and/or eating the fetuses of pregnant young girls'.[13]

These rumours are one aspect of a widespread preoccupation with evil and its manifestations in daily life. In markets all over the continent, pamphlets on the problem of evil, written by Africans and published locally, are best-sellers.[14] There are widespread accounts of a spiritual underworld where people may make money through contracts that promise worldly riches in return for a pact with the devil. Stories of witches and sinister ghosts and spirits are popular in television soap operas and video cassettes and are discussed in radio phone-ins. They are a common topic of conversation. In short, there is a widespread perception that evil is pervasive and palpable. This state of affairs may be regrettable, but it certainly does not reflect a view of life that is frivolous or superficial. Nor does the spiritual dimension displace more prosaic explanations for Africa's problems, such as poor governance or an unjust world order. Rather, many people merge religious and secular modes of explanation, so that secular forces like imperialism or neo-colonialism are assumed to have a spiritual component.

Although there is evidence that Africans have thought about the world in terms of a spirit idiom throughout recorded history, they have not always had such a bleak view as in recent years. One may ask why this has come about. There are at least three reasons why people have come to see the traditional spirit world increasingly as a source of almost undiluted evil. The first of these, as we have discussed,[15] is that there has been a gradual demonisation of the spirit world over a long period, dating back to the nineteenth-century evangelisation of Africa by foreign missionaries. As a result, the traditional spirit world has lost much of its original morally neutral character. Second, the traditional religious specialists who used to have the authority to regulate relations between the human and the spirit worlds have seen their influence dwindle during the twentieth century. Factors that have eroded it include the institution of a secular state apparatus; social changes that undermine the standing of the village elders and notables who officiate in traditional religious cults; and Western education, secular or Christian. Traditional experts today are often ridiculed by younger people and despised by adherents of new religious movements, including Islamists and 'born-again' Christians. There are raging debates between advocates of a return to tradition and those, including the more radical Pentecostals, who maintain that indigenous practices, or indeed any religious actions not based on explicit scriptural authority, are evil. Third, since the spirit world is to some extent a reflection of the material world, it is hardly surprising that it mirrors the adverse conditions of so many African countries today. After a century of rapid and profound change, there is considerable confusion about what precisely constitutes good and evil, including in such important matters as making war,[16] while in many countries there is no consensus on which authorities are competent to pronounce on such matters. The old techniques no longer work. Nowadays, the traditional spirit world itself is often seen as inherently evil.

Thus people have lost the means to resolve the many problems that they attribute to evil spirits and witches. This has been widely noted by Western anthropologists among others, who have in recent years produced a series of works on witchcraft in Africa[17] and on the theologies of evil in charismatic churches.[18] The same processes have also been extensively described by African experts on religion and theology, whose work has received little attention from Western scholars.[19] Accusations of witchcraft often arise when people find their vitality waning without any obvious reason, to the extent that they fear their very essence is being consumed. They conclude that the cause lies in the relationship with another person, whom they suspect of using evil powers. The notion that every living being contains a life-force has been recorded over many decades from all parts of Africa.[20] It is common for people who use a spirit idiom to think of the power residing inside themselves as an autonomous force, which some believe to reside in a physical object contained in the stomach. Others conceive of it as a purely abstract notion. Witches are often suspected of stealing or 'eating' the life-force of others to enhance their own vitality. People suspected of using witchcraft are liable to the cruellest treatment.

Although it is impossible to know for sure whether witchcraft accusations are more frequent now than in the past, it is hard to avoid the impression that they have reached epidemic proportions in some countries. People who are believed to manipulate the spirit world for selfish purposes include politicians and plutocrats. Above all, though, witchcraft accusations concern neighbours and family members. For example, in Congo there has recently been an epidemic of witchcraft accusations made by parents against their own children.[21] Criminal gangs working in the international prostitution and drugs trades exploit traditional beliefs to bind young girls whom they then exploit as sex-slaves for profit.[22] This perversion of traditional morality reflects both a social and a spiritual confusion.

Hence it is not surprising that so many people are constantly searching for power that will effectively protect them. This is one important reason for the popularity of new religious movements that promise original solutions for contemporary problems. Just as harm is thought to be caused by those who manipulate the spirit world for their own selfish purposes, it is to the same arena that people turn for effective remedies, in the form of powers and medicines that can protect and heal them. The concept of medicine implies more than just a medium for curing a physical ailment. A medicine is an instrument for channelling power from the spirit world, which may be either harmful or protective according to the ambivalent nature of the spirit world itself. There are 'good' medicines designed to cure illness and amulets to ward off danger, but also 'bad' medicines that transmit harmful forces that are used for offensive purposes. Both good and bad medicines are often popularly referred to as 'magical charms', *juju* and so on.

Where it is widely believed that a spirit world exists, people may seek intensive contact with individual spirits in times of crisis, just as a family crisis might provoke urgent discussions with relatives and neighbours. A typical circumstance calling for closer contact with the spirit world could be a serious illness or infertility or impotence, but it could also be something as mundane as long-term unemployment or other forms of 'bad luck'. By the same token, good luck may be sought actively from the spirit world, such as for safe travel or success in school exams. Not only do African footballers routinely pray when they take the field for a match, but they are also known for taking a range of other spiritual measures intended to secure victory. Riots have occurred when a team or its supporters find evidence of counter-measures by the opposing team, such as burying *juju* objects under the goal-mouth designed to attract the ball into the net.[23] Entire sports teams may consult healers before matches.

Since health and prosperity are considered to include the moral and spiritual as well as physical aspects of life, it is logical that remedies also extend into these areas. G. L. Chavunduka, former vice-chancellor of the University of Zimbabwe, himself a practising healer as well as a social scientist, speaks of the need for 'holistic medicine', which treats the whole person and not only that part of the body which ails.[24] He applies several analytical distinctions within this holistic approach. Disease, according to Chavunduka, is a word that properly refers to the medical aspect of ill health, defined in terms of biological or physiological malfunctioning; illness refers to an element of social dysfunction; and sickness refers to the subjective experience of an individual condition.[25]

People who claim some expertise in healing routinely advertise their services in the press, through handbills, on billboards and by word of mouth, generally claiming to be able to cure physical ailments without any self-evident cause, like headaches and back pain, but also troubles that in Western medicine would be regarded as partly or wholly psychological, such as disturbing dreams and impotence. Many of the best healers combine a deep knowledge of medicinal plants with acute psychiatric skill expressed in a spirit idiom. A person suffering from insomnia, for example, may be diagnosed as being troubled by the spirit of a deceased parent who needs to be placated. Rather typical is the Zambian healer whose price-list includes remedies for bad luck, unemployment, and other problems regarded in Western clinical practice as entirely non-medical. The healer, one Dr R. Vongo, offers advice on such matters as death, theft or loss, and treatment for rheumatism, blood pressure disorders, heavy or irregular menstrual periods, sore eyes, asthma, but also[26]

> Directions on how to thank your ancestor spirits
> Have your worrying dreams explained
> Love smoke, preparing for important discussions, interviews or meetings
> Travellers' charm
> Magic pen for exams class
> Lucky cuttings on 4 sides of the head
> Bowel cleaner to remove dirty or acid or gass [*sic*]
> Improve your sexual powers (super class and middle class)
> Lucky, especially for job seekers
> Remove bad spirits
> House protection from enemies

...as well as 'Hamurabbi style (an eye for an eye)', which appears to be a counter-attack against malicious spells.

These days, such advertisements are to be found also in many large cities outside Africa where Africans have settled. Moreover, in cities like Paris with large African populations, many indigenous whites also resort to African healers. The migration of African people to the West has not effaced the migrants' perception of the causality of sickness and the necessity for healing. Africans who have lived in the West for years, including university graduates, lawyers and other professionals, continue to consider health with reference to both the spiritual and material realms. Both sickness and health are seen as manifestations of a spiritual power that may invest a person and either add to or diminish his vital force. 'A person who is oppressed, who must daily face injustices and affronts to his personal dignity, is a person who lacks power',[27] the South African theologian Allan Anderson has noted. Use of the word 'power' in this sense is as common in religious circles as it is in politics. During the 1980s, anti-apartheid militants in South Africa were known for their chanting of the slogan *amandla!* ('power') or *amandla ngawethu!* ('the power is ours'). Its use is echoed in African-initiated churches, even overseas. For example, an African pastor in Europe, using a clenched-fist gesture reminiscent of the liberation struggle, may shout 'Jesus!', while the congregation responds with 'power!' In this case, the congregation, of course, is being enjoined not to overthrow a government but to draw upon the power of Jesus through the Holy Spirit. Power is required in many situations, from living under apartheid to the difficulties of life in Europe, where the greatest problem for African immigrants is to acquire legal documentation.[28]

The power acquired by individuals implies their ability to live and to have an abundant life, to be healthy, and to avoid poverty and all the other misfortunes that trouble everyone from time to time.[29] Anderson summarises the idea widespread in Africa that all forms of sickness and misfortune are related to a lack of power as a whole, in the statement: 'our life, our very existence is inextricably tied up with power. To live is to have power, to be sick or to die is to have less of it'.[30] It is in order to achieve a condition of wholeness that people feel the need to consult religious specialists like Dr Vongo for what might be called self-empowerment. Spiritual power, for this reason, is described by Anderson as 'enabling power', which allows people to take control of situations they are otherwise unable to master. The ability of power in general to shape people's lives is recognised in many parts of the world, and indeed many definitions of political power include some consideration of its ability to transform those over whom it is exercised.[31]

Accessing spiritual power is deemed to be a field in which women excel, and many so-called 'medicine-men' are women. At the heart of women's perceived spiritual qualities is the belief that they are by nature closer than men to the spirit world due to their ability to produce life. This observation is not unique to Africa either. Elsewhere in the world there is evidence that people think there to be a connection between women's fertility and a dimension of spiritual knowledge from which men are excluded, causing them to respect and fear women in equal measure.[32] This is probably one reason why women are more likely than men to be accused of witchcraft. The capacity of women to produce new life by bearing children is shared by deities, which in some traditions are also considered able to reproduce by creating new versions of themselves that can be transported from a 'mother' shrine to a new site.[33]

Women are prominent as leaders of the thousands of independent churches in Africa that are known particularly for their healing activities. West Africa even has female Muslim sheikhs.[34] One new religious group in Ghana, Zetaheal Mission, combines elements of both Christianity and Islam, and is led by a woman.[35] Typically, such movements start when a person, male or female, is recognised as being called by a powerful spirit, and then goes on to become established as a religious specialist. In Christian belief, such a calling is seen as the work of the Holy Spirit. The historical mainline churches—those that emerged from the experience of European mission—tend to accord a far less prominent role to this spirit than African indigenous churches, more familiar with spirit belief, generally do. In mainline churches the power of the spirit is usually mediated by professional, male functionaries, who may doubt the legitimacy of any unregulated vocation. Women leaders are not easily accommodated into these churches, as the continuing debate on women's ordination in the Catholic Church indicates, hence women are more likely to establish their own independent congregations.

Indeed, it is rare for women in Africa to hold high public office in any field, although this is becoming more frequent under the influence of international feminism. Since independence, there has been only one female head of state in Africa. This was Ruth Perry of Liberia, who occupied the position only as a makeweight for a few weeks in 1996 while rival warlords battled one another. Nevertheless, women may assert real influence on politics by indirect means through their privileged access to spiritual power. That this is not without risk has been illustrated by I. M. Lewis. In his discussion of *zar* possession in Somalia, he shows how women, by becoming possessed, may create legitimate space for themselves in which they may make political and economic claims that would not normally be admissible. Those who go too far in this direction, however, risk being accused of witchcraft, turning this spiritual power into an illegitimate force. In short, the use of spiritual power by women can be dangerous if it trangresses the limits set by men.[36]

Just how redoubtable the power of a woman leader may become is illustrated by Alice Lakwena, a Ugandan prophetess (Lakwena means 'messenger' in Acholi) who in the 1980s made common cause with some defeated army officers to create an important military movement.[37] Her case is all the more notable in that no institution of state has been more male-dominated than the armed forces, which have been a key factor in Africa's postcolonial history. This is only one of several well-known cases of a process whereby religious and political power merge: politicians and others often try to co-opt religious leaders, like Mary Akatsa in Kenya.[38] Hence, politicians are constantly aware of the potential offered by spiritual power. This can be articulated by African prophets who can emerge, sometimes with astonishing speed, from the most obscure corners of society. Sometimes, new prophets can attract massive followings with formidable political and even military consequences.

Thus does spiritual power enter the world of *realpolitik*.

## Power and institutions

Various forms of power are connected to some degree in most societies. Even where state and church are formally separated, and where government is divided into legislative, executive and judicial branches, and where there is a high degree of respect for legal convention, powers may overlap. In the United States, leading politicians command very large sums of money and, conversely, wealthy people can acquire considerable political influence. Hence, the observation that politicians and wealthy business people in Africa are widely believed to have more spiritual power than the average person is not particularly surprising. Our point, however, goes further than this: the tendency for politicians to seek spiritual power, and for spiritual leaders to develop substantial material power, shows distinctive patterns in continuity with systems and ideas rooted deep in Africa's history.

Colonial rule was intended as a rupture with many aspects of that history. Briefly, colonial administrators believed that government should be through the modern, bureaucratic organs of a state whose core function is to maintain a monopoly of violence. In a modern state this is achieved by promulgating a rational system of law. Such states also implement rational policies that depend on material inputs for the satisfaction of specific aims deemed to be in the common good. The latter is identified, in the last resort, by political authorities who in colonial times were situated in European metropoles but today are located in Africa's capitals. This colonial concept of government is almost identical to that of 'good governance' so much in vogue among donors today. Nowadays, some of the difficulties people experience in regulating their dealings with the spirit world arise from the condition of Africa's public institutions, which were originally established by the colonial powers in conformity with the norms applying in Europe at that time.

Colonial states also used indigenous rulers in a system of indirect rule (largely because it was cheap), and this stimulated the mutual assimilation of imported and indigenous ideas of government. The erosion of Africa's public institutions in the last two decades has revealed the extent to which, throughout colonial rule, power was being incorporated into religious patterns of thought. Hence, many of Africa's new religious movements are attempts to revive known sources of power. In effect, many forms of religious revival challenge the very bases of legitimacy of states that operate through institutions and norms of governance originally created in colonial times. The rather sudden and radical political changes in Africa in the 1990s encouraged the irruption of spiritual movements into political space as people sought alternative sources of authority and at the same time were freed from institutional constraints previously imposed by single-party governments. Seen in this light, the reoccupation of public space by religious movements expresses in a spirit idiom a concern with poor governance. This is clearly the case with neo-pentecostal movements, whose central concern is the presence of evil in society. Although they have existed in Africa for much of the last century, their recent extraordinary increase is certainly connected to the opening up of political space through the democratisation movement.[39] This is also broadly true of the Islamic revival movements witnessed from Cape Town to Algiers. Something similar could be said of traditional religions in Africa.[40]

Whether religious or political in nature, no power can endure without institutional foundation. According to Max Weber,[41] power is subject to a permanent tension between that asserted by the personal authority of leaders whom he calls charismatic, and that of bureaucracies, where power resides more in the office than in the individual. The distinction he makes between personal and institutional charisma ('charisma of the office') can be seen as the two extremes of a continuum. Sooner or later, if it is to

endure, personal charisma is bound to become subject to a form of insti-
tutionalisation, during which the charismatic characteristics are transferred
from the unique personality, or the unstructured group, to an institutional
order. The specific charismatic aspects are dissipated as they become integrated into the orderly, regular routine of social organisation. This insight
is helpful in a number of ways. First, it explains the tensions between highly
organised religious institutions, such as historical mainline churches, and
the charismatic leaders that are a feature of Africa's indigenous traditions.
Second, it casts light on the reasons why politicians try to associate themselves with charismatic religious leaders, in the hope that spiritual power
will be reflected on themselves. This is likely to lead to some unprecedented configurations of power in years to come. Third, it suggests that
the search for spiritual power, so prominent in Africa's new religious movements, must find institutional channels if it is to endure.

We may see these processes at work in the history of Ghana, with which
this chapter began. Secular leaders there have regularly tried to co-opt
religious power. Successive political leaders after President Nkrumah
emphasised their credentials as Christians or God-fearing people with a
view to maximising electoral support.[42] Meanwhile, some religious leaders
have tried to create new institutions independent of their colonial antecedents. A particularly interesting example concerns Vincent Damuah,
also known by his Ghanaian name Kwabena Damuah. In addition, he
used two traditional titles, *osofo* and *okomfo*, which both designate a person
having a special relationship with the spirit world. Ordained as a Roman
Catholic priest in 1957, the year of Ghana's independence, Damuah
became increasingly dissatisfied over the years with the failure of the
Catholic Church to take full account of what he saw as African spirituality.
As Ghana underwent a drastic economic and political decline under a
series of corrupt military governments, Damuah became close to various
left-wing intellectuals and activists. In 1981 a young air force officer, Flight-
Lieutenant Jerry Rawlings, took power in his second coup, this time at the
head of a wide and unstable coalition of left-leaning political forces including radical soldiers, civilian intellectuals and pan-Africanist revolutionaries. The dashing Rawlings proclaimed himself chairman of a broad-based
committee intended to hold the ring while a radical new system was put in
place. Father Damuah was one of the eight people appointed to the ruling
committee, known as the Provisional National Defence Council.

It is in itself interesting that the PNDC government should have considered a dissident Catholic priest such as Damuah to have enough political
weight to merit a place in the ruling council. His Africanist ideas seem to

have chimed with the anti-Western thinking of some of the more orthodox Marxists and the assorted admirers of revolutionary Libya, Nicaragua
and Ethiopia gathered around Rawlings. Meanwhile, Damuah pressed
on with his ambition of founding a new African religion. In late 1982 he
resigned from the ruling council and renounced his Catholic ministry to
take up his new project: 'to re-activate the African Traditional Religion to
take its leading role among the religions of the world'.[43] He called the new
religion Afrikania Mission or Godian religion. Damuah described Godianism, allegedly rooted in the African experience, as a way of life and as a
spiritual revolution that aims to create a new world order based on God,
on 'positive conscientism' (a clear reference to Kwame Nkrumah's political philosophy of similar name) and on spiritual equilibrium. Godianism
would fight for the religious and cultural emancipation of the black person. It rejects the claim of Christianity as the only way to salvation. Damuah
demanded compensation from the former colonial rulers and missionaries
of Africa for distorting the continent's religion and imposing 'unnecessary'
doctrines. He even wanted foreign journalists to compensate 'the African'
for their misleading writings and criminal representation of Africa as the
Dark Continent. The whole thrust of his radical career was, Damuah
wrote, to advance not just the Ghanaian revolution, but the 'total African
Liberation Movement and all the struggling people of the world'.[44]

There is nothing new in religious leaders associating themselves with
politics and even accepting formal office, sometimes in governments known
for their corruption or repression. Reverend Canaan Banana, a Methodist
church minister, was no less than the first president of independent Zimbabwe. He retained his position throughout the 1980s while the government of Prime Minister Robert Mugabe was organising the systematic
killing of thousands of people in the west of the country. Kenya's President arap Moi was particularly adept at gaining the support of independent church leaders, and appointed Archbishop Ondiek of the Legio Maria
Church as a minister in his government.[45] In overwhelmingly Muslim
Senegal, successive presidents since independence have courted the leaders of Sufi brotherhoods, which have on occasion explicitly recommended
their followers to vote for a particular party.

## *Religion and democracy*

Ghana's decline from the Black Star of Africa to economic and political
basket-case in just two-and-a-half decades, until its stabilisation under
Rawlings after he had done a deal with the International Monetary Fund

(IMF) and the World Bank, was dramatic. It was, alas, not unique. By the late 1980s, many Africans, including notably from the urban middle classes, had grown dissatisfied with the undemocratic, and often single-party, political systems that had become the norm in many parts of the continent and had presided over the years of decline. Everywhere there was a feeling that political power, which in the 1960s had been promised to whole nations, had been confiscated by cliques that used it in their own interest with little regard for formal checks and balances. After the extraordinary upheavals in Eastern Europe in 1989, a similar point of view was also gaining ground among the providers of development aid, that is to say the world's richest countries and the most powerful development institutions such as the IMF and the World Bank. From late 1989 onwards, most African countries were under intense pressure to carry out political reforms. When Nelson Mandela was released from prison in February 1990, all over Africa people wondered aloud whether, if the hated apartheid government could prove itself capable of change, then why not a host of other tyrants?

A rough consensus soon emerged between African reformers and international development technocrats as to what form these reforms should take: countries wishing to continue receiving development aid and to gain a stamp of international approval in the new, post-cold war world would be expected to hold regular parliamentary and presidential elections and to allow free political competition and freedom of expression. This was the democratisation process that was such a prominent feature of African politics in the early 1990s, inspiring hundreds of academic books and articles and thousands of newspaper reports.

But Africa's democratisation soon began to produce results quite different from those its supporters had intended or imagined. Outside South Africa, there were few unambiguous triumphs for democracy. In some places, incumbent heads of state were thrown out of office after losing democratic elections but were replaced by newcomers who manifested many of the same characteristics as their predecessors. More surprising were the heads of state, including some of Africa's most notoriously corrupt dictators, who managed to hold on to power even after allowing an opposition to emerge. Presidents Eyadéma (Togo), Bongo (Gabon), and Biya (Cameroon) are all prime examples. Presidents Houphouët-Boigny (Côte d'Ivoire) and Mobutu (Zaire) achieved the same feat but were undone by age and sickness, the former dying in 1993 and the latter, brought down as much by cancer as by his enemies, in 1997. In Madagascar and Benin, two old-style political dinosaurs accepted defeat in democratic elections and then, in an astonishing turn-around, got themselves elected in a subsequent poll.

It is instructive to see how such political veterans managed to stay in power into a democratic era. All of them used an array of techniques, including straightforward bribery of opposition politicians so as to divide their parties, propaganda through state-owned media, and the creation of legal formalities calculated to hamper opponents, such as requirements for a minimum number of party members in each region of the country. Ethnicity emerged as a redoubtable mechanism for mobilising support in the new democratic dispensation. In the old days of one-party states, politicians had often organised their support on ethnic lines but were obliged to do so surreptitiously, respecting official injunctions to eschew ethnic particularism and build a new nation. Now, leaders could openly exhort members of a particular ethnic group to support them. In some cases, the existence of ethnic political blocs reflected a long history of political or cultural community, while in others these units resulted more than anything from colonial practices of indirect rule, which encouraged the construction of tribal units for administrative purposes. In the most extreme cases, today's ethnic units are new formations that have emerged as a result of political imperatives and on the basis of administrative divisions only in the last two or three decades. Modern political ethnicity in Africa—sometimes known as tribalism—is not an ancient form of organisation that is re-emerging as a result of state collapse. Rather, as an American anthropologist was correct in noting, '"tribalism", the avowed enemy of national unity, has been a product of...nationalisation itself'.[46] Only rarely do today's political-ethnic blocks demand secession. In most cases they are instruments for demanding an increased role in existing national politics.

Ethnicity and nationality have both been subject to the complex interplay of formal and informal political methods that has become characteristic of African public life in general. In Zambia and Côte d'Ivoire, changes to the constitution or to electoral laws have been made by incumbent governments to exclude particular presidential candidates from future elections on the grounds of foreign parentage. In both cases this ploy was a blatant piece of opportunism as the intended targets of these rule changes—Kenneth Kaunda in Zambia and Alassane Ouattara in Côte d'Ivoire—had already served as head of state and head of government respectively. The argument about who is or is not really from a native-born family, in countries that generally did not exist as sovereign entities before the 1960s, has become a very hot topic. In numerous countries, it has been rumoured that even the longest-serving heads of state are not really nationals of the countries they rule. According to many versions of *radio trottoir*, Houphouët-Boigny was in fact a Ghanaian, Mobutu was born in the Central African Republic, José Eduardo dos Santos of Angola is from Saõ Tomé, Hastings Banda was really an American, and so on. Rumours of this sort are so widespread that they appear to represent a fundamental conviction about the nature of heads of state, namely that they are basically aliens.

This illustrates a fundamental principle of rule in Africa and indeed in many other parts of the world. Where there are ruling castes, families or dynasties these often claim or justify their privileges partly on the grounds that they are a sort of people different from the rest of the population. This has been central, for example, to the character of royal houses in Europe, which have traditionally married into other familes of similar status, or at least foreigners, rather than commoners of their own countries. The underlying principle until very recently was that the crowned heads of Europe were somehow related (which in any case many actually were, through intermarriage), and that they were literally of a different breed from commoners. Traditions of monarchy in other parts of the world insist that the founders of a dynasty have their origin in a figure who descends from heaven, or is the product of a union between a mortal and a deity or a spirit, like the emperor of Japan. Not for nothing did the French revolutionary orator Saint-Just denounce the monarchy that he and his colleagues were brutally ending as 'an unnatural being'.[47] Precolonial ruling dynasties in central Africa often promulgated genealogies and myths of origin that emphasised their origins among divinely-inspired strangers.[48] The ambiguous nature of these founder-kings has been reproduced by more recent rulers.

The most skilful African presidents have not discouraged rumours that their origins are mysterious, since the notion that they are from elsewhere helps them to govern ethnically diverse populations by dissociating themselves from any single ethnic group.[49] So, to return to our discussion of democratisation in the 1990s, many presidents navigated the dangers democratisation posed to them by encouraging the belief—already contained in the personality cults of the old one-party states—that the head of state is the repository of great mystical power that originates elsewhere. The simultaneous use of death-squads and clandestine thuggery of all types encouraged the belief that presidents were not only even more powerful than people had presumed, but that this power was of an essentially sinister type.[50] In Zaire, fief of arguably the most innovative and Machiavellian of all African dictators, there were more than ever stories of President Mobutu surrounding himself with marabouts and magicians who conferred miraculous powers on him. Spiritual power is a vital political reality.

'Reputation of power, is Power', Thomas Hobbes wrote over three centuries ago, 'because it bringeth with it the adhærence of those that need protection'.[51] This insight goes some way to explaining why, during the democratisation process of the 1990s, many African politicians took a fresh interest in religious movements that were already in existence. For the sake of what in advertising jargon is called a public image, political leaders must always pay attention not only to their own reputations, but also to those of others in society.

Also in the 1990s, discussion of who really is or is not from a particular territory emerged more strongly than before as a basic element of politics almost all over Africa. In law, of course, citizens are equal in rights and may live in any part of the national territory that they wish. But there has been a spate of arguments, that can all too often turn violent, about which ethnic groups may actually live in particular places within a country. This has led to forms of ethnic cleansing over large areas of the continent, such as in central Nigeria, in Kenya, and in Zimbabwe. In most cases these result from a mixture of ethnic mobilisation fuelled by the new multi-party politics and fears about the loss of land provoked by moves to liberalise land ownership laws. Democratisation, debates about ethnic allegiance, the growth of a free market in land and other factors have all combined to cause arguments such as whether people of Sahelian origin are really Ivorians, whether the Tiv should live in certain federal states of central Nigeria (on land they have occupied for centuries), whether Mandingoes may live in Liberia and, most tragically, whether Tutsis really have a right to live in Rwanda. People soon manufacture or remember myths that they claim to have historical validity, such as that all Tutsis originate in Ethiopia and are thus foreign.[52] One may consider in the same bracket the argument that white Zimbabwean citizens of local birth are not 'really' Zimbabwean. Moreover, this is part of an international debate, as white Europeans wonder whether German, British or Dutch citizens of Middle Eastern or African origin are 'really' nationals, even when they are born and bred in the country and have legal title.

When ethnic mobilisation becomes a strategy for political organisation, it can lead to violence as fault-lines of conflict become apparent. When this in turn occurs in societies where certain forms of religious allegiance are associated with particular ethnic groups or regions, then religion can become associated with violence. In general, there has been rather little violence on religious grounds in African conflicts, even where the population is thoroughly diverse, including Christians, Muslims and others. Violence organised along religious lines is most closely associated with Sudan and Nigeria. In both cases, memories of enslavement by Muslim state-builders in precolonial times make religious allegiance a matter always likely to raise passions. In Nigeria, although parts of the country have a history of Islam being used for purposes of government over centuries, the modern incidence of religiously-related massacres really dates back only to the 1980s. Also in both cases, such violence is more a strategy in a political struggle than a religiously-inspired action in itself. Properly speaking, there are no religious wars in Africa south of the Sahara.

Ethnic and religious mobilisation in a democracy can be a strategy that favours either the government or the opposition, depending on the precise circumstances. In general, the experience of democratisation in the 1990s showed the great advantages of incumbency in giving access to a whole range of politically useful instruments. Presidents control the state bureaucracy and official media and can use the sovereign rights of the state to their advantage, such as to print money and boost the economy just before elections. Many other methods, however, rely on a purely informal exercise of power, at times flagrantly criminal, such as using thugs or personal militias to murder opponents or stir up ethnic hatred. An important part of many winning strategies in the 1990s was for a president simultaneously to cultivate an image as a head of state and father of the nation who is formally above party politics, rather like a constitutional monarch, while actually using informal means to engage in the most vicious political manoeuvres. The fact that the dirtiest methods were informal meant that they were also deniable. It greatly encouraged the popular belief that power tends to be exercised in secret and has become inherently evil.

Indeed, an emphasis on institutional reforms, limited to the formal political realm, was one of the reasons for the widespread failure of democratisation to produce a more equitable spread of power. Among its other failings, liberal democracy could not formally encompass spiritual power. This may be one explanation why so many of the national conferences held in Africa in the early 1990s chose bishops as their presidents, people who could appeal to sources of power unavailable to discredited politicians but who were unlikely to turn their office into the base for a presidential campaign.[53] This is another example of how the political space opened by democratisation encouraged religious revival. Inasmuch as the established Christian churches (the former missionary or mainline churches), with the best international connections, have been widely observed to have encouraged the democratisation movement, they did so through formal channels. The Vatican, for example, appealed to a number of national Commissions for Justice and Peace in Africa to lobby for the democratisation of their governments. This message soon reached grassroot level through the structures of basic Christian communities. A secondary effect was a call for more democracy in the day-to-day affairs of local Catholic churches themselves.[54] Attempts to regulate power by imposing new rules have in many cases resulted in formal institutions being voided of power, which instead is conducted along informal channels. The religious sphere has become subject to a similar phenomenon as the political sphere, with a massive growth of unregulated activity.

Churches in Africa have been criticised by Western academics for their failure to speak out against corruption and injustice and for their willingness even to make common cause with disreputable regimes.[55] Leaders of the latest generation of independent churches, including those of a charismatic variety, are sometimes regarded as particularly susceptible to lending their support to regimes considered unsavoury in liberal quarters. Presidents Taylor (Liberia), Chiluba (Zambia), Kérékou (Benin) and Obasanjo (Nigeria) have all made political capital out of publicly declaring themselves to be born-again Christians. Some Catholic clerics actually participated in the 1994 genocide in Rwanda. Religious organisations and media have also been berated for their relative failure to advance explicitly the cause of democracy in Africa by organising support for, or opposition to, particular parties or leaders or commenting on specific political issues.[56] The most explicit political comment to emanate from religious circles has generally been from the mainline churches, the ones most closely associated with European missionaries and most closely resembling European institutions. Liberal church leaders sometimes lament that leaders of independent churches will actually sing the praises of the worst tyrants and warlords, perhaps in return for cash or favours. Some critics have suggested that healing churches are especially prone to being politically acquiescent, presumably because their energies are turned towards the spiritual healing of individuals rather than towards political action aimed at restoring the health of society as a whole.[57]

These observations require an explanation. To some degree, religious people may believe that any means for advancing their cause is legitimate, and those churches without income from foreign sources may be easily swayed by promises of funding, even when these come from disreputable politicians. It is perhaps useful to compare the situation of African churches not with that of churches in the West, but with the position of foreign aid-donors. Foreign donors have worked with and funded even such notorious dictators as President Mobutu of Zaire, feeling that they have no other choice if they wish to continue operating. African church leaders may follow roughly the same logic. Some may themselves be hypocrites or fraudsters, but it would be unwise to work on the assumption that most are. African Christians, who often interpret the Bible literally, may believe that they are required to work with any incumbent government. Many seem to believe that a president owes his position to God, and that continued incumbency is a sign that the president has continuing divine support, as presidents themselves often argue. Western governments and former mission churches regard power as vested in institutions, whereas Africans are generally more likely to see it as emanating directly from the spirit world. For them, spiritual power, unlike political power as such, draws its strength not from institutions themselves, nor from the will of the people, but from the world of the invisible.

The travails of democratisation, and its introduction at a time when many countries were confronted with enormous political and economic problems, have contributed to an impression that the exercise of supreme political power has become so intrinsically vicious as to be quite literally the work of the devil. This may lead people to wonder about the spiritual sources of the power wielded by politicians. There were so many rumours of devil-worship in Kenya, for example, that the government commissioned an official inquiry into satanism. Its report was not published, giving rise to rumours among the opposition that the reason for this was a finding that senior officials were themselves satanists.[58] In all parts of Africa, presidents are rumoured to maintain coteries of sinister advisors. Zambia's Archbishop Emmanuel Milingo attests that he has actually received confessions from politicians and business people who admit to having made diabolic pacts in return for earthly power and riches.[59] The most striking aspect of these stories is the widespread supposition that the most powerful politicians wield a power that is evil by nature, meaning that it will be consistently used not for the general good, but for the most perverted and selfish purposes. In some cases—Nigeria under Abacha, say, or Zaire under Mobutu—this is indeed a reasonable description of how power was actually used. But it becomes a dangerous self-fulfilment when citizens *expect* power to be abused, and feel vindicated when they see evidence emerging.

The preoccupation with evil that has become evident in politics in recent years may be found in other areas of public life. Some of the political space opened up by democratic reforms has been filled with organisations widely regarded as self-seeking and anti-social, a character also expressed in a spirit idiom. In recent years, we have noted already, there has been a sharp rise on some university campuses of clubs in which students are initiated. Some of these societies are widely regarded as satanic. They often exist in areas where in precolonial times traditional secret societies, in which initiates had religious powers over life and death, have never entirely disappeared, despite being discouraged or outlawed by colonial governments. Some student societies have arrogated to themselves similarly alarming powers.[60] If national governments and armies use their powers for purposes of self-enrichment and law-breaking, it is hardly surprising if students do the same. Student societies in Nigeria for example have been manipulated by military governments as a way of undermining university trade unions and the activities of liberal lecturers.

The growth in unregulated power has resulted in the erosion of what in modern Western thought is regarded as the principal duty and even definition of a state, namely its vocation to monopolise violence within its defined territory. There is now hardly a country in Africa that does not have more or less organised vigilante movements, from Mapogo in South Africa's Limpopo Province, to the gangs of Nairobi, to the many militias and private armies in West Africa. These groups can be situated roughly on a scale, at one end of which are guards formed by small communities with the aim of preventing crime, in the absence of a reliable police force, and armed generally with clubs or bows and arrows and such like. They often closely resemble the armed bands of precolonial times, when young men belonging to a particular age-set would be expected to fight on behalf of their villages in time of trouble. At the other end of the spectrum are thousands-strong warlord armies with artillery and automatic weapons. Many such groups have used methods of recruitment and organisation borrowed from traditional secret societies, and some, like the famous *kamajors* of Sierra Leone, claim to have originated from traditional hunters' guilds. But in just about every case, although they do articulate some historical continuity, such bodies are not romantic resurgences of tradition so much as the creations of modern politicians.[61] One thing all vigilante groups, large or small, defensive or aggressive, have in common is a spiritual component, expressed in ritual and the use of medicines.

## *Religious literature as political comment*

Perhaps the most obvious of the new liberties emerging from Africa's democratisation is a greater freedom of expression. Where the old one-party states kept a tight grip on published or broadcast material, and could even intimidate *radio trottoir* into discretion, new media flowers now blossom. Democracy has opened up a space where ideas are expressed and power is fought for, but not always with respect for empirical truth and professional standards of accuracy or fairness. The new freedom of expression is open to exploitation by incumbent presidents, political heavyweights and assorted entrepreneurs interested less in the objective recording of events than in using the press for purposes of party propaganda, libel and blackmail. Senior politicians have the money to fund their own newspapers and radio stations and may have no inhibitions about bribing or intimidating independent operators. Meanwhile, religious leaders and organisations have also emerged as important broadcasters and publishers, sponsoring newspapers and radio and television programmes, while many pamphlets and videos are produced by individual religious activists. This makes African media extraordinarily interesting as a mirror of what is happening in society, but less dependable as sources of facts or objective reporting, as we have discussed in chapter two. Many popular religious pamphlets that take no position on formal politics are nonetheless heavy with political implications in a broader sense, offering trenchant opinions on society and connecting these with a moral view derived from religious beliefs. Some of these publications, we have argued, can be interpreted as having a political meaning expressed in a spirit idiom. Literature that may appear at first sight to be entirely religious in nature may be usefully read as a critique of power, and of its uses and abuses in politics and society.

One such tract was published in 1995 by Ernest Pianim, a minister in one of the pentecostal churches in Ghana which has branches overseas.[62] Pianim uses biblical imagery and allusions to criticise the past military regimes of Ghana, including the Rawlings government, which was in power when he published his work. It is described in the booklet as 'terrifying, frightening and powerful', and more aggressive in its approach than any previous government. This, the author states, can be seen in the brutal way the government treated students, but also in its efforts to oppose Christian progress, such as by the introduction of the Religious Bodies Decree. But the 'rule of the saints' is coming nearer, he says, as is evidenced by the revival of Christianity in Ghana and among Ghanaians overseas that has taken place since the mid-1970s. Never before, Pianim argues, have so many Ghanaians travelled to all parts of the world as in present times. The explanation for this extraordinary situation is that God is preparing an army of saints both at home and abroad to lead His crusade at the appointed time. When that day dawns, those living abroad will return home to rebuild Ghana using all the knowledge and skills acquired overseas. Then the prophecy for Ghana will be fulfilled. Peace and stability will reign and the country will prosper again.

Whatever one's opinion of such an interpretation of history, it is interesting to see how a religious frame of reference can assimilate and incorporate reflection on important secular developments, including international migration. Pianim's tract is one of several produced in Africa that do not concern only domestic or African themes but also comment on the world as a whole. In this case, Pianim identifies the European Union as the Anti-Christ. This opinion he bases on an evangelical reading of the Bible, beginning with the Old Testament story recording the vision of the prophet Daniel. Chapter eight of the Book of Daniel tells the story of the second of the prophet's visions, that of the ram and the goat. After this vision, which concerns the end of the world, the angel Gabriel comes to Daniel to explain its exact meaning. The two-horned ram represents the two powerful kingdoms of Daniel's time, Medea and Persia, which are overthrown by the Greeks, represented by the goat with its superior horns. The angel then prophesies the end of this kingdom by an unnamed king who, in Pianim's interpretation, is taken to be the ruler of the later Roman Empire. The theme of the horned beasts is taken up once more in the Book of Revelation, which Pianim sees as a continuation of the earlier prophecy about the end of the world. According to Revelation, one last powerful government will come and rule the world. Pianim refers to this regime as the Revived Roman Empire, which he identifies with the European Union, based as it is on the Treaty of Rome. This new government, whose geographical location—not by coincidence but by design, according to Pianim—coincides with the former Holy Roman Empire, will dominate world politics. During that time the Anti-Christ, in the person of the World President, will emerge from the European Union to pose as the world's saviour. Under his reign the rapture of the saints will take place and God will intervene to expose the World President as the Anti-Christ, after which the reign of God will begin, joined by the saints, that is, those who have been born again in Christ.

Religious stories like these, which contain a more or less clear critique of politics expressed in a spirit idiom, may be placed in a tradition where religious practices form the sinews of political allegiances, and where translations of the Bible in local languages are often read as political messages of great potency. In European history too it has been well described how translation of the Bible into vernacular languages gave this religious book a capacity for forming a political ideology, such as in seventeenth-century England.[63] The same tendency is still more clear in Islam, in that

Islam, unlike Christianity, offers a specific view of government in the form of theocratic rule.

These are examples from different continents of how religious thought may inform political action. Religious ideology provides believers with a level of understanding that they consider to be deeper than explanations that limit power to its material aspect. In Africa and elsewhere where people adhere overwhelmingly to religious ideologies, these modes of understanding have a real effect on politics. This is notable in current Islamist groups and more generally in movements often classified as 'fundamentalist'. For this reason, the characteristics that believers attribute to the invisible world become a matter of direct political importance.

Some classic works of European history and sociology describe how the religious ideas that emerged from the debates of the seventeenth century were to have enormous consequences not only for politics but also for economics, as they encouraged types of behaviour that had clear economic outcomes such as the virtues of self-sufficiency, of parsimony and saving, of strict accounting and rigorous codes of borrowing and lending.[64] These too may be expressed in a spirit idiom, as we will see next.

# 6

# WEALTH

Iyke Nathan Uzorma was born in a small town in Imo State, Nigeria, in 1964. People in his home area traditionally believe it to be under the authority of a spirit known as Njaba that is reckoned to have protected it from war and famine during the civil war of 1967–70.[1] There are many other local cults too.

Looking back on his life, Uzorma realises that he was initiated into esoteric cults over many years. 'My partial initiation started in the dream state when I was three years old', he writes. 'In the early part of 1967 I began to have strange dreams, mostly of being turned into a python', widely recognised as an animal closely associated with the spirit world. In adult life, when he had become a senior official of a cult called Okonkor, he learned how to go into trance and make contact with spirits. He used these skills to make money. 'I was empowered by higher sprits to be making money through occult manipulations', he recalls. 'Consequently, I had a mystical handkerchief (Lakshmi Jacha) prepared with the blood of a hunch-back man, with which I made 1,000.00 [nairas] daily'. There were various rules attached to making money by such means, including that he must spend the money only on himself, that the money must be destroyed if not used on the day of its acquisition, and that he would have to kill a pigeon every ninety days and use its blood to revive the powers in the handkerchief. So successful was the handkerchief, with its spiritual power, that it ensured his success in several frauds. By his own admission, among those he succeeded in cheating out of money were a banker in Port Harcourt, a businessman in Kano, an army officer in Lagos and businessmen from Britain and the United States. He also accepted money from those who wanted him to use his special powers to cast deadly spells on their enemies. Uzorma now believes that the spiritual powers he acquired, attested by diplomas from colleges in India and England, were demonic. He converted to Christianity and has become a popular writer and preacher.[2]

Uzorma's story of how he used the spirit world to make money touches upon some aspects of money and wealth that reflect religious beliefs widely held in Africa. These echo ideas that have preoccupied thinkers over the ages, from the ancient Greeks onwards. Chief among the mysteries of money, or of its close associates wealth and capital, are how to acquire it and how to cause it to reproduce by growing in value. These are eminently moral questions, for not all ways of acquiring money are equally respectable.

Curiously, perhaps, the modern obsession with economics, the main preoccupation of Western politicians and a staple of newspaper and television reporting, tends to overlook some of the most basic but also most puzzling aspects of wealth. Modern economic theory tends to consider money in terms of a set of technical problems rather than as a series of philosophical or moral issues. 'Much discussion of money involves a heavy overlay of priestly incantation', one of the most civilised economists tells us, with a sharp dig at his professional colleagues. 'There is nothing about money that cannot be understood by the person of reasonable curiosity, diligence and intelligence'.[3]

## *Money, credit and wealth*

Money is 'what is commonly offered or received for the purchase or sale of goods, services or other things'.[4] It can be banknotes, coins, bank deposits or anything else that is readily used to obtain goods and services which have a value. In industrialised countries, money in these forms or, increasingly, in the form of credit cards, has become so ubiquitous, and so necessary, as to appear almost a natural resource, like air or water. Most money in its modern forms is actually credit issued by lending institutions. Credit itself has a market value based on market traders' trust in the institutions that offer it or guarantee it,[5] including, in the end, the government and the central bank that underpin a country's entire system of credit. Therefore, the value of money reflects quite closely the confidence people have in the states that govern them. There are other sources of wealth than money alone, in the form of valuable assets like land or buildings. In order for these eventually to be translated into money, however, various forms of social and legal transaction are necessary. These generally take time to effect and, in some circumstances, they might be difficult to complete.

There is thus a range of instruments to convey capital, which can potentially be converted to credit and money. Although capital is at the heart of the world's financial and economic system, it is not itself visible. Like a spirit, capital is an abstraction, a concept, that may acquire material form. Capital becomes most easily visible in the form of money. 'Capital is now confused with money', notes the Peruvian economist Hernando de Soto, 'which is only one of the many forms in which it travels. It is always easier to remember a difficult concept in one of its tangible manifestations than in its essence'.[6] Capital itself, he tells us, is 'that part of a country's assets that initiates surplus production and increases productivity.'[7] It is not itself visible to the naked eye, hidden as it is in the property systems of developed nations. In this respect, systems of property-holding designed to regulate the movement of that mysterious entity, capital, are comparable to systems for regulating communication with the world of spirits.

De Soto argues that capital cannot be created, nor freed from the relations and assets in which its potential is contained, unless the right social and legal climate exists. He shows that in many countries capital cannot be mobilised due to the existence of complicated and outdated property laws that prevent many people from using their assets, such as the house they live in, as collateral for loans. The efficacy of a legal system is in turn connected to such vague and diffuse factors as the degree of individualism present in a society, the efficiency of the organs of government, and so on. In an advanced modern economy, all sorts of assets can be turned into credit and thus into money, making a huge range of objects and even personal relationships into potential sources of money. Natural resources, including even air and water, can all be connected in this way. 'Indeed', notes a writer who has studied the political economy of oil and diamonds in Angola, 'the transformation of nature into tradeable commodities is a deeply political process, involving the definition of property rights, the organisation of labour, and the allocation of profits'.[8] Trading is another essential strand of the modern global economy that is subject to an invisible element inasmuch as the knowledge of comparable transactions elsewhere has a bearing on the price of the goods and services on offer. Adam Smith famously described as a 'hidden hand' the real but invisible mechanism that affects prices in free market transactions.[9]

People over the centuries have thought hard about the unusual properties of wealth and especially its most tangible expression, money. Money is notable for what one recent writer calls its 'potential to fulfill any mortal purpose and convey any mortal desire', either instantly or at a time convenient to the person who has it. It is this which can cause the possession of money to become 'the absolute purpose and the object of the most intense desire'.[10] The philosopher Schopenhauer called money 'human happiness in abstract'.[11] It has an awesome capacity to transform people's relationships with others and with their surroundings in any society that admits its general use, which today means everywhere. This was noted by Shakespeare, who referred to gold as that which 'will make black white, foul fair, wrong right, base noble, old young, coward valiant'. It would, he thought, 'place thieves, and give them title, knee, and approbation with senators on the bench'.[12] Conventions that attribute a monetary value to property and social relationships can have an extraordinarily dynamic effect, as Marx and Engels noted in a famous passage in which they wrote that 'all that is solid melts into air' as the logic of capitalism unfolds inexorably.[13] It is because of the power of money to transform people and social relations that it has been an object of suspicion since antiquity, and that a long line of philosophers and political activists, from Plato to the Khmer Rouge, has imagined moneyless utopias.[14] In Africa too the transforming power of money, as the most obvious form of wealth, as well as its ambiguity, is widely recognised. One African philosopher has noted that money is itself rather like a traditional medicine in being inherently neither good nor bad.[15] In this respect it could be said that it is also like the traditional spirit world more generally.

We all have in our heads a jumble of ideas, many of them contradictory, about how the world works. Most of the time, performing familiar daily actions, we give no thought to these inconsistencies. Exceptionally curious individuals may do so, and others occasionally reflect on the topic in times of crisis. We could perhaps take the example of Americans, who care little where the dollars in their pocket come from but may stop and think when they learn that their savings have been wiped out by a collapse in the stock market, or that the managers of dot-com companies can make vast sums by pure manipulation. In this respect, Africans are not unusual in probably giving little thought to the nature of money most of the time. But when they learn about people getting rich overnight, at the same time as they see their own wealth being destroyed by inflation or collapsing commodity prices, they may begin to wonder a little more about the nature of wealth, and how it can be created or destroyed overnight.

Related to the transforming power of money are questions raised by thinkers the world over as to its naturalness. Humans are the only animals that create their sustenance rather than finding it, and this creativity is one of the distinguishing features of humanity. Even hunter-gatherers use traps and other stratagems. Is money, then, to be considered something essentially artificial, made by humans and governed by whatever rules they may care to devise? Or is money, like speech, naturally inherent in man? Money in the form of naturally occurring elements such as gold and silver has provoked fewer doubts than systems of interest-generation and credit, where wealth creation is divorced from precious metals or other

natural commodities themselves. This has retained the attention of many
thinkers and religious authorities. Aristotle called interest 'the birth of
money from money', which he considered 'unnatural'.[16] Usury was forbidden or restricted among Christians in medieval Europe, as it is widely
among Muslims to this day on account of those verses in the Qur'an that
cast doubt on the theological soundness of interest. Even today there are
Christian movements in the United States that consider credit cards and
paper money not backed by gold or silver bullion as satanic.[17]

Money in its modern forms was hardly known before colonial times in
some parts of Africa, while elsewhere it was used in certain sectors of the
economy only. Nowhere in precolonial Africa had a capitalist economy in
the sense of a pervasive system whereby credit could be obtained through
the alienation of private property valued in monetary terms. In general,
the inclusion of Africa in such a system has been a far from straightforward process. Colonial governments wanted Africans to use money and
pay taxes, but were careful to regulate the credit available to them. Western
banks have lent money to Africa, but have also collaborated in the capital
flight that is widely seen as one of the continent's greatest problems.

## People and wealth in Africa

People's attitudes to the generation of wealth are connected to the ways in
which they make a living. In the forest regions of Africa especially, where
hunting remains even today a staple activity, there are indications that
many people think of wealth, including in the form of money, as something that needs to be hunted, like game for the cooking-pot. This is an
activity that requires courage, skill and stealth. Hunting is widely recognised to contain a spiritual element. The hunt 'is something other than
mere hunting', in hunting communities all over the world, but 'rather, it is
part of a vitally important relationship'. Hugh Brody explains:[18]

> The people depend on the animals, and the animals allow themselves to
> be killed. An animal's agreement to become food is secured through the
> respect that hunters and their families show to the land in general and
> to animals in particular. If animals and hunters are on good terms, then
> the hunters are successful.

The relationship between hunters and animals is a prime example of the
kind of relationship that is classically governed by spirits in African thought.
In areas where hunting has been, or even still is, not a sport but a liveli-
hood, these ideas retain a strong influence. In southwest Congo a constant

stream of young men from the region and from Kinshasa heads south to the diamond-fields of northern Angola. Digging for diamonds is one of the few ways open to a young man to earn an income, and it holds out the infinitely distant prospect of making really big money through discovery of a large diamond. The young Congolese men who make this trip are aware that it is a very risky undertaking, during which some are sure to be killed either by minefields sown along the border area, or in the Wild West conditions of the diamond-fields themselves. They see it as being similar to a hunting-expedition, using many of the same words associated with stalking and 'capturing' their quarry.[19] Indeed, diamond-digging is so fraught with risk and uncertainty that the comparison is quite appropriate.

The fields that the young diggers head for are not modern mines, deep underground, but alluvial deposits, old river-beds where diamonds are mixed with stones and soil just a few feet under the surface. A typical alluvial diamond-field, mined by hand, is a large clearing, perhaps a couple of times the size of a football-field, pockmarked with holes containing stagnant brown water, and surrounded by piles of gravel. Teams of diggers stand waist-deep in water, using shovels to dig out the earth and grit that other teams process by passing it through a series of sieves, until there is a flat panful of fine gravel that can be sorted by hand to look for a diamond that might be no bigger than a little toenail. It is back-breaking work. The control of alluvial diamond-fields in central and West Africa is often in the hands of armed bands that either organise the workings themselves or take a large cut of the profits made on the stones that are found. These are sold to professional diamond-traders with international connections, who are quite often Lebanese or Israeli but also include some specialised groups, such as the Malinke traders from West Africa who travel as far as Angola on business and are to be seen in the hotels of the Pelikaanstraat, Antwerp's diamond district. The connection between this type of diamond-mining and marketing and the control of violence has received extensive attention in recent times through the international campaign against 'blood diamonds'.[20]

Although not every part of Africa has such a strong tradition of hunting as the forest-areas of central and West Africa, there is a general tendency to consider wealth as natural, to be understood in the same terms as other things that exist in nature. Interest is often considered as the offspring of money, so that the word for it in Malagasy is *zana-bola*, literally 'the child of money'.[21] Similar expressions are to be found in some other African languages, indicating a widespread view that money, like almost everything else in the agrarian economies that dominated Africa until recently, is subject to what are seen as general rules governing nature and fertility. Real wealth in such an environment cannot be produced out of nothing, or merely by multiplying paper, but only through birth, planting, or a similar act of creation. All of these processes are presumed to have an important religious element since they involve the creation of new life. Normally speaking, there is no need to wonder where wealth and money emanate from as it is usually obvious that it comes from whatever a person's habitual work may be. Some ordinary people clearly think deeply about such matters, such as the Nuer cattle-herder from the Sudan who asked a visiting anthropologist about the ultimate origin of money. 'But there's something I still don't understand about money', he said. 'Money's not like the cow because the cow has blood and breath and, like people, gives birth. But money does not. So, tell me, do you know whether God or man creates money?'[22]

In the type of farming or herding societies that prevailed in Africa until the mid-twentieth century, the total wealth of a community was generally regarded as being finite. Although one person might be a better farmer or hunter and more skillful trader than another, the capacity to use these talents to generate extra wealth would normally be quite limited. In any event, the source of any new wealth was generally pretty obvious to everyone in a smallish community, and if such wealth was not acquired externally (such as through migrant labour or a long-distance trading expedition or an armed raid), then people were liable to assume that a sudden or unexplained increase in the wealth of one person could only be at the expense of another, by means of theft or trickery. This is an idea characteristic of the moral economy of peasant cultures, in which all wealth is seen as being at the expense of others.[23] Over the last two or three generations, the general spread of paper money has caused many Africans to wonder what exactly is the nature of the wealth it represents, although most people still probably give the matter little thought for as long as they are handling small quantities of money only.

Wealth in Africa's precolonial societies was classically measured in living beings, able to reproduce. Among herders this was cattle or other animals, while among farmers it was more likely to be people. In most farming communities male family heads aimed to attract the largest possible number of dependents, including wives, slaves and other clients, both as a mark of status and as labour-power. Successful rulers usually strove to extend their power over the greatest number of people, except perhaps in resource-poor communities such as among nomads in desert areas, where a different logic might apply. In these circumstances, many transactions consisted in an exchange of wealth involving rights over people.[24] Dependents could be acquired in various ways involving pawnship, obligation, bondage or slavery, and of course marriage, with female dependents being valued particularly for their precious ability to produce children. Transactions involving fertile women were typically regulated by the payment of bride-wealth, a form of compensating a family for the loss of a daughter upon marriage in those societies where it was customary for a bride to live with her husband's family, and a major channel for wealth redistribution. Politicians and other members of Africa's elites today still negotiate relationships with or through women as forms of alliance, such as the famous *deuxièmes bureaux* ('second offices', an untranslatable play on words), a euphemism for the mistresses and concubines of successful men in central Africa. They use women to seal political deals, like President Houphouët-Boigny who gave one of his numerous god-daughters in marriage to the son of Liberia's President Tolbert, or the son of the president of Nigeria who, according to *radio trottoir*, took a sister of President Charles Taylor as his mistress. Likewise President Mobutu is said to have systematically demanded sexual rights over the wives of his cabinet ministers.

The Atlantic slave trade, before it grew hugely in the seventeenth and eighteenth centuries, was quite easily understandable in terms of such a system, in that the Europeans who offered wealth in the form of imported goods required people in exchange. It is possible that, for as long as the demand was small-scale, few Africans wondered why Europeans should want to buy slaves.[25] But certainly when it grew, Africans did question what was happening. There are reports from places thousands of miles apart suggesting that when the slave trade became large-scale, people in the communities that provided slaves wondered why Europeans should ship them overseas in such numbers, and often drew the most alarming conclusions. '[The people] had the idea that the Europeans are Cannibals, and that it is the above which compels them to come up…for to buy slaves that they may eat them in their own Countries' wrote a Malagasy chronicler, referring to ideas current at the height of the slave trade.[26] For people accustomed only to Africa's low-producing agrarian economies, it was hard to think of any explanation for the voracious European appetite for slaves other than that they were required as food.

Although people today may carry out everyday transactions without much further thought, there remain traces of the slave trade in attitudes towards extraordinary wealth whose origin is unclear. Along a large stretch of Africa's Atlantic coast, the acquisition of exceptional wealth is often assumed to involve the activities of a water spirit known in English as

Mammy Wata (with variant spellings). She is represented as a beautiful woman who is light-skinned, perhaps even part-European, and very sexy.[27] She usually appears to men in a dream in the form of a mermaid, seducing them into living with her. A man who dreams of Mammy Wata may feel that he has entered into contact with a living spirit. He will be tempted by her known ability to give money to her human lovers. But Mammy Wata is unable to bear children. Further, she is thought to demand the life of a child in exchange for the money she can provide to her human lovers. The relationship, then, is in most respects like a conventional one between man and wife, except that Mammy Wata lives in the underwater world and is invisible other than in dreams. There is, however, a further difference between having a relationship with Mammy Wata and with a woman in the visible world. Whereas a normal woman is acquired by payment of bride-wealth and then provides her husband with children, the system works the other way round with Mammy Wata: the suitor gives a child to the spirit world and receives money from his ghostly lover. Everything is the wrong way round, as is usually the case in the underworld.[28] Mammy Wata, the half-European woman who comes from the sea and is the source of wealth, seems to articulate the spirit of the Atlantic slave trade. She is very much alive today, and was rumoured to have appeared in person in Brazzaville, close to the mausoleum of the late president of the country, just one week before the outbreak of civil war in June 1997, in a premonition of the orgy of looting that was shortly to occur.[29]

Most commercial transactions do not involve any spiritual element, and usually people give little thought to the spirit world when they daily take money from their pockets. Someone is likely to feel a need to enter into an economic arrangement with the spirit world only to perform an extraordinary transaction, perhaps before borrowing a really large sum of money for example. In such a case, the same basic rules apply as in a material transaction, in the sense that a bargain has to be reached and payment made in some form. This is sometimes stated quite explicitly in the popular literature concerning people's experiences of the spirit world. For example, in one pamphlet, published in 1994 in Brazzaville, a man who records his experiences working for what he calls '*un sorcier*' claims that his boss demanded that, in return for employment, he should supply his employer with human flesh. So, he concludes, 'as we can see, in both the visible and invisible worlds, the law of work and payment is a living reality',[30] illustrating that the acquisition of money is subject to the normal rules of exchange even when it involves the spirit world.

The association between acquiring wealth and making a payment to a spiritual being, including even in the form of a human life, can be found in popular literature, rumours and stories from just about every part of Africa south of the Sahara. South Africa is one country where it is widely believed that it is possible to steal a person's soul and turn the victim into a zombie, whose life-force has been acquired by someone else.[31] The victim becomes a physical shell with no autonomous spirit.

Sometimes people who grow rich without obvious cause, such as a farmer whose crops flourish while those of his neighbours do not, are accused of having turned someone into a zombie to work for them at night. There are people who complain of waking up in the mornings feeling extremely tired and therefore suspect that their own souls have been taken to work as night-time zombies, accounting for their lack of refreshing sleep. In the South African lowveld, white people are thought to be adept at acquiring money by sucking blood from a human body, like the *nwam-lambo*, a snake-like witches' familiar which provides its owner with cash in exchange for blood.[32] In regard to West Africa, the antiquity of zombie beliefs is testified by the fact that they were taken to the Americas by African slaves and have become a technique for wielding political power in some Caribbean and South American countries to this day.[33]

New conditions of life and new ways of earning a living and making money have obliged people to think anew about fundamental ideas that previously went unquestioned. In many communities, wealth is no longer primarily held in people and in beings able to reproduce, such as cattle. Nor are children always investments for the future. It is quite possible that the changed place of children in societies where millions of people now live together in cities has had a major effect on adults' attitudes to children, and this may help explain the growing tendency to recruit youngsters as soldiers. A general inflation of the symbols of wealth can be expected to result in devaluation of the medium in which transactions are made. It is logical that this maxim of economics should apply to wealth considered in people as much as to wealth in any other form.

## Bargaining with the spirit world

Religious believers the world over may go for considerable amounts of time without feeling any great need to communicate with the spirit world, or they may interact periodically, simply as a matter of routine. In many religions, people habitually leave small offerings, such as food and drink intended for the spirits of ancestors that are thought to need these for sustenance, pretty much as they did when alive. Without such attention the spirits will themselves grow weak, not to mention annoyed, and will be of less use in future. It is quite common for a spirit to require an element of life-force as payment, perhaps in the form of a domestic animal that is killed by the human party to the deal. The basic idea is to transfer the life-force of the animal to the spirit that is being negotiated with in exchange for a service required from that spirit, or simply for its continuing goodwill.

If an exceptional service is required, then an extraordinary sort of exchange may be needed. This is subject to negotiation and agreement on payment in return for the goods or services requested, much the same as in any market. For extraordinary services that require spiritual intervention, such as the acquisition of a substantial amount of money or some other major advantage, payment may involve the life-force of a human being. This is the logic behind the use of human blood or vital human body-parts, such as genital organs, in certain transactions with the spirit world. Human body-parts or blood may also be used in the most powerful amulets or 'medicines'. *Radio trottoir* and African newspapers often contain reports of children especially being kidnapped and, allegedly, killed in order to pay a blood debt to a spirit or to make an amulet that is believed to bring wealth or power.[34] Transactions in which life-force is exchanged for power and money are often described in African newspapers and by academic authors as 'sacrifices' or 'ritual murders'. However, they are best understood primarily as forms of exchange.

Given beliefs in the efficacy of spiritual transactions such as these, it is not surprising that sometimes quite innocent activities can generate the most disturbing rumours. In 1959, in the Belgian Congo, amid the febrile atmosphere of an ill-prepared decolonisation, riots erupted when people learned of the arrival of a shipment of preserved meat in tins labelled with a picture of a smiling baby. It was rumoured that the tins contained the flesh of African children preserved for consumption by European cannibals.[35] In Malawi, a similar scare was inadvertently caused by the first president, Hastings Banda, a qualified medical doctor who had practised in Britain for many years before turning to politics only in middle age. After becoming head of state, he cultivated a reputation as a man of great and inscrutable power. He was a staunch ally of apartheid South Africa. When he tried to set up a national blood transfusion service and appealed for blood donors, the wildest rumours swept Malawi, usually along the lines that the president wanted to sell blood to South Africa where it was required for some magical purpose. When there was a series of killings and disappearances in Malawi in 1969, 'rumours circulated that men were being killed to provide what was quite literally "blood money" to the South African government in return for its assistance to Dr Banda'. These rumours were 'an updated version of an ancient and terrible fear among the Malawi people',[36] namely that Europeans are addicted to drinking human blood. This notion, which probably dates from the era of the slave trade, is still current. In 2002, Reuters press agency reported the existence of 'a bizarre rumour that Malawi's Government is colluding with vampires to collect human blood for international aid agencies in exchange for food', which had led to 'a rash of vigilante violence', in the latest appearance of the story of people being traded for wealth and money.[37]

The idea that prosperity flows from a good relationship with the invisible world, which may require nurturing like any social relationship, is common among religious believers all over the world, although not always in the sense of involving specific transactions like these. In theory, it is possible to trace the genealogy of such ideas in any society, in the form of a history of religious thought. In the case of Africa, southern Nigeria offers a good focus for a rapid survey of how spiritual ideas and practices in relation to wealth have changed over time because its history has been relatively well documented over quite a long period. The quality of this documentation is largely due to the intensive commercial relationship of some groups in this area with foreign traders in precolonial times. Some of the southwestern city-states of modern Nigeria impressed European visitors by their prosperity even in the seventeenth century. Until the nineteenth century, the most common ways of acquiring substantial sums of money in this region were through the exercise of political power and through trade, including the slave trade that flourished there for over two centuries.

Before the twentieth century, what is now southern Nigeria was subject to a wide variety of political arrangements, varying from the city-states of the Yoruba area to the stateless societies of Igboland. All of these had in common the tendency for kings, chiefs, 'big men' and other notables to be associated with elite religious organisations and secret societies. Some of these are said to have performed blood rituals, possibly including the use of human blood, which no doubt strengthened the supposition of a connection between wealth and power and payment of life-force to the spirit world, the ultimate source of material power.[38] A leading Nigerian historian suggests that in precolonial and colonial times it was generally assumed that anyone who acquired money exceptionally quickly or without obvious material cause must have done so either through theft or through interaction with the spirit world.[39] Millions of Yoruba people today gener-

ally consider money to be connected to the invisible world insofar as it is
seen as a medium by which individuals can realise their destiny in life,
which is known in the spirit world.[40] The fact that generations of Yoruba
have believed that money, and wealth more generally, has a mystical
aspect does not imply that everyone in southwestern Nigeria regards every
minor transaction as a religious act, but it does bear witness to the resil-
ience of the idea that the generation of unusual wealth has a spiritual and
often mystical component, and that the acquisition of very sudden and
spectacular wealth is associated with the exchange of human life, a belief
partly rooted in the historical experience of the slave trade. Similar ideas
are to be found also in other areas of Africa, especially those from which
slaves were exported not only to the Americas but also to North Africa
and the Middle East, where the export of people was the main means of
procuring imported goods.[41]

A particularity of Nigeria is the oil-boom that followed the massive rise
in world oil-prices in the 1970s, when Nigeria emerged as a leading world
producer. This, allied to the country's other resources and its large and
dynamic population, led many intellectuals and politicians to make
extravagant plans for the country's emergence as a world power and a natural leader of Africa. But Nigeria has never lived up to its huge potential.
Rather, the mixture of a massive rise in oil earnings plus an arrogant
assumption that Nigeria was destined to become an African superpower
has proved disastrous.[42] Oil created a class of immensely rich entrepreneurs, usually people in government and the army or with good official
connections. This system has been cynically described by one retired general as 'a government of contractors, by contractors, for contractors'.[43]
From the start of the oil boom, Nigerians have generally understood well
enough that it is through the manipulation of oil contracts and procure-
ment or other government contracts that the massive infusion of new
wealth has benefitted relatively few people. What seems to Nigerians most
in need of explanation is why providence should endow such enormous
wealth on a rather small number of people, sometimes quite young and as
often as not unendowed with any particular qualifications or wisdom or
even talent for anything but manoeuvre. Nigerians' frequent assumption is
that these plutocrats must have access to special spiritual power. A British
academic who worked with popular theatre troupes in southwestern Nigeria in the 1980s noted how the spectacle of rapid enrichment was reflected
in drama, such as in the stock character of the rich man who acquires his
wealth by stealing children.[44]

The implication of views like these, recorded among Nigerians, is that
the modern state and its associated businesses are run by people whose

massive wealth and power is connected with the manipulation of spiritual forces, and it is supposed that cultivation of these may involve taking the lives of children.[45] 'Many children disappear in many parts of Nigeria in mysterious circumstances and ritual murders are often suspected by the police' wrote a Nigerian researcher in the 1980s.[46] Whether rumours of child-stealing for use in a bargain with the spirit world are more or less prevalent now than they were in the past in any particular town or area of Nigeria is difficult to ascertain. What can be said with more confidence is that the volatility of money and the inequalities of wealth have increased massively since the 1970s, and that this may cause people to resort to extra-ordinary means both to acquire money and to keep it, such as through negotiating with the spirit world. If so, this could imply a greater number of human lives than in the past. Currency devaluation, so common throughout Africa, implies a general inflation of payment, and perhaps this is reflected in people's ideas about the frequency of blood-payments too.

The scale of corruption among Nigerian generals and politicians is staggering.[47] This, plus the oil boom, has produced an environment in which fraud and other forms of commercial crime can flourish. Nigerians have acquired an unenviable reputation for criminal behaviour world-wide, and Nigerian passport-holders complain of the extreme prejudice shown against them by customs, police and immigration services every-where, affecting many honest and hard-working people, as they rightly complain. It must also be said that Nigeria's reputation is not baseless, and there is evidence of the success of some Nigerians in forms of crime that have gone international. Thus, in a 1991 study in Britain of 899 people imprisoned for importing illegal drugs, 30 per cent of those surveyed were Nigerians.[48] In the mid-1990s the US authorities estimated that 58 per-cent of fraudulent insurance claims in their country were made by Nigeri-ans, and that Nigerian fraudsters were responsible for some 20–26 billion dollars' worth of fraud each year in the United States alone.[49] (It may be noted, however, that even this figure is small compared to the amounts defrauded by Enron and other major companies in the US stock-market boom of the late 1990s.) The notorious Nigerian advance-fee frauds known as '419' after the relevant article of the Nigerian criminal code are estimated to be worth several hundred million dollars a year, and to have netted a total of five billion US dollars as of 1986.[50] British police in 1997 received from members of the public 68,000 reports of '419' letters sent by Nigerian gangs, with very many more being circulated but never made known to the police.[51] Since then, the spread of e-mail has led to a massive increase.[52] No doubt many readers of this book will have received their very own 419 e-mails.

Some criminal entrepreneurs like these certainly make use of spiritual resources that are thought to ensure success. One such person was Iyke Nathan Uzorma, whose confessions were quoted at the beginning of this chapter, before he found Christ and, he tells us, abandoned his dishonest ways.

## Regulating money

The general insolvency of two decades has had a radical effect on attitudes towards money and time throughout Africa, in populations whose average age is under eighteen. The economic and political environment is generally unpredictable throughout Africa. Fortunes can be gained and lost with extraordinary speed. Enjoyment is increasingly seen as instantaneous and fleeting.[53] What started as a financial crisis throughout Africa in the late 1970s has been followed by radical economic reforms that have left many people extremely poor, while those fortunate enough to have plenty of money have often acquired it by means that are unclear to the great majority of the population. These conditions challenge people's received ideas about money and wealth and how they may legitimately be gained. These days, many people no longer earn money through farming, with its familiar cycles of planting and harvesting, but often through occasional trading or small jobs. Decent salaries are rare. There is little foreign investment to create new jobs. Sometimes people may work to mine commodities that were without value until very recently, such as the mineral columbite-tantalite ('coltan'), that can be processed to maintain an electric charge in a computer chip and is thus useful for mobile phones. Its price in recent years has been up to $200,000 per ton, only a tiny fraction of which is actually received by the Congolese who mine it.[54] The miners themselves are powerless to negotiate a higher percentage of the returns from the sale of coltan on international markets to which they have no access.

If capital will not come to where there is labour, then labour must move to where there is capital. The best option for many young people today is to emigrate to an industrialised country to find work, often with a view to returning once they have made enough money to build a house or start a viable business back home. Emigration to the European Union, North America and Australia is now very difficult for most people, but still they may try to enter clandestinely, entrusting themselves to unscrupulous people-smuggling gangs and taking enormous risks to reach the promised land. This is such a risky business that it, too, demands a high investment in spiritual protection. The millions of Africans who leave their home countries in search of work make use of the spiritual resources at their disposal for the arduous challenge of reaching their countries of destination and living as migrants in often difficult circumstances. Enough Africans have succeeded in making some money in the rich world that for many African countries external remittances are now one of the main sources of national income. Total remittances to Africa have been estimated at $ 20 billion per year. Even if this figure were inaccurate, remittances are in any case likely to be much greater than the annual inflow of international aid to the sub-continent.[55]

People who make money overseas, then, are expected to send some of it back to their families at home, including in the villages that most Africans still identify as their ultimate point of attachment. For many of the 34 per cent of people who now live in the towns and cities of sub-Saharan Africa, the ancestral village remains the moral point of reference. Even people living in Chicago or London may have special regard for the village where their ancestors lived maybe one or two generations ago, rather as the first waves of Italian or Irish immigrants to the United States used to have. Those who have made money may try to legitimise their gains, as it were, not only by redistribution among the extended family to whom they acknowledge a moral obligation, but also by building ostentatious tombs, churches or mosques in their villages, rather like those rich merchants in medieval Europe who contributed to the building of the great cathedrals in the belief that this would absolve them of any suspicion of improper or immoral gain,[56] or, indeed, US billionaires who give money for charitable causes. Perhaps the best known example is that of Félix Houphouët-Boigny, the late president of Côte d'Ivoire, who built an imitation of Rome's basilica of St Peter in his home town with some of the vast wealth he had acquired.[57] There are good reasons for laundering wealth in this way, for a suspicion that it has been acquired by mysterious and illegitimate means can easily become the ground for one person to suspect another of a mystical assault, normally translated into English as 'witchcraft'. Political and economic changes in recent decades have greatly increased the propensity for people to suspect sinister dealings of this type, making it more important than ever for individuals to find ways of demonstrating that their wealth is legitimate if they wish to avoid being accused of witchcraft.

Throughout West Africa especially, an area integrated into systems of long-distance trade for centuries, both overseas and across the Sahara, the morality of exchange has long been associated with markets.[58] West African markets are real meeting-places, not just virtual or technical places of exchange. Some are regulated by sophisticated conventions on the pricing and sale of goods. They are rather like the *agora* of the ancient Greeks, places to meet friends and talk as well as to do business, of fundamental social importance. It is small wonder that they are also classic sites of *radio trottoir*. It is in recognition of the social aspect of trading that bargaining over a transaction, so strange and apparently pointless for first-time visitors to Africa, is designed for there to be no loser. If a price has been negotiated face-to-face, it has therefore been freely accepted by both parties. Money in such circumstances does not have a fixed value but one that is dependent on the status of the two contracting parties and on the relations they have. Thus, whereas in advanced capitalist countries it is generally seen as virtuous to offer goods at a fixed price, irrespective of the customer's identity, in West African market tradition virtue consists in setting the price appropriate to the nature of the relationship between seller and buyer.[59]

The whole continent has nowadays been inserted into markets in a more abstract sense, those of which economists speak in reference to commercial systems for the transfer of assets, organised on a global scale. Generally speaking, the main avenue to really substantial wealth in Africa, and to entry into major global markets, still goes through some sort of association with the state, with exceptions such as South Africa, which has the continent's largest Western-style private business sector. Although since the onset of economic reform in the 1980s African states have been obliged to privatise large areas of activity, political elites have nevertheless managed to keep pervasive control over liberalised business, often through informal methods akin to those they have used to mobilise political support. In economies that remain very open to external trade, most ways of making big money involve the use of foreign connections associated with the state, or at least with those informal channels where politicians have undue influence, such as in import-export.[60] This remains the case even with the new donor emphasis on 'civil society'. Knowing the right people is all-important.

In a modern economy, such crucial but invisible elements as capital and the hidden hand of the market are regulated by states, by central banks or by various other corporations that have rules of operation and ethical codes enforceable ultimately by law. These rules, and the institutions that uphold them, have grown up over time. How this came about in European history is well known, as is the process by which the medieval suspicion of usury, considered immoral, gave way over time to a religious concept that certain forms of interest imply virtue and even godliness.[61] It is instructive to compare this history, however well known it is, with some aspects of economic life and ideas in contemporary Africa, and to reflect on the way in which new theological thinking played such an important role in the development of modern economic instruments in seventeenth-century Netherlands and Britain, including through the invention of multinational companies, futures markets, long-term credit, a stock exchange, joint-stock companies and central banking. Seventeenth-century writers did not fail to note the link between the emerging institutions of a dynamic new economic system, later to be dubbed capitalism, and the political regimes that facilitated it, most particularly constitutional monarchy or republicanism. Contemporaries associated the use of paper money and advanced systems of credit with Protestant states, while Catholic monarchies even in the eighteenth century preferred gold and silver, for reasons both political and theological.[62]

We must emphasise here that the point of considering briefly the evolution of financial and economic systems in Europe, the role of religious thought in their invention, and their association with certain types of political regime, is not in order to argue that every part of the world must follow the same path and solve the same technical problems by the same methods in the same sequence. We are not arguing that Africa is undergoing an inevitable historical phase with a three-century time-lag. There is a general agreement among historians and social scientists that it is neither accurate nor helpful to think of all societies as being destined to follow the same linear path. There are successful capitalist countries or groups today that have achieved success by original methods.[63] Interestingly, these include some examples from Africa of societies that have successfully integrated aspects of capitalist economics into their own traditions, such as the Bamiléké of Cameroon, famous for their commercial skills, whose achievement in this respect is attributed to the integration of personal wealth with moral ideas stemming from religious thought and practice.[64] The interest of comparative historical examples is simply to throw light on the current situation that, in much of Africa, is dominated by an economic Bermuda triangle of unconstrained political rulers, untrustworthy institutions and lack of viable credit.

One could summarise the evolution of economic thought in Europe and North America over four centuries by saying that faith in God has been replaced by faith in credit, an entity no more visible than the deity. According to one analyst, this mental shift was apparent in England in a single generation, in the mid-seventeenth century.[65] Famous episodes of the time such as the Dutch tulip mania can be seen as marking revolutions in thought, including the discovery of 'a monetary reality behind appearances',[66] that would soon be applied to all manner of commodities and resources. The development of a new way of thinking about the relationship between the visible and invisible worlds was set in motion by the theological and political revolution of the Reformation. It was soon to lead to new ways of thinking about uncertainty in general, leading to the creation of life insurance, and insurance against fire and accident. Protestant theology tended to regard gambling as immoral not least because it left the decision of who would win to chance, rather than to the providence of a rational God who would reward those who respected the order of his creation by using rational methods for calculating risk, such as by investing money in viable commercial ventures. Theology was the basis of new ideas about the virtue of self-improvement and personal property. From this has evolved a view of the natural order in which money is the key instrument. In modern economies, money is applied to time, in the form of hourly rates, per diems, monthly salaries, and 'that redemptive eternity that economists call "the long run"'.[67] The religious notion of providence has been replaced with that of statistical probability, which, with compound interest, has become 'essentially, the theology of modernity'.[68]

## *Wild economies*

Academics, bankers and many others agree that the infrastructure of states and institutions necessary to run a modern economy is deficient in Africa today. It is a debatable point how far this and other shortcomings are the result of wrong-headed policies implemented by African governments in the first decade after independence, to what extent they are the product of ill-conceived attempts at reform implemented by the international financial institutions since the 1980s, and how they may be understood in the context of a long historical evolution that includes the colonial experience.

On one point at least, *radio trottoir* concords with the latest academic literature in political science and economics: all agree that Africa's elites cannot be regarded by and large as managing their economies soundly in the national interest. Stories of grand corruption are numerous. Some plutocrats and politicians actually make money not just by skimming bribes or kickbacks from contracts but also from activities more associated with organised crime, such as trading in drugs, forgery, and so forth.[69] Rich people, knowing better than anyone just how insecure this environment is, prefer to keep their money where it can earn interest, in European or North American banks. This can be done only with the complicity of international bankers. One World Bank economist reckons that 39 per cent of Africa's capital is held offshore, while a former US assistant secretary of state has suggested a tentative figure of $150 billion in offshore holdings.[70] The president of Nigeria has quoted a figure of $140 billion held offshore by African leaders and politicians.[71] If even one-tenth of these sums were invested in Africa annually, it would exceed current foreign investment flows. Meanwhile, impoverished African states borrow money from donors. There is a brutal political logic to this system. The debt-and-loan nexus gives rich countries a hold over African governments. Within Africa itself, money regulates the circulation not only of goods, but also of people, in time-honoured fashion, and so politicians have every reason to see economic policy primarily as the wherewithal to build a clientele. Hence, government ministers who have little choice, apart from delaying tactics, other than officially to accept the economic reforms imposed on them by international financial institutions feel themselves impelled nevertheless to turn the new measures to political advantage, for example by ensuring that useful parts of the privatised economy are run by their friends and protégés and by draining of power both the formal economy and the formal state system generally. It is in recognition of this logic that Uganda's President Yoweri Museveni is reported to have referred to financial aid as 'a life-support system for brain-dead regimes'.[72]

It is remarkable that there are nevertheless certain financial techniques in Africa that work well. It is striking that perhaps the best example is an institution that is entirely informal, namely the unofficial savings clubs, known in French as *tontines*, that exist in all parts of the continent. These work as follows: a group of people who generally know each other contribute to the same fund, each putting in a set amount per week or per month. Some may operate with very small sums, the equivalent of a few US cents per week, while others are used by wealthy traders who may put in hundreds of dollars per week, so that in effect people can participate in a club at their own level. A treasurer keeps the cash on behalf of the group in return for a small payment. Members of the association take it in turns to receive the whole pot, which provides them with a capital sum that they can use for a business venture, to finance a wedding or funeral, or whatever they want. There are few reports of savings-clubs collapsing, such as because a dishonest treasurer has run off with all the money. They seem to work, generally, because people are investing in a personal relationship with the other members of the club, whom they may meet face to face. The fact that savings-clubs simply provide money in rotation apparently strikes most people as more moral than if they were to pay regular interest on individual accounts. Other popular associations with specific aims, such as burial societies, work in much the same way.

The pervasive atmosphere of financial uncertainty, often including high inflation, means that those who have a little money are desperate to find some means of using it to ensure that it keeps or even multiplies its value. The big problem is how to do this, in an environment that discourages investment, where banks cannot be relied upon, and where there is little trust. One consequence is that people try speculative methods. Lotteries and games of chance of all sorts have become wildly popular. Here, a distinct religious element enters into people's calculations as they try to control the element of risk. According to the director of the national lottery in Niger, 'people consider games of chance as though they were a *tontine*, where everyone takes part to gain what you might call a place in line for the luck of a prize'.[73] He explains that people consider a lottery to be like a *tontine*, but with the addition of an element of chance that, he implies, may be influenced by interaction with the spirit world.

This is particularly interesting because it reflects a spiritual reasoning— not along the same lines, of course, but in the same idiom—such as was followed by the grave and sober gentlemen who pioneered the institutions of modern capitalism in northern Europe. Similarly, the charlatans and gamblers in Africa that prey on people who must trade to survive recall the eighteenth-century British hucksters of wild speculative ventures and shares in bogus companies, so difficult to distinguish from the real thing, or even their contemporary American equivalents, the executives of companies raising share capital by fictive accounting. What unites all these examples is the moral value that is attributed to that notoriously invisible entity, luck. In this respect, the property and casualty insurance companies that were major in the development of European capitalism are the precise opposite of a lottery. Both have in common that they 'imagine a cataclysm, of vanishingly small probability, value it in money and distribute it around a population so as to mitigate its force'.[74] The vital difference between an insurance fund and a lottery is the role each attributes to chance, or what a statistician might call probability, and a religious believer might call providence. An insurance company works on a precise calculation of chance that a Protestant cleric of the early modern period could attribute to the wondrously precise and rational ways of the Creator but that an atheist would simply call mathematics. A lottery or other game of chance works on a calculation about the likelihood of getting the winning ticket. A person who believes that the spirit world can be manipulated may be convinced that, with the right technique, he can win the big prize. For puritan Christians, this is an illusion inspired by Satan, the master of ruse, in collaboration with dishonest people who exploit it for their own enrichment. In such a view, the God-fearing person should avoid all such schemes and stick to compound interest. It is in this way that theological views inform techniques for spreading risk.

For people living in an economic climate where saving and productive investment are discouraged, and who do not have the resources to open bank accounts abroad, the options are limited. It is not only the investment climate that is uncertain; there is even a lack of confidence in the nature of goods on offer, such as pharmaceuticals advertised as manufactured by reputable international companies but that are in fact pirated copies. Pharmaceutical companies have been known to profit from this uncertainty by dumping on African markets drugs declared unsafe in the West, or pills that are past their sell-by date.[75] In Lagos, there are so many crooked real estate agents, some of whom have succeeded in obtaining money for the phoney sale of houses to which they have no legal title, that people have taken to painting on their houses 'THIS HOUSE IS NOT FOR SALE'. Every type of trickery is to be found at just about every level, and the buyer must beware. Some people have internalised the atmosphere of frenetic consumption and insecurity, turning life into a permanent carnival. Such are the *sapeurs*, the dandies of Brazzaville and Kinshasa who cultivate an outrageously extravagant form of elegance, while priding themselves on having no visible means of support. They resemble the beaux of regency England, while the milieu they inhabit recalls the cults of gambling, cheating, and whoring in eighteenth-century London.[76] In Cameroon, the name 'feymen' has been invented for a category of fraudsters renowned for their skill in acquiring money through deception, often just simple persuasion, with extraordinary skill. The king of the Cameroonian feymen, Donatien Koagne, is said to have cheated presidents and entire governments, inside and outside Africa, out of millions of dollars.[77] Newspapers sometimes contain stories of 'money-doublers', fraudsters who convince the gullible that they have a mystical power to turn one banknote into two. They work by persuading a victim to part with a high-denomination note for doubling and then simply absconding with it. Some Nigerian money-doublers have moved into the international field through the worldwide 419 scams, while a Congolese fraudster, one Richard Mwamba, is reported to have delivered some 150 million US dollars' worth of forged Bahreini bank notes to the Iranian secret services, receiving some $ 3 million of genuine US dollars in commission. A veteran forger, he is said to have once imported counterfeit banknotes to his home country in a lot weighing no less than 30 tonnes.[78] Successful tricksters like these are widely admired by young people for their skill and the supposed spiritual power that makes them successful. There are certainly older and wiser voices that regret all this dishonesty, as popular literature attests. In northern Nigeria, also an area with a long commercial history, there is a thriving social criticism in Hausa-language books, such as in the novel *Turmin Danya*, a critique of the rapacious and immoral new class of government contractors.[79]

Frauds of the sort discussed, mind-boggling in their audacity, are all too easy to perpetrate in the absence of more trustworthy ways of causing money to multiply by bearing interest. The mere presence of corporations that collect deposits and make loans is not enough to produce a viable banking system. Even in highly regulated environments, when bankers are unscrupulous they can get away with massive frauds, such as the Bank of Credit and Commerce International, which collapsed in the biggest bank failure in history. BCCI, with a presence in the City of London and in other world financial capitals, prided itself on being a third world bank, and opened more branches in Africa than in any other continent.[80] Since all banks depend on lending money far in excess of their capital assets, there is nothing intrinsically odd about the idea of collecting deposits from small savers for re-lending to others. Small savers depend on effective state regulation for the protection of their deposits. In a poorly-regulated environment, it becomes almost impossible for the general public to tell the difference between a genuine bank and a crooked one. A spate of bank failures in Russia in the 1990s and ruinous pyramid schemes in Albania, Rumania and other parts of Eastern Europe all occurred in situations where regulation was ineffective and where publics unfamiliar with the ways of the market were easy to dupe. There have been many similar scams in Africa, such as the Bindo and *Panier de la Ménagère* pyramid schemes that rocked Zaire in the early 1990s.[81] It is impossible to tell the difference between a pyramid fraud and a genuine bank without considerable access to information about a bank's inner workings, which ordinary people do not have. The public must have confidence in decisions taken by government departments and banking authorities. In 1990s Botswana, one of Africa's best-regulated business environments, there was sharp criticism of the government among some newspapers and the general public for closing down pyramid scams. Some members of the public, attracted by the high interest rates offered by the fraudsters, thought they were being cheated out of an opportunity to make money by some sort of elite manipulation.[82] There is no doubt that reliable banking requires management that can generate a belief in its reliability and, hence, a feeling of trust. It is no coincidence that many early capitalist banking ventures in Europe arose out of religious networks, of Jews or Quakers, for example, that combined probity with financial acumen.

This last observation finds echoes in Africa. Many of the most dynamic religious movements in Africa devote considerable attention to making money, like the Mourides, probably the fastest-growing Sufi brotherhood in Senegal, whose members have also become successful entrepreneurs overseas.[83] Some of the new breed of charismatic and pentecostal churches also energetically promote the proposition that God can make his people rich. Africa's most populous country, Nigeria, is the foremost example. The pentecostal churches established in the south of the country since the 1930s were generally regarded as 'holiness churches', and until the 1980s were characterised by an ascetic morality. The 'pentecostal explosion' in Nigeria, as it has been dubbed, coinciding with the massive influx of petro-dollars, has changed this, with some of the new churches gaining a reputation for fabulous wealth. Religion is becoming a fast-growing economic activity. Churches trade in video tapes, books and other merchandise, often establishing themselves in empty warehouses and industrial premises in Lagos. The Faith Tabernacle chapel at Ota seats 50,000 people and is said to be the world's largest church auditorium. The Faith Tabernacle has members in Europe and America, managed by a mission organisation with some 2,000 employees.[84] The Synagogue Church of All Nations also has a global following, partly on the strength of the reputation as a healer of its founder, Prophet T. B. Joshua, who attracts people from all over the world. Several of the new-breed evangelists are immensely rich, since they exhort their followers to pay tithes to the church, promising them that God will deliver massive riches in return.[85] Perhaps the most famous of all Nigerian pentecostalist preachers, the late Benson Idahosa, was buried in a coffin imported specially from the United States, carried to his $ 120,000 tomb in a funeral cortege full of expensive cars and well-dressed people, and followed by a crowd of 30,000 mourners. The property of his church, the Church of God Mission International Incorporated, went not to his former assistant but to his wife, reputed more for her business sense than her knowledge of scripture.[86]

The connection of some of the most dynamic religious movements in Africa with extreme wealth, most notably some neo-pentecostal churches, has attracted considerable controversy. Many criticisms of what is sometimes disparagingly referred to as the 'prosperity gospel' and of the unseemly wealth of new Christian leaders refer to Nigerian examples. The extravagance of Nigerian churches is characteristic of a country where attitudes to wealth are extreme, as we have seen. Christianity in Africa has always had an association with social success and economic advancement, and it grew so rapidly during colonial times in part because it was associated with material advancement through schooling, learning European languages, and employment in the state sector,[87] just as Islam all over sub-Saharan Africa has historically been associated with successful trading.

It is well established in the history of Europe, we have said, that material prosperity is apt to be considered by religious believers as a sign of virtue and of divine blessing, and so it is among many Africans. And yet, curiously, many scholars studying new religious movements in Africa today consider that the charismatic cultivation of wealth carries a suspicion of hypocrisy or deception not just in marginal cases, or in the cases of the charlatans who are attracted to the scent of money in every field, including religion, but in general. The thinking behind this appears to be that making money through conventional financial operations, such as buying and selling shares, is moral because it is generally an entirely secular transaction, bearing no trace of religion; the latter, presumably, should be occupied with matters other than the creation or distribution of wealth despite its historical importance in this regard. But, as the Ghanaian theologian Kingsley Larbi points out, 'prosperity' refers to 'the ability to live a happy and balanced life without the problem of having to think what to eat, where to sleep, what to wear; how to meet one's social expectations, like school fees, children's education and the ability to contribute to the needs of one's community'.[88] The religious message, he argues, must be placed within the social and economic realities of a country, and understood in terms of traditional concepts of life, for it to be appreciated. There is an undeniable relation between the visible and invisible worlds in the sense that a person who is in a good state of spiritual health can also expect to prosper materially.[89]

Some scholars seek to explain the obsession with material prosperity in some of the new pentecostal churches in Africa, and their equally frequent concern with evil, in terms of the impact of global capitalism. Pentecostals, according to this view, consider the modern global economy to be enchanted, and see themselves as agents of disenchantment. They use the power of prayer to cause commodities to cease acting as 'fetishes' that threaten the personal integrity and identity of their owners. Pentecostalism, it is argued, thus helps people to handle globalisation and to control foreign commodities in such a way that these can be consumed without danger.[90] In such an analysis, the designation of certain goods as 'devilish' is interpreted as a metaphor designed to help people cope with the global economy.[91] However, this interpretation is based on sparse evidence and contains several doubtful assumptions. As some critics have noted,[92] it is at bottom based on the nineteenth-century view that Africa, stubbornly clinging to its own authentic character, is fundamentally opposed to modernity. Another recent theory is advanced by the American anthropologists Jean and John Comaroff, who start from the numerous reports of people seeking to acquire wealth through negotiation with the invisible world, and place these in the context of a new style of capitalism in which vast sums of money are traded daily for purely speculative purposes. They suggest that Africa is witnessing the emergence of what they call 'occult economies' characterised by attempts to conjure wealth out of nothing. These, they argue, are created by 'the Second Coming of Capitalism'. The Comaroffs note that late twentieth-century capitalism is marked by a concern with consumption rather than production, and a celebration of risk rather than its strict regulation. New religious movements worldwide, in their view, 'may be seen as the apotheosis of the occult economies of which we have been speaking'.[93] Elsewhere, they describe new religious movements as 'holy-owned [sic] subsidiaries' of occult economies.[94] In short, they suggest that new religious movements are a consequence of recent changes in the international economy. We find this interpretation unsatisfactory because it neglects to place current attempts by Africans to acquire wealth by negotiation with the spirit world into a longer history of religious thought, traditionally closely linked to the maintenance of material prosperity, or into the economic context of a continent that has become steadily less agrarian. The use of spiritual techniques in pursuit of prosperity also occurs in countries that have generally done well out of capitalism, such as in East Asia and, for that matter, the United States.

People in a great variety of cultures and epochs have used religion in the pursuit of worldly health, prosperity and well-being generally. A fully satisfactory explanation for the use in Africa of spiritual techniques intended to create or capture wealth would need to take account of this fact. Material conditions and spiritual ideas appear to have a bearing on each other in many contexts, but this does not mean that the one determines the other. Rather, there is a dynamic relationship between the two. Africa's recent history has led to an extreme degree of uncertainty and unpredictability in many spheres of life. The latter are reflected in people's perceptions of the spirit world, itself destabilised by more than a century of historical change precipitated by colonial government and missionary education. An overall result is a confusion of the spirit world as it is perceived by many people today, the mirror of a volatile material world. Africans are faced with a bewildering variety of purported spiritual experts, among them prophets, priests, healers and diviners of every sort, including quacks and charlatans. Such conditions have also created an economic field wide open to cheats and frauds, as well as opportunities for would-be political messiahs.

Intelligent and well-informed people in Africa may understand economics and finance but still seek an explanation for the extreme unpredictability of the environment they live in, as many Europeans and Americans did in the depression of the 1930s. How people are to find their way in this moral maze is another problem.

# 7

# MORALITY

'I am an African leader', Liberia's President Charles Taylor once proclaimed in a radio interview, 'and I can do as I wish.'[1]

Many people would probably refer to the lack of accountability of African heads of state if they were asked to give some reasons for the continent's political problems. The many presidents who have stolen and squandered vast sums of money, who have changed constitutions to perpetuate their rule, and ruined their countries for the sake of a few more years in power, are too well known to need repeating. But this is far from a full explanation. Although people with a scrupulous respect for the law do not easily advance in African politics, that does not mean that all the continent's politicians lack integrity. Africa includes among its leaders Nelson Mandela, probably the most admired statesman in the world at the beginning of the twentieth-first century. Some of his fellow-heads of state have spurned personal wealth. Like politicians elsewhere in the world, some have made terrible mistakes with the best of intentions. But whether or not they are temperamentally inclined to be tyrants, Africa's heads of state have been surrounded by courtiers, relatives and supporters whose interests they cannot afford to ignore. Some presidents have actually been the captives of their entourages, to the point that they may run a risk of being murdered if they go against the wishes of the cliques that appear to serve but in reality dominate them, like the notorious *akazu* faction that organised the 1994 genocide in Rwanda while hiding in the shadow of President Juvénal Habyarimana. If only in this form, every African politician faces real constraints on his power. It would thus be more accurate to describe the lack of accountability for which African politics are notorious by saying that few African heads of state are bound by moral codes that have been translated into constitutions and law codes so rigorously and objectively enforced as to be implacable.

Liberal commentators often suppose that the relative absence of the rule of law is the Achilles heel of governance and politics in Africa. This was one of the themes underlying the moves to democratise African governments in the 1990s. If the attempt to reform the political systems of an entire continent demonstrated any single thing, though, it was that the rule of law is not achieved simply by promulgating a suitable code of laws and arranging for regular elections to a parliament that forms the legislative branch of government. We have described how politicians found it relatively easy to sidestep formal checks and balances, encouraging the general informalisation of political and economic life and even the privatisation of the state itself.[2]

Impeccably liberal law codes, investment codes and constitutions are of small use if they do not repose upon a corpus of moral values, expressed in social convention and internalised by individual civil servants and voters who see their ethical beliefs reflected in the formal rules governing the conduct of state affairs and enforced by institutions. Such a system depends on the bulk of a community subscribing to more or less agreed criteria of what constitutes right and wrong, which vary from place to place and time to time. Among African philosophers and other writers[3] on the subject, there appears to be a consensus that African traditions of morality have different points of emphasis than those of Europe. The Ghanaian philosopher Kwasi Wiredu points out that among the Akan people, moral constraints are defined primarily in human rather than divine terms. The only exception he can identify is in regard to taboos, such as those forbidding people to work on certain days. These are conceived of as stemming from 'the will of an extra-human being'.[4] Elsewhere, Wiredu writes that 'one of the safest generalizations about African ways of thought is that morality is founded therein purely upon the necessity for the reciprocal adjustment of the interests of the individual to the interests of the community'. Therefore, he points out, 'moral rightness or wrongness, on this showing, is understood in terms of human interests'.[5] It is widely agreed by African philosophers that 'a moral rule is articulated on the basis of its ability to meet human needs in the communal setting'.[6]

In Europe, however, moral beliefs have become, over the centuries, so closely associated with the idea of law that is has become difficult to imagine any system of public morality that is not upheld by a written code promulgated by a state. Africa's historical trajectory has been rather different.

## Law, justice and morality

The colonial occupation of Africa followed two or three centuries during which European traders had been doing business on Africa's coasts without generally aspiring to settle in the continent (other than at its southern tip) and without feeling the need to establish a permanent military presence other than in a few forts. But conditions changed during the later nineteenth century, leading to the partition of Africa. In Europe itself, a new generation of bankers was prepared to lend money anywhere in the world. They preferred ideally to negotiate loans with people or corporations that carried no risk of defaulting and in situations where disputes could be settled in a court of law. According to a Victorian editor of the *Economist* magazine, this new situation required a particular political climate: 'The primary conditions of national good faith are three', he wrote in 1867: 'a continuous polity; a fixed political morality; and a constant possession of money'.[7] Large manufacturers required regular supplies of raw materials at steady prices. European diplomats, particularly after the emergence of a united Germany in 1871, wanted to be able to sign binding treaties anywhere in the world, implying a strong preference for what the same editor called a 'continuous political morality' that 'hardly penetrates to oriental despotisms'.[8]

For these reasons, the emerging complex of economic, financial and diplomatic interests found it inconvenient to do business with 'oriental despots' or with 'big men', individual rulers or traders whose jurisdiction was unclear and who, however trustworthy they might be as individuals, could not guarantee that arrangements they had made would be respected after their death or demise. Such interests needed the continuous political morality of a bureaucracy; this requirement was one of the main reasons for Africa's colonisation. The establishment of Western-style jurisdictions with territorial boundaries agreed in international law permitted Africa's wholesale entry into the world of capitalist business and diplomacy even if these boundaries had no existence on the ground. Foreign bankers could henceforth loan money to colonial governments that, unlike individual big men, would guarantee the security of a loan over long periods, beyond the span of one political life. The same bankers could seriously contemplate investment in mines and railways, safe in the knowledge that these assets were located in a specific jurisdiction.[9] These are the conditions necessary for capitalist investment and production, very different from the circumstances permitting import-export trade, which had previously been carried on in the absence of a Victorian concept of continuous political morality.

Colonial government was not a just order. Some colonial administrations were responsible for the greatest injustices imaginable. Yet it was based on the idea that a centralised state apparatus must be responsible for promulgating a code of laws, usually in written form, that has a binding force on society and on the state itself. This approach to government continues to be reflected in the modern African states that have succeeded their colonial predecessors and that aspire, formally at least, to uphold the rule of law. It is important to stress what this does not mean: it does not mean that in Africa today public life is always governed by the consistent application of written laws. The key point is that it is *in theory* governed by the consistent application of such laws. The continuing importance of the formal mantle of legality in countries that have undergone the colonial experience is illustrated by the case of Zimbabwe, where President Robert Mugabe has gone to great lengths to ensure that many of the extraordinary measures he has taken are supported by appropriate changes to the law, however unfair they may be. This is a continuation of a colonial practice in which measures considered unjust by the majority of the population are nonetheless carried out in conformity with the law of the state. A formal commitment to upholding the rule of law, in circumstances where much political and economic business is transacted informally, gives to African politicians and their foreign partners an opportunity to manipulate the gap between theory and reality to their advantage. In extreme cases the rule of law is little more than a facade.[10]

Nor should consideration of how colonial governments established the convention of ruling by reference to written codes be taken to mean that African societies before colonial times were ungoverned. While any functioning society must have a notion of norms and standard procedures, these do not always take the form of written laws—or even of unwritten ones—in the sense of a body of rules that is consistently applied, at least in theory, including to those who implement the code. Colonial officials, seeking to understand how African societies worked, often attempted to identify their authentic rules of operation in the form of so-called customary law or tradition. Colonial scholars set out to investigate small-scale societies and, generally by careful interviewing, to discover the unwritten rules that chiefs and elders had used to administer justice in the past. The sub-discipline of legal anthropology was based on this principle. It formed part of the enterprise, fairly typical of anthropology in colonial Africa, of identifying individual ethnic groups and fitting all the relevant data associated with each one of them into a coherent system, so that each ethnic group as far as possible was identified as having its own religion, its system of law, its succession rights, and so on, like a European nation in miniature. Since rather little was known about Africa's history, and it was generally presumed that individual ethnic groups had not changed much over time, colonial officials and researchers came to consider the customary law they believed themselves to have identified as being more or less set in granite.[11]

It has gradually become clear that the characteristic colonial view of Africa as consisting of distinct ethnic groups, each governed by a static, codified, corpus of tradition and customary law, was not altogether accurate. It tended to portray precolonial societies as frozen in time, whereas there is every reason to suppose that this has never been the case.[12] What is called 'tradition' in regard to precolonial African societies was not so much a corpus of rules as a way of thinking about change. Tradition can function in this way when people assimilate new developments by integrating them into oral histories and into their customs. Thus, colonial officials were in practice often frustrated to find that people in villages persisted in doing things in ways that did not accord with the monographs on ethnic tradition that were being printed on the basis of expert research, and that chiefs often did not apply the customary laws that had been identified. Rather, chiefs and others were constantly updating custom in light of new circumstances. Even in postcolonial Africa, the same process continues, as officials of some central governments continue to uphold a bureaucratic notion of proper customary law that differs from what people actually do, or what might be called 'living' law.[13]

In precolonial societies without writing, all rights and duties had to be remembered. They were often brought to mind through ritual performances and the oral transmission of myths and histories. There were at all times claims and counter-claims about who owned what or had which rights, including very often to the succession to chiefdom titles. Unlike in Europe, with its highly legalistic tradition of succession by the eldest son, the identification of a legitimate ruler was often not obvious. A successful ruler was one who became legitimate over time, including by being able to demonstrate a right to office by reference to the past, but also by ruling in a way that most people found acceptable. The various counter-claims about a chief's right to succession would go unmentioned if he ruled well, but would soon be revived if important people were dissatisfied with his actual conduct of affairs. This too was often expressed through ritual action. The most important exception to these generalisations about the nature of governance and justice in precolonial Africa concerns societies where writing was known and used for official purposes. This concerns especially places with a significant Muslim presence, in some of which shari'a law was enforced. In one of the clearest such cases, in northern Nigeria, British colonial governors tried to preserve as much as possible of government by Muslim emirs and sultans, subject only to the requirements of colonial administration and the banning of legal punishments that the British deemed to be cruel. Shari'a was retained for purposes of civil law but replaced by a new colonial law in criminal cases.

In general it is helpful to think of precolonial African societies as having been ruled by justice rather than by law. Justice is a moral concept; law has become a bureaucratic one. While Africa today frequently lacks the effective rule of law, this situation reflects the absence of an efficient bureaucracy more than it does the lack of any morality. In the past, justice was the prerogative of a ruler acting in accordance with what could be represented as tradition, although there was actually no single body of tradition but a mass of memories, all of which reflected to some extent current claims to status and power. In almost every case, tradition was transmitted largely through religious belief and action, often directed by ritual experts. This constituted a system that in effect imposed the equivalent of constitutional checks and balances on a ruler. It depended on a perception that the spirit world itself had a known order and that there were people who had recognised authority to interpret the invisible world. In this way even societies without regular codes of law could be well governed in having an atmosphere of public order and a pervasive sense of justice. Such a community was able to reproduce itself over time. Perhaps the outstanding feature of a system like this was its extreme flexibility. The lack of writing and of bureaucratic rules and laws was precisely what enabled oral societies to absorb even radical innovations. At the same time, it was because judicial decision-making devolved upon the person of a leader, a king or a chief, normally acting in council, and not upon a fixed code, and that rules were often embedded in rituals, that it had become unsuitable for European purposes by the late nineteenth century.

Today, there are analysts who see the type of legal-bureaucratic regime introduced by colonialism as a Western transplant that never really took root in the African soil.[14] This reflects a romantic view inasmuch as it can be taken to imply that there is an authentic African way of doing things, as opposed to patterns of behaviour that are more or less influenced by history. It is a recurrent feature of much Western writing on Africa (and an idea occasionally used by Africans also) to assert that there exists a timeless Africa, in an almost transcendent meaning of a continent with qualities that are proper to itself only. This is different from a description of structures, institutions or patterns of behaviour that are African in the sense that they can be shown to have existed in the sub-continent over a long period, and therefore to have deep historical roots. The idea of an Africa outside of time was implicit in quite a lot of early twentieth-century writing.[15] Moreover, it appears still to be alive today. It is tempting to detect such a view of an Africa outside history in occasional quests to identify political systems that are 'really' African, or to lament the creation of colonial borders that are said to have done violence to the 'real' human geography of the continent. That systems of government and political borders were imposed by Europeans in the last hundred years or so is a historical fact with consequences for both Africans and non-Africans. Specific arrangements made in regard to government—the choice of an electoral system, for example, a particular policy, or the fixing of a national boundary—may have effects either positive or negative, depending on one's standard of measurement. The point is that there are no political systems that are authentically African: there are only systems that have a history in Africa, longer or shorter. The most fundamental historical patterns, those of the *longue durée*, change slowest of all, in Africa like everywhere else.

It was in self-interested pursuit of what they regarded as the authentic nature of individual tribes that all the European colonial powers, to greater or lesser extent, set up a centralised administration in each colony and appointed 'traditional' African rulers in systems of indirect rule. In most cases this involved freezing many of the dynamic processes of local government, permitting local rulers to dispense with many of the more subtle checks and balances that had traditionally operated. In some cases the result was the conversion of chieftaincies into 'decentralised despotisms'.[16] This change does not automatically make today's chiefs illegitimate, but indicates only that they have adapted to changing circumstances. Consideration of how this occurred does, however, destroy the idea that there ever were 'pure' ethnic traditions. New influences have always been absorbed to produce new combinations. By the same token, European colonial administrations, even where they were staffed at their senior levels entirely by Europeans, assimilated aspects of African political practice. This process of reciprocal assimilation[17] was speeded up once African nationalists began to take control of national governments, typically in the 1950s.

Western missionaries who began to settle in the interior of Africa in the nineteenth century were also imbued with a mission to change the morals of Africans, whom they considered primitive and in need of education. Many nineteenth- and twentieth-century missionaries were convinced that their charges' moral and spiritual upliftment should be accompanied by an infusion of modern patterns of work, time-keeping and consumption. Good Christians would live in houses, the men wearing trousers and the women dresses; they would read books, earn money, and pay taxes.

Some of these ideas were not merely encouraged but rigorously enforced by colonial governments. Existing practices that were in due course restricted or outlawed, or which were the subject of strong moral disapproval by churches, included forms of bodily mutilation (such as female circumcision or ritual scarification); polygamy; capital punishment involving techniques that Europeans thought cruel; forms of ritual considered by missionaries as idolatry or fetishism; certain types of dress, and so on. In summary, Europeans made an intensive effort, in the name of humanity, development and civilised behaviour, to persuade Africans that quite widely held ideas were backward, and that the practices associated with them must cease. This campaign to renounce long-held ideas about right and wrong and the forms of behaviour associated with them, and to adopt instead standards suggested by people from outside the continent, especially Europe, was often referred to as 'the civilising mission'.

These days, the colonial civilising mission is criticised from every point of the political compass, including by progressives who feel that the whole attempt to transform Africa was misguided or even criminal; by romantics who lament the destruction of a purer, more 'authentic' Africa; and by African nationalists who resent that such interference ever came from outside. But in spite of this almost universal condemnation of the civilising mission, the imposition of discipline on Africans continues today much as before. World Bank experts calling on them to adopt the virtues of 'good governance' and offering them financial incentives, ecologists telling them to conserve the environment, feminists scandalised by female genital cutting, and humanitarians moved by the cruelty of war: all of these, however sincere or commendable their causes, seek to impose on Africans a particular view of what is right and wrong. The point at issue is not whether any of the above are desirable concepts. It is hard to disagree with the proposition that certain benefits should ideally be available to everyone. The point, rather, is that outsiders have rarely sought to negotiate these and other ideas with Africans other than in a token manner, from early colonial times to this day. Even today, little attempt is made to link new ideas to indigenous concepts that are rooted in local traditions.

Nowadays, there are some Africans who share certain of these ideas, and others who do not. The sustained effort to impose new morals on Africa has had an effect both on outsiders and on Africans themselves, reflected in the attitudes of politicians towards their constituents and of citizens towards their rulers. What this century-and-a-half-long campaign has only rarely achieved is a wide consensus that is conducive to providing real checks and balances on the way in which politicians use power. This can come about if the majority of the population, including the executive branch of government, proceeds from a similar set of ideas about what constitutes a right and just way to act. Given the predominantly religious world-view in Africa, many important discussions relating to the development of new moral codes take place in religious language.[18] People's attempts to create for themselves a clear distinction between good and evil can be seen as one of the motive forces in the striking growth of neo-pentecostal and charismatic churches. The same is true of Islamic revivalist movements, with the reintroduction of shari'a into the code of criminal law in northern Nigeria being welcomed by many Muslims there as a statement of moral principle.[19] The lack of justice in African societies, whether expressed in the effective rule of law or in different form, is widely conceived of in a spirit idiom.

## The concept of witchcraft

Some of the clearest expressions of a search for justice expressed in a spirit idiom are the discourses of 'witchcraft' that are so widespread in Africa today. In popular speech, 'witchcraft' has become shorthand for many situations in which mystical powers are believed to be at work.[20] The word 'witchcraft', in its classic use in English, designates a perception of spiritual power employed in an evil manner or for evil purposes. This is the way in which it was used by Evans-Pritchard, the founder of modern anthropological studies in this field, in his work on the Azande of Sudan.[21] Accordingly, we may define witchcraft as 'a manifestation of evil believed to come from a human source'.[22] The moral aspect of the forces subsumed in the term 'witchcraft' is of great importance in the discussion. For analytical purposes it is desirable to restrict the use of the word 'witchcraft' in this way so as to establish some order in the linguistic confusion that has grown over time in the use of the term. Only by defining witchcraft by reference to its moral dimension can we appreciate the significance of the debates it generates. The way in which people speak about witchcraft in many parts of Africa today is so vague as to require qualification if it is to be used by academics. It is equally important to make an analytical distinction between witchcraft beliefs—the content of which, as with other forms of spiritual belief, cannot be empirically tested—and witchcraft accusations that may follow from such belief. Witchcraft accusations, unlike witchcraft beliefs, can be empirically observed, and the ensuing actions analysed.

There has been a revival in witchcraft studies among Western anthropologists in recent years.[23] This is helpful inasmuch as it focusses attention on an important expression of deep moral concern. But it is precisely because they often devote insufficient attention to the moral aspects of witchcraft that academic studies may risk contributing to the stigmatisation of people who are accused of being witches, with sometimes fatal consequences. Scholars who perpetuate witchcraft discourse uncritically in their own work may unwittingly help in the construction of witchcraft in Africa as a social fact.

Both the state and well-established religious authorities in large parts of Africa lack the means to deal with witchcraft accusations in a legitimate manner. Hence, if people see *prima facie* evidence of what they take to be witchcraft, and if there is no legitimate authority that proposes to look into the matter, they are all too likely to take the law into their own hands. Unscrupulous elements may use this as an opportunity for self-advancement, accusing others of witchcraft in order to eliminate political opponents or simply anyone against whom they hold a grudge.[24] Popular beliefs in witchcraft have become a convenient cover for cynical political manipulations. This process shows obvious similarities with mechanisms in the great variety of societies in the world that recognise a category of officially-labelled deviance, to which are consigned 'those who commit acts perceived as transgressing the fundamental moral axioms on which human nature, and hence social life, is based'.[25] The behaviour of such perceived dangerous and anti-social wrong-doers is often thought to be the mirror-image of what is considered desirable in terms of sexual behaviour, eating habits and ideological orientation.

Such categories of infamy are conceived within a dominant ideology or discourse. Whether the prevailing ideology is religious or secular, the subsequent pursuit of scapegoats shows remarkable similarities across societies. An authoritative account of Stalinist purges in the 1930s Soviet Union explicitly notes the 'many similarities' between that episode and earlier European witch-hunting.[26] A study of the persecution of alleged sexual deviants in modern Britain makes a similar analogy.[27] Although neither of these cases concerns so-called witches, they are comparable inasmuch as they concern the use of power to label certain people as deviants and to hound them, often to their deaths. Even in a wealthy and highly ordered society such as the Netherlands, this scapegoating mechanism operates. A typical example was reported in the Dutch press during the epidemic of foot and mouth disease in 2001, when people in a village accused one farmer of having deliberately introduced the virus into the local community, allegedly from Africa. His family was threatened and forced to leave the village.[28]

Before the establishment of colonial states whose institutions were designed on a European model, witchcraft belief in Africa might result in accusations against individuals and in their condemnation and even execution. This would normally take place in a context where there was a degree of consensus concerning which authorities could legitimately decide on such matters. Occasional 'anti-witchcraft' drives aimed to cleanse communities by identifying suspected witches and rendering them harmless, often through some form of ritual purification.[29] However, there are also historical examples of lethal witch-hunts in precolonial Africa in exceptional circumstances. In the days of the overseas slave trade, the common practice of selling alleged witches gave an incentive to unscrupulous chiefs to abuse their powers. The betrayals, suspicions and opportunities for gain created by commercial slavery encouraged accusations of witchcraft generally.[30]

In precolonial times, the use of mystical power as a weapon was seen as legitimate in certain circumstances. For example, the manipulation of such power in order to cause harm was generally seen as justified if it was for morally proper purposes, such as to detect thieves or to wage war, in which case it was no different from any other weapon. It could also play a role in the regulation of economic activity. An accusation of witchcraft was often made against a person whose source of wealth seemed inexplicable and who was therefore assumed to have used mystical power to become rich, probably at the expense of others and therefore in an immoral manner. As we have seen in the previous chapter, in precolonial African societies individuals had few ways to accumulate wealth. Economic relations were subsumed in social relations. Even today, wealth can be reckoned not only in material terms but also in spiritual terms. Hence, a person advanced in age and knowledge may be seen as having accumulated spiritual wealth. This may be one reason why old people are often liable to be accused of witchcraft. Women, by reason of their ability to produce life, as well as diviners and other ritual experts, are particularly vulnerable in this respect. Witchcraft accusations are almost impossible to refute since they refer to a belief rather than an action.

Today, witchcraft accusations can have dramatic social and political consequences in the form of assault, killing and expulsion. In some places people named as witches flee in fear of their lives to special settlements. These 'witch camps', as they are called in Ghana, or 'witch villages' as they are known in South Africa's Limpopo Province, are places of destitution. The Limpopo Province of South Africa is a prime example of a place where witchcraft accusations cause immense harm. This area, one of the poorest regions of a country which is nevertheless Africa's premier economic power, has been plagued for almost two decades by witchcraft accusations resulting in hundreds of gruesome deaths, many expulsions, and untold misery.[31] The people of this area have always believed in witchcraft, but, at least in the most closely-studied areas, such as Green Valley, these beliefs rarely resulted in the deaths of those accused until the 1960s or later. This is no longer the case. It has become all too easy to spread gossip about a person who then falls victim to a witchcraft accusation, even when the charge is connected to the basest of motives, such as the desire of a neighbour to confiscate a piece of land, jealousy, political rivalry, and so on. The frequent occurrence of lightning strikes in the thunderstorms that are a natural feature of the lowveld is very often the occasion for an accusation, as people wonder why a particular person has been struck. Nobody is immune, but the targets of such accusations are often older people. They may also include the relatively prosperous members of communities that are generally poor. Accusations are now typically made by young people, who traditionally were not allowed to accuse others of witchcraft. Neither the police, nor local chiefs, nor traditional healers, nor Christian pastors seem able to control these accusations. When the weight of an accusation reaches a certain level, the victim has little choice other than to flee the area or face murder. In the 1990s this was often done through the 'necklacing' method made notorious during the last years of apartheid.

The frequent and uncontrolled use of witchcraft accusations has led in a number of African countries to discussions on the position of the law in this regard. During colonial times anti-witchcraft legislation was widely introduced as a means of regulating such accusations. In practice, colonial magistrates often ended up condemning the accusers, regarding them as perjurors or troublemakers. Some Africans in colonial times, therefore, believing in the reality of witchcraft as a mystical force, were alarmed that the government was failing to provide a proper form of regulation. Accusations, counter-accusations and subsequent processes of adjudication went underground in the sense of taking place in a sphere outside the formal scope of the law and the state. Today, with colonial rule long gone, several African governments have introduced new measures to deal with the perceived problem of witchcraft. In Cameroon, for example, new legislation empowers the state to prosecute alleged witches.[32] In South Africa, a similar debate is taking place, which equally proposes to make witchcraft a criminal offence, permitting the state to prosecute anyone accused of it. This is remarkably similar to developments in Europe four hundred years ago, where states, by taking it upon themselves to prosecute witches, contributed to the construction of witchcraft as a social fact rather than considering it a matter of belief. The result was the judicial killing, over a period of two centuries, of perhaps 40–50,000 people considered by courts of law to be witches.[33]

At almost every step of the process, the judicial prosecution of witchcraft as a criminal offence is directly contrary to the classical precepts of law. Witchcraft is a private discourse characterised by gossip and hearsay, that can easily be hidden and malicious, whereas the judicial system properly operates on written rules and adheres to explicit procedures and standards. While witchcraft accusations are highly dependent on personal relationships, the law is equal for all. Witchcraft discourse addresses existential problems, whereas law enforcement addresses concrete offences. Divining cases of witchcraft depends on personal interpretations, whereas proof in law has to be factual. People accused of witchcraft are in effect held to be guilty unless proved innocent, which infringes against a basic principle of law. Hearsay evidence is regarded as proof.[34] In sum, if the idea of legislating against witchcraft were to be pursued, it is likely only to multiply current injustices.

Discussions in Africa on how to deal with witchcraft accusations often take on a culturalist tone that some people feel to be appropriate in a postcolonial age. There are those who claim that witchcraft is an authentically African belief and that it 'really' exists in Africa. It is therefore logical—or so it is argued—for Africa's sovereign states to devise appropriate home-grown solutions through the instruments at their disposal, which means the police and the law courts.[35] In South Africa, only recently freed from the rule of a white minority, this approach is sometimes said to be in keeping with the idea of an African Renaissance, launched by the government as a project for the regeneration of the continent. In practice, little substantial intellectual or political content has been given to the vague notion that South Africa is, or should be, undergoing such a process. The letters pages of South African newspapers sometimes contain communications from readers claiming that all sorts of illiberal attitudes are authentically African and therefore justifiable in the new age. Nevertheless, the state cannot simply ignore the witchcraft fears that lead to such social upheaval and suffering. The most desirable course might be for the state to retain the principle of religious freedom, including the freedom of people to believe in witchcraft as in any other religious construct. This demonstrates in concrete terms the importance of making an analytical distinction between witchcraft belief and witchcraft accusations, as was discussed above. The state would be well advised, thus, to observe debates on witch-

craft beliefs with a view to intervening when there seems to be a real risk of
a criminal action such as physical assault. For witchcraft discourses do not
necessarily result in violence, as many examples from other societies attest.
A cross-cultural comparison of witchcraft beliefs and accusations suggests
a model of escalation, in which administrative interventions are feasible
before matters get so out of hand that serious injuries occur.[36]

## Political morality

For all the liberal constitutions hammered out in the 1990s, there are still
very many African heads of state who gained their positions through military coups or palace intrigues. Guinea, Burkina Faso, Benin, Togo, Uganda,
Mali, Chad, Congo-Brazzaville, Congo-Kinshasa, Sudan and other countries have leaders of this sort. Even if they have subsequently managed to
get themselves elected in civilian guise, the coercive methods originally
used by such leaders are not forgotten by the population. So discredited is
the profession of politics that even civilians who are elected after long
campaigning risk being cynically regarded as intriguers or parvenus who
have succeeded by cunning and trickery rather than as representatives
of a truly national constituency. In the Wolof language, the word 'politig'
has come to mean lying or deception, while in the Lingala language of
Congo, 'coop', derived from the notion of cooperation much used by international donors, has come to mean a bargain of dubious morality.[37] At
worst, politicians are seen as a clique of witches, agents of the devil in
human form.[38]

   At various levels, an inescapable connection arises between illegitimate
political regimes, whatever the precise technical means they use to come to
power, and the type of spiritual power on which they are believed to
repose. Power is usually defined as the ability of a person to induce others
to act in a desired manner.[39] Many great minds have expressed the conviction that the possession of great power tempts its holders to immorality,
or at the very least confronts them with dilemmas that demand profound
choices concerning good and evil, normally considered the prerogative of
gods. Nietzsche noted that 'every high degree of power always involves a
corresponding degree of freedom from good and evil'.[40]

   Politics in Africa today appears to many people as the ultimate form of
individual activity, in which power and wealth are conjured out of nothing
and used for selfish purposes. Many politicians display a self-belief that is
reckless in the extreme, being prepared to contemplate almost any measure that is calculated to increase their power. According to Moses Nagbe,

a Liberian academic and novelist who also declares himself an agnostic in religious matters, a politician typically believes that the spirit world will save him from the consequences of his most selfish actions: 'God, he believes, will pull a magic formula and all will be improved, without touching his weakness in spending'.[41] Those who wield power often claim that actions in conformity with a destiny decided in the spirit world must therefore be moral; success is its own justification. 'Even though I cannot have access to God's computer, I believe I have still some programme', claims Umaru Dikko, once regarded as Nigeria's most corrupt politician, who survived an attempted kidnap by air-freighting him in a packing-crate from his place of exile in Britain. 'Otherwise I would have perished in that crate. I feel thankful to God that he has given me this opportunity. He wouldn't have given it to me if I had seemed bad in His sight'.[42] South Africa's apartheid-era intelligence chief, Hendrik van den Bergh, claimed that a divine mission had been revealed to him after he had accidentally electrocuted himself while he was welding on his farm. 'I could feel I was dying', he recalled. 'Then I realised I was dead, and on the other side, for I heard God say "Hendrik, your life's work is not finished—I need you back on Earth", and I was restored to life'. His servant Johannes had had the presence of mind to run and shut off the main electricity supply.[43]

The ruthless and self-interested nature of the political struggle is commented upon in ostensibly religious texts. A Brazzaville pamphleteer who claims to have been to hell and back records that 'the Universe contains various spirits of different status and type. There are higher infernal spirits who govern the spirit world from inter-stellar space'. Among these devils is 'the Emperor Lucifer, the prince of darkness Asmode', and a secretary-general of evil spirits, one Lucifuge Rofocale. Lesser spirits are divided into political-military grades, the whole resembling uncannily the author's home country of Congo-Brazzaville during its Marxist period.[44] In another popular tract, an analogy is made by a young pentecostal preacher in Nigeria. Seeking to explain the origin of evil in the world, he compares the story of the revolt of the angel Lucifer against God to an attempted coup in heaven. He refers to God as the commander-in-chief of heaven and Jesus as his second-in-command, while Lucifer, before his fall, had the rank of general officer commanding the host of angels. The following is his account of the battle in heaven when Lucifer launches his coup:[45]

> The day for the coup came. Lucifer and his followers got more than they bargained for. Their logistic and strategic plans failed. They were defeated almost before the coup execution started!
>
> The announcement was brief. A group of dissident angels led by Lucifer, the Commander-in-chief of the heavenly angels, had attempted

to overthrow the kingdom of our Lord. The dissidents have been rounded up. All peace loving angels should go about their normal duties as every situation is under control. There would be no need for curfew as all the dissidents were arrested at less than the first second of the coup. The prince of peace is in firm control of every situation.

This description is adapted to a Nigerian public all too familiar with hearing radio broadcasts interrupted by martial music and a coup announcement.

The assertion by religious writers from countries with long experience of military rule that evil originated in a coup in heaven, or that the evil spirits are organised like an army in power, is eloquent, since the equation can easily be reversed—if hell is like a military government, then military governments are also connected to the world of devils. A successful political intriguer is widely assumed to have access to a source of immense spiritual power that translates into actions likely to be selfish and immoral. Many of Africa's military coups have been carried out by young men, sometimes not even thirty years old. The moral implications of coups like these are all the more pronounced in societies where age has traditionally been a key qualification for power. One Beninese journalist was asked whether this meant that all politicians, even the revered Nelson Mandela, were therefore dishonest. He replied that Mandela languished for twenty-seven years in prison and had been seen to demonstrate moral behaviour. He had waited for power to be given to him rather than grabbing it. Therefore, he concluded, Mandela can only have received power from a benign spiritual force.[46] A Mandela, in other words, is granted power by a beneficent force, whereas an upstart army officer who seizes power is assumed to have enlisted the services of a more sinister one.

The connection between political power and spiritual force felt by politicians may take very particular forms, implying distinct moral choices. We may cite an example from Liberia, Africa's oldest republic, created in 1847 but ruled until 1980 by an elite largely drawn from people of African American origin who claimed to have a mission to westernise those of their fellow-Liberians who were of purely African origin, often known as 'country people' or 'tribal people'. Yakpawolo Kollie was born into an indigenous Liberian family in the mid-twentieth century.[47] Since his father was a chief, Kollie was educated in traditional practices with a view to his inheriting the chiefdom title in due course. His training included attending an initiation school in which, like other adolescents in his area, he was confined to a secluded place in the forest for some months and taken through a series of initiation rituals interspersed with instruction on the traditional history of his people and the moral values of his community.

After initiation Kollie returned to the Christian school where he was receiving a conventional American-style education. He was baptised as a Christian and assumed the name James Paye. Later, he went to America and took a PhD degree at an American university. On returning to Liberia he was elected to the Senate. Various of his supporters and friends began to suggest that he would need to carry out a blood sacrifice in order to acquire the power to be an effective senator. He was even told that this might mean taking someone's life, 'in order to purify him for the jobs ahead'.[48] His grandfather appeared to him in dreams, urging him to follow the way of his ancestors. For James Paye, respectful of his ancestral tradition but also a Christian, this was a moral dilemma. Was he to cause someone's death in the interests of his career? Or was he to see his political career becalmed, and risk being seen by some of his family and friends as a failure, who had lost faith with the culture that had sustained him from birth?

Comparable dilemmas are quite common, in the sense that there are many Africans who, educated in the West and returning home with ideas they have acquired in Europe or America, have been ridiculed, even by their own families, if they choose not to follow what are presented to them as local cultural conventions in matters of political morality. This can involve attitudes to life and death, but perhaps more commonly relates to the combination of public office and personal enrichment known as corruption. 'Former public officials or civil servants who do not have booties [sic] to show for their period of service are ridiculed and decried as failures', writes an expatriate Liberian. 'They are scorned and bad mouthed, simply because they failed to do the "cultural thing": to exploit the public coffers'.[49]

Most of the young men who have shot or manipulated their way to power have claimed to be acting for the good of the nation, to bring freedom or stamp out corruption. Many are wildly acclaimed at first. Second thoughts may follow when a regime turns out to be less moral than it at first proclaimed. The true nature of a regime is hard to detect, but people may reflect from rueful experience that there are tell-tale signs of its true nature. The difficulty of discerning these may be compared to the difficulty of distinguishing between true and false prophets, that is religiously inspired people who claim to bring revelations of a deeper truth that they have gleaned from the spirit world. The full nature of a prophet can be known only in retrospect, by the accuracy or otherwise of the prophecy. So too in politics, an army officer, a guerrilla leader and a politician all arrive in power proclaiming freedom and prosperity. People have learned from hard experience to wait and see what they bring. The moral nature of power lies in the manner of its exercise.

## Morality and the state

Colonial systems of government, depending on rules and laws necessary for bureaucratic consistency, found it convenient to lump Africans into groups of rather uniform status for administrative purposes. This was generally done by identifying people as members of a particular 'tribe' or ethnic group, depending perhaps on their mother tongue or the area of their birth, and then assigning them to the control of an African official regarded as the tribal or village chief. The British were particularly fond of indirect rule, but it was used by every colonial regime. Some Africans developed vested interests in the system and learned how it could be turned to advantage. Although nationalist movements in their heyday from the 1950s to the 1970s were quite effective in convincing diverse populations that they were all members of a wider, national community, often represented by a single party, the nationalist programme was ambiguous in the sense that politicians nevertheless continued to appeal to ethnic constituencies, while intellectuals often romanticised ethnic communities as examples of an authentic African culture and history. Postcolonial states, formally based on the same rational-legal principles as their colonial forebears, have found it equally convenient to deal with clusters of people identified by a collective label, ethnic or regional.

It is instructive to consider the moral basis on which appeals for ethnic solidarity are commonly made. In Africa as in most other parts of the world, it is regarded as virtuous for people to form bonds of obligation towards those closest to them, such as members of their immediate family. These are small-scale relationships, typically shared by those who know one another intimately and who join in numerous daily activities. The British historian John Lonsdale refers to these as 'moral ethnicity'.[50] Describing a relationship as moral does not mean that it is without elements of coercion and inequality. Many African communities in precolonial times were adept at integrating newcomers into such relationships, not always by any means in pleasant ways, since they included slavery and bondage. Political tribalism, on the other hand, posits the existence of an obligation to a leader who claims to represent a substantial community of people, tens of thousands or even millions in number, too many to know each other personally or to have any real relationship beyond an imagined one. Politicians invoke such imagined communities to form constituencies that they can mobilise in their quest for national power, by means varying from rhetorical appeal to the threat or practice of violence. They use the language of moral ethnicity to facilitate the use of a political tribalism that is exclusive. Groups that lose out in the political logic of the ethnic mobilisation process in Africa include Tutsis in Rwanda in 1994, Mandingoes in Liberia, whites in Zimbabwe, northerners in Côte d'Ivoire, and so on. The moral point of reference of the ethnic community becomes twisted into a justification for expulsion and even, in the most extreme cases, genocide. In fact, many countries in the world use similar methods to exclude parts of their population considered illegal or not having full rights. Thus the language of ethnic or national exclusion may be justified by reference to democracy, majority rule, and international order. In Europe, for example, nations that have thought of themselves as consisting of more or less integrated blocks are today struggling to accommodate substantial numbers of immigrants with different backgrounds, calling into question some generally held assumptions about political values.

The use, or abuse, of deep-seated ideas about moral rights and obligations also underpins the phenomenon of corruption. This word can hardly be used without some reference to morality, for while corruption is generally thought to involve using a public position for private benefit, the relatives or clients of an office-holder may consider this to be morally justified. In Africa, this is often based on an argument that a political patron has a duty to extend physical protection and to redistribute material rewards to those associated with him, according to the logic of clientelist politics. The duty of the dependents, in return, is to praise the leader, support him, vote for him, even fight for him. This reflects a core ingredient of all political systems, which essentially turn on coercion, exchange of services, and the way in which relations between leaders and followers are represented. Opinion polls as well as more anecdotal evidence suggest that Africans are often deeply ambiguous about the resulting relationships. For example, in one opinion poll in Kenya, 95.7 per cent of those interviewed thought that corruption was practised in government offices, and 94.6 per cent thought politicians were corrupt.[51] This did not prevent many Kenyans from voting for President Daniel arap Moi and his party in numerous elections until the electoral defeat of both president and party in 2002. People admire rich and powerful patrons for their success, it seems, the more so when they are generous in redistributing wealth. Political relationships are often described in terms of a family, as though a president or other leader were a father to his people. He is expected to be generous although he may also be stern, and he demands loyalty.[52] At the same time people may sometimes express resentment of the corruption of those in power as a class, the more so if they themselves feel excluded. In this way, a traditional value—generosity to one's kin and dependents— sits awkwardly with what is touted as a universal commitment to bureaucratic efficiency and an idealised rectitude known as good governance. It may be cynical, but it is not inaccurate, to note that good governance was of little concern to Western governments when they were deriving satisfactory political or economic benefits from African political systems. By the same token, Africans could be accused of equal cynicism, but a common human tendency to accommodation, if they tolerate all sorts of immorality for as long as these deliver the goods of political stability and economic prosperity. It is when things start to go bad that people become most critical.

Many observers believe that corruption has become far more widespread in Africa in recent years.[53] If so, there are obvious reasons for this, since most civil servants are not paid a living wage and a fend-for-yourself atmosphere has become widespread. Politicians, civil servants and managers derive economic opportunities from the bureaucracies they run, which is hardly a phenomenon unique to Africa, but which occurs there in a context of extreme poverty and unpredictability. It is little wonder, then, that those who use public services will resort to any means to get what they need. Members of the public who have to acquire an official document from a vast and impenetrable administration will typically seek a friend or relative in the appropriate office and appeal to a sense of moral solidarity as a way of getting the rubber stamp or piece of paper that is required. Such appeals to 'moral ethnicity' rarely make sense in Western societies where the loyalties of personal relationships have to a large extent been subjugated to loyalty to the law and the impersonal organs of the national state. For their general well-being in a range of matters, Westerners are no longer dependent on their relatives but on the state to provide for their basic needs. In Africa, on the other hand, people cannot rely on the state in the same way. It is essential for them to maintain a wide network of personal connections, with the ensuing rights and obligations, for success or even for survival. This range of personal relationships and accompanying duties extends into the spirit world.

The need for a new moral approach is widely commented on by African intellectuals.[54] Many people are concerned to investigate relevant aspects of their traditions for this purpose, in the conviction that they have to start with the material at hand. As in debates about witchcraft, some people see this as a cultural issue primarily, suggesting there is a unique and authentic quality to African ways of life which makes the continent different from everywhere else. At bottom, Africans who wonder which of their cultural traditions might be developed for constructive purposes are participating in a worldwide debate that takes so many forms that people in different countries may not realise they are engaged in fundamentally the same discussion. The tendency to emphasise differences between cultures rather than to focus on what may bind them invites the question whether cultural particularism breeds moral particularism. In other words, if one is to argue for the primacy of cultural diversity, on the grounds that there exists a range of separate cultural identities, is it possible at the same time to uphold the existence of moral standards which override a particular cultural tradition, such as those embedded in the Universal Declaration of Human Rights?[55] Thus, in many developed countries including the European Union, Australia and the United States, there are heated discussions about which foreigners have a right to enter the country and which migrants have no such right. In the EU, a policy of rigorous exclusion has led to the creation of an under-class of foreigners classified as illegal, including many Africans. 'Illegals' are people with few rights. In other countries, such as Malaysia, Iran and China, governments sometimes refuse to countenance international codes of human rights on the grounds that these are not culturally appropriate. Meanwhile, in many parts of Africa small-scale village chauvinisms exclude people coming from a different part of the same country.[56] All these cases are concerned with the question whom to include within a network of moral bonds and, therefore, to whom one has moral obligations.

The limits of inclusion and exclusion in regard to any modern state are defined by law. However, legal definitions are not necessarily seen as morally legitimate, as the citizens of a particular country may decide that a law enacted in their name is nevertheless unjust. Moral bonds are not always identical with legal rules. There are many examples of states taking certain measures on moral grounds, but of the law being widely flouted because it does not conform to the moral sentiments of the general public. This was the case with the prohibition of alcohol in the United States in the 1920s. Something similar may apply with regard to the definition of who is a citizen. That is, people who are legally qualified for admission to a community may nonetheless be excluded on moral grounds, such as those black migrants to Europe who have valid papers but who, even so, find themselves socially excluded. By the same token, people formally excluded may believe themselves to have a moral right to belong. Moral arguments, it is clear, may be used as much to exclude as to include.

Africa has been particularly prey to an excess of legalism, with over a hundred years of colonial and postcolonial legislation designed to change moral beliefs and practices, but with a very mixed record of effectiveness. So many laws have lacked legitimacy that many Africans have been left with a distinct lack of respect for the law of the land they live in. At the same time, the process of trying to change people's moral beliefs through legislation and bureaucratic action has brought into question many values that people may privately hold. Hence, many Africans feel a need to create new moral bonds, irrespective of the law.

# 8

# TRANSFORMATIONS

While bombs fell on London during the Second World War, George Orwell was working on an essay about the nature of Englishness. Grasping for an analogy to help convey his sense of how the England of 1940 contained certain elements that it had inherited directly from the England of 1840, even though it had changed enormously in the intervening century, he compared the nation to an individual, asking his readers: 'What have you in common with the child of five whose photograph your mother keeps on the mantelpiece?' and replying: 'Nothing, except that you happen to be the same person'.[1]

This most commonplace of observations—that both individuals and groups of people are subject to continuity and change—is key to a series of questions that need to be asked about the nature of human beings and of the history they collectively make. In the case of Africa, an investigation on these lines is often deceptively difficult because of the dominant conceptions associated with the rise of modern states, which have made it hard to imagine processes of social change in which the state does not play a central role. It could be said that modern states exist for no other purpose than to manage change; this, each state does by such means as defending its physical integrity through armies and police forces and by ensuring its own economic prosperity and that of at least a critical mass of the society it aspires to govern, through organs of financial and economic management. Like all professional managers, public functionaries abhor uncertainty.[2] Most parts of Africa have acquired states of this type only rather recently, as we have seen in the previous chapter. If we are to place interactions between religion and politics in Africa in time perspective, we have to reconstruct histories of change in societies where bureaucratic states have not assumed a privileged role, and where religion has been a more important technique for managing change. Nor is Africa unique in this respect. India, Indonesia, Egypt and many other former colonies have ancient state traditions, but not ones that exactly resemble those of Europe.

Understanding the new interactions between religion and politics in Africa and many other parts of the world requires taking the histories of those places seriously. In particular, it demands that we think of processes of social change without placing states always at the centre of the narrative. But it is not satisfactory to consider such local histories as if they were isolated from the broad sweep of human affairs; they need to be considered in a global context, as aspects of a world history in which the lives of colonised and colonisers have become inseparable. Thinking about the role of religion is crucial to this historiographical enterprise. For, together with politics, religion has proved over time to be one of the two most important mechanisms for managing change in any society, in individuals and *en masse*. In many parts of the world before the nineteenth and twentieth centuries, religion played a far more important role in managing both personal and collective change than is allowed for in modern statecraft. Hence, in the many parts of the world where European forms of government were imported or imposed, the grafting of modern states over the last two centuries connects with older traditions concerning the government of both the soul[3] and the body. This chapter will examine the theoretical aspects of this process, with the aim of elucidating the nature of current transformations in Africa. Further, it throws an original light on processes now taking place in many other parts of the world also, including Europe and North America.

Considering trajectories of change through the prism of religion provides a useful vantage point on African history. First, it reflects the importance of religion, as defined in this book, as a medium for managing change in African societies over centuries. Second, the study of religion is facilitated by an abundant literature, much of it written by Africans, that in some respects challenges conventional ideas current in Western universities. Examining African history through the prism of religion collapses many conventional distinctions, such as those regarding tradition and modernity as an opposed pair; concerning the division of history into precolonial, colonial and postcolonial periods; and in regard to enduring patterns of interaction and exchange between individuals and communities that, we noted above, are a dynamic feature of African religion.[4] Third, it places the recent growth of religious movements in a long perspective. The aspiration of some religions to attain a global reach, starting with Christianity and Islam, has been linking Africans to people in other parts of the world for centuries. Today, the process has simply accelerated. Finally, considering change through the lens of religion throws new light on the ways in which ideas and practices rooted in local societies may come into conflict with the legal-bureaucratic type of states created in the age of colonialism. This has been much commented on recently inasmuch as it may take the shape of formal, religiously-inspired political movements, often referred to as fundamentalist.

The friction that may emerge when religion and politics compete with each other reflects a deeper potential for rivalry between these two basic fields of human thought and action. Actors in both fields attempt to manage change in ways that affect individuals and collectivities. Accordingly, in this chapter we discuss the relation between individual and social change, before examining the role of state and religion in their management, with regard to Africa but also more generally. The aim is to arrive at a closer understanding of the nature of change in African societies today, in which religious ideas play such an important role. Our point of departure is a theoretical discussion of aspects of personal and social change, especially those that are so radical as to qualify as transformations. The latter is a term that may be applied to certain perceptions or experiences of the nature of personhood that can be situated on a scale of continuity and change in human life. We explore these ideas in more detail in the following section. Transformations are dramatic and sudden changes, so radical as to require a recategorisation of the individual concerned. As we have seen in earlier chapters, people may consider such changes to take place in a variety of social, political and economic contexts.[5]

## Aspects of personal and collective change

As Orwell's analogy shows, any person who lives for more than a few years undergoes profound changes that are experienced subjectively. Everyone changes over the course of a lifetime, proceeding from childhood into adulthood and old age, often through marriage and parenthood, unless the process is cut short by premature death. All societies recognise the importance of the transitions that mark the course of a human life, often doing so through rites of passage, in which the change of phase is managed by public or semi-public performances that are frequently religious in content. So powerful can be the perception that the true nature of a person changes when he or she moves from one state or condition of life to another, that it is quite commonly believed that the former person 'dies' when passing through such a phase, and is 'reborn' in a new category, marked for example by a change of name.

Consideration of how personal change is to be categorised reflects a more general conundrum that presents itself when people classify the things they perceive in the world, as they must do. While there may be room for debate as to whether a particular piece of furniture is a table or a chair, for example, depending perhaps on its size, its function, and the material from which it is made, once the matter has been decided there is no further need for reclassification as the object will not change its nature. Animate beings, on the other hand, go through a cycle of life and death, changing their nature over time. If this nature is thought to have changed substantially, it may become appropriate to call the being in question by a new name. Any thing that ceases to exist in one category, and which may more appropriately be assigned to another category as a result of the changes it has undergone, may thus be considered to have 'died' in the first category, even while some element of its previous nature is transferred to its new existence. It is this last which enables life to be experienced as having some continuity, and not consisting of phases utterly unrelated one to another.

In many religious traditions, certain forms of existence—particularly human life, but sometimes animals, plants and trees and even inanimate objects—are believed not to expire but to undergo a radical change of nature at the moment of death or physical destruction. Death is considered to be accompanied by a change of form or external appearance, but with some part of the original essence surviving. Essence, according to Karl Popper, is 'that which remains unchanged during change'.[6] Most religious thought is acutely sensitive to the perception that the nature of a person can change over time, but that its essence can survive even the most radical change of appearance, such as the death of the physical body. Changes this radical may be called transformations.

Transformations contain a subjective element in that individuals may believe themselves to be transformed, either temporarily or permanently, when they experience a sensation of being occupied or guided by a spirit, leaving them persuaded that they have become in some sense 'new' people, even if only for a limited period. Michel Foucault includes personal transformations among what he calls 'techniques of the self'. These he defines as techniques that 'enable individuals to effect, by themselves, a certain number of operations on their body, their soul, their thought, their behaviour, and to do so in such a way as to produce in them a transformation, a modification, and to attain a certain state of perfection, of happiness, of purity and of supernatural power'.[7] Modern examples of such reshaping of the self by means of religion include 'born-again' Christianity and new Islamic movements that emphasise the transformation of the self. Both are particularly popular in Africa today.

The social element in transformation is at least as important as the personal one, since if others also perceive a transformation to have taken place, they may regard a transformed person as different from his or her previous self. Such a perception may be marked by rituals or in words, for example in changing the name of the person who has been transformed. It is on this principle that, in many societies, a child may adopt a new name on reaching puberty, or a woman may adopt a new name on becoming married. Special clothes may be worn to indicate that a person has undergone a radical change. Such a transformation is different from a mere change of role, as for example when a person switches professions, since transformation not only implies a profound change in personal or subjective feeling, but also in social recognition.

Many religious traditions maintain that other sorts of change in a person's nature, less radical than death, may occur. Examples include spirit possession, experiences of rebirth, shamanism, and similar mystical experiences of journeys through space and time. Another concerns people perceived to be witches. They may look no different from their neighbours, but are believed to harbour evil powers. These endow an alleged witch with a supposed ability to effect the most astonishing transformations, such as into an animal. All of these, and others, are concepts widely encountered in many parts of the world and in the history of every continent. Such perceived types of change are often radical and abrupt. They occur today not only in agricultural communities steeped in tradition, such as in rural areas of what was formerly called the third world, the setting of many classic anthropological studies, but also in some industrialised countries.[8] Everybody knows that life involves change, but perceptions of the limits within which change occurs, and the ways in which people think about it, differ greatly.

Under some circumstances, a whole group may be considered to cease to exist in its original form and to acquire a new character, marked by a different name, if a profound change occurs in its circumstances. A case in point concerns an insurrection that occurred in Uganda in the late 1980s. The government led by President Yoweri Museveni—intent on rebuilding the country after two decades of turmoil under Idi Amin and Milton Obote—was faced with a serious political and military threat in the Gulu district of the far north. An organisation known as the Holy Spirit Movement, led by a young woman with no military or political experience, posed such a formidable threat that it at one point advanced to within a few dozen miles of the capital, Kampala, before being repulsed. The rebel leader, Alice, widely known as Lakwena or 'messenger' in the Acholi language of northern Uganda, was regarded by her followers as a prophetess possessed by powerful spirits. She was thought to have the ability to transform her followers in such a way as to make them invincible in battle.[9] Many of her enemies—government soldiers—probably believed this as well, which caused them to retreat in the face of her army.

The history of Alice Lakwena shows how the concept of transformation may be applied not only to individuals but also to groups of people. It also indicates the political and even military consequences that collective transformation can imply. If enough individuals collectively undergo a personal experience of change sufficiently profound as to alter their very perception of who they really are, or if the perception that one prominent individual has changed in this way is held very strongly by many members of the same social group or community, then the whole society may be said to have undergone a type of transformation. Whole communities may experience rapid change from one class of society to another, such as from commoner to noble, or from slave to free. Entire families may change from the status of respectable citizens to an inferior position as outcasts or refugees. As we have seen, among the most powerful catalysts for such changes is money.[10] In all such cases, the same observation applies to groups as to individuals and things: when such transitions are perceived either by those who undergo them or by onlookers as being sufficiently sudden and radical, they may be deemed to represent not merely a change but a qualitative re-ordering, a transformation, in the group thus affected. This typically affects not only the external appearance of such a group of people, but above all their subjective feelings concerning their condition.

The change that all human beings experience in their lives, if only that from childhood to adulthood, is generally subject to various forms of institutional control, notably through religion and politics. If religious and political institutions cannot manage change effectively, they are particularly liable to consider radical changes in the personalities of individuals and groups as subversive. In exploring how societies institutionally regulate highly subjective experiences of personal transformation, we now consider, first, the ways in which states manage change in different historical traditions, and second, the importance of religion as an institution of management. Although the argument is theoretical, it is punctuated with specific examples, the cases chosen for illustration being drawn from Africa as well as other parts of the world.

## States and the management of change

During the nineteenth and twentieth centuries, the world's most advanced industrialised countries developed forms of social intervention in matters such as public education and public health in order to manage change more comprehensively. Since then, social engineering[11] has become one of the hallmarks of modern states. This remains true even in an age where market economies and free trade have become the international norm, as states still aim to manage the societies they aspire to govern, although they now prefer to do so more by indirect means.

Governments that wish to effect a radical change in a society may be called 'revolutionary', by themselves or by others. This term has gone so thoroughly out of political fashion since the 1980s that one might be tempted to believe that the great age of revolutionary states, namely those that derive their sense of purpose from the desire to effect a transformation of the society they govern, in the tradition of the late eighteenth-century Enlightenment, is now past. Only a handful of states today proclaim a revolution or a transformation of society as a whole as their formal purpose. The most important of these, China, hardly gives an impression of ideological dynamism. Nevertheless, the decline of self-proclaimed revolutionary states is probably less significant than may first appear. Even in states with no such ambitions, officials ceaselessly design and implement policies in the hope of limiting changes to which they are averse or, alternatively, encouraging those they consider desirable. States employ rhetoric, coercion, and financial incentive in pursuit of such aims.

It is now widely accepted in modern social theory that power in the modern age has come to work 'through what we know as "the social", or the construction of a space of free social exchange, and through the construction of a subjectivity normally experienced as the source of free will and rational agency'.[12] This insight is most closely associated with the work of Michel Foucault, who makes a helpful connection between the techniques that individual people in all societies use to discipline their own minds—'techniques of the self'—and those techniques that states or other corporations enjoying a position of power use to impose discipline on those subject to their control. The point at which these two sets of disciplines meet—those known as 'techniques of the self'[13] and those associated with state control—is precisely the place where people form their own subjectivity, that is to say the manner in which they think about themselves, or even the way they think in general. It also defines the characteristics of a society's 'governmentality', in Foucault's vocabulary. Hence, the techniques of the self and those used by the state have an effect upon each other.[14] Nevertheless, an appreciation of the way power is shaped by discourse should not blind us to the continuing importance of state bureaucracies and of their coercive power, even where those in power aspire to reduce the incidence of social and economic interventions. A striking example is the United States, where an ideology of minimum state social intervention coexists with massive use of some of the bluntest and most ruthless of the state's powers of repression, in the form of a record level of imprisonment.[15]

Massive social intervention, then, is not a technique limited to the revolutionary and totalitarian states whose heyday was the mid-twentieth century, even if it took some of the most extreme forms there. On the contrary, it is a basic characteristic of the state in all those countries that have succeeded in effecting or managing the type of economic and social change that Karl Polanyi called, in a telling phrase, 'the great transformation'.[16] The systematic, bureaucratic management of social affairs, whether or not applied in the service of an explicitly revolutionary ideology, is inherent in the very concept of the modern state.

Modern methods of bureaucratic social management and the technologies associated with them have enabled hundreds of millions of people in the rich world to achieve a degree of personal security and an avoidance of risk undreamed of in earlier ages, reflected in statistics on life expectancy. Men and women who have grown up in such an environment can predict the course of their lives and make plans with relative certainty, secure in the knowledge that, statistically speaking, their existence will probably not be cut prematurely short by accident, disease or war, and that they are largely immune from the sudden changes in condition associated with major upheaval. It is the modern state that has done this, enabled to do so by the constant dialectic between administrative action and the various intellectual disciplines that make possible bureaucratic power on this scale. This great bureaucratic power also has a negative face, very evident in the twentieth century. Many people have drawn attention to the less attractive aspects of modern states, such as the ruthlessness with which they treat groups regarded as deviant, or the way in which they handle their affairs with the wider world.

Politicians and civil servants concerned with managing society concentrate their efforts on whole sectors rather than on individuals. This they do, as is appropriate to their purpose, not by exploring each individual psyche, in the manner of a psychiatrist, a healer or a priest-confessor, but by engineering the external aspects of individual lives through taxation, policing and the regulation of material resources. Modern state functionaries regulate the main events in the lives of individuals, such as by requiring the official registration of births, deaths and marriages. Still, such powers remain bureaucratic and impersonal. If the difference between modern and pre-modern governance can be summed up in any single aspect, then it consists in the intimacy of the rapport between the ruler and the individuals whom he governs.

In addition to their more coercive powers, modern bureaucrats and managers, both inside and outside state employment, use rhetoric intended to persuade people towards particular ways of thinking. It is here that modern communications media play such an important role. The twentieth century saw the development of a new and massively powerful instrument for influencing people in the most intimate aspects of emotion and personality, in the form of the mass media that had already become a major instrument of government by the 1920s. Mass media made possible the phenomenon of totalitarian government, sometimes considered to be the only genuinely new form of rule introduced in the world since Aristotle's time, 'probably the only distinctively modern type of rule'.[17] In Nazi Germany, so intrusive were mass media that they were able to penetrate the dream-world of individuals.[18] Since then, media for information, advertisement and entertainment have become ever more pervasive and now constitute to a great extent the environment as it is perceived by individuals, what was described even in the 1920s as a 'pseudo-environment'.[19] States and the economic elites with which they work so closely have developed techniques to regulate the individual psyche via pervasive mass communication media, including advertising and public relations, to such a degree that modern, bureaucratic elites, often linked to the state, can control very large populations perhaps more effectively and more completely than any type of regime known to history.

Religion provides little obstacle to state regulation if it can be relegated to a private, non-political domain of society. Nevertheless, the relationship between religion and the modern state is more complex than is sometimes thought. Totalitarian states did not merely abhor organised religion, in the same way they despised any autonomous social sector. Rather, they co-opted or reproduced key religious ideas and rituals in their own service, creating 'coercive utopias'[20] that largely replaced religion. During the nineteenth and twentieth centuries, states began increasingly to mimic religion. The notion that the decline of religion in Europe has led to a sacralisation of politics has been a subject of discussion from the French revolution until today.[21]

Aware of how modern states have equipped themselves to manage change, including by assimilating techniques previously falling within the religious domain, it is instructive to reconsider the recent history of what used to be called the third world. Since the 1950s and 1960s, when three-quarters of the member-states of the United Nations acquired sovereign status as they threw off colonial rule, almost every government in Africa, South America and Asia has proclaimed national socio-economic transformation in the form of 'development' to be its central objective. All have used bureaucratic management to try to control the massive social changes entailed by the implementation of such development policies. In Africa particularly, the development agenda has often disguised the redistribution of power on a vast scale.[22] Development, in fact, is one such 'coercive utopia' that has been imposed by modern states.

## Religion and the management of change

The course of world affairs over the last three decades suggests that there are now pressing reasons to reassess ideas concerning the relationship between secularisation and development.[23] It is now clear that the ambition to create a world of efficient modern states, which seemed on the road to realisation in the third quarter of the twentieth century, has become an illusion. Nor is it surprising that where the state can no longer convince people of its ability to deliver prosperity through development, religious ideas are likely to gain a renewed attractiveness. For religion, too, has a redoubtable capacity to manage change at both individual and social levels.

The ability of religion to manage change is now re-emerging in many parts of the world, including in Africa, where it was a central element of governance in precolonial times. One of the features of the religious and socially-based networks that remain pervasive in Africa is that they aspire to regulate people not only through impersonal bureaucracies, in the modern manner, but also through personal networks. This occurs in a context where people have a much broader idea than in Europe about which transformations of the personality are legitimate, for example through trances, dreams and visions. The political importance of such techniques shows no sign of disappearing, and has become of greater salience over recent decades.[24] While many traces of this tradition of governance survive or have been revived or reinvented, they have also been synthesised with political institutions, ideas and instruments imported from Europe.[25] People undergoing experiences of transformation may be regarded as potentially dangerous, because they do not fit into any stable category. They are in a liminal condition, passing from one state of being to another.[26] This exceptional condition is often marked by ritual drama, which is in effect an attempt to manage change through religion. One example of what can happen when such transformations are poorly managed was seen in the Liberian civil war of the 1990s, when adolescent boys committed terrible atrocities while dressed in women's clothing. Their transvestite behaviour was drawn from the repertoire of traditional initiation rituals in which youngsters on the verge of adulthood display symbols of the opposite gender to indicate their indeterminate status.[27]

The rites of passage by which religious institutions in almost every culture regulate and mediate the transformations that every human being undergoes bear a close resemblance to drama. Indeed, such rites *are* drama, performed not for amusement or intellectual edification alone, but for a religious purpose, as were the ancient Greek tragedies. Acting and transformation of the person[28] are two closely allied concepts in the sense that an actor imagines himself to be someone else for a period of time. The greatest actors are considered to have the ability not just to mimic the gestures of the person they aspire to represent, but actually to become that person for the duration of the performance, or, to put it another way, to transform themselves temporarily. The fact that politicians employ similar techniques, in the sense of staging rituals of power, and sometimes represent themselves as having a character that they have studied for the purpose, testifies to the great importance of drama and ritual in human life. It also hints at the esoteric or mysterious element that power always has, even in those societies that have gone furthest in stripping it down to its material aspects.

Religious techniques for managing radical change have been analysed most insightfully by Elias Canetti. He has pointed out that the continuum of form and nature that we discussed above in the context of humans' ability to transform themselves can also be applied to the public powers that govern society.[29] He describes how the control of societal transformations may be achieved by authorities using techniques that can be classified according to their tendency towards mobility or immobility. At one end of the scale is the master-transformer or shaman; at the other end is the divine king. The shaman is a religious specialist who is believed to be so adept at negotiating relations with the spirit world that others are obliged to respect his authority. The special character of the shaman is his perceived ability to assume any shape at will, to appear or disappear, and to travel astounding distances in an instant. Many shamans are people who are thought to have died during their initiation and to have returned at a higher level of being. In some parts of Africa, an important role in governing transformations is played by a masked figure. The mask is used not only to hide the identity of a person performing a ritual, but also to express the unchanging identity of the invisible force or spirit that is thought to be invoked through the mask and that transforms people during initiation into adulthood, for example. Spiritual authority remains quite a prominent feature of local communities and even of public life in a wider sense in many parts of the world. In Europe, on the other hand, spiritual authority of all types has long been subject to bureaucratic control by the churches. The more dramatic aspects of religion have been gradually abandoned and mainline churches have adopted a convention whereby mediation between the individual and the invisible world, if and when it occurs at all, takes place with great discretion. Religious communication has adopted a very limited range of forms, of which silent prayer is perhaps the most common. This and other forms of religious communication in the West are generally conducted privately, behind doors rather than in the street or in public space, although the rise of television evangelism and charismatic belief is providing an interesting new development in this regard.

At the other end of Canetti's spectrum of authorities that can control transformation is the divine king, who does not change, 'to whom all *self-transformation* is forbidden, though he is a continual fount of commands which transform others'. This figure, Canetti notes, 'has had a decisive influence on our whole modern conception of power. The non-transformer has been set on a pedestal at a fixed height in a fixed and permanent place'. An authority of this type 'who is himself denied all transformation can transform others as he pleases'.[30] Modern states fulfil this function. Institutional, implacable, they present a massive solidity that endures over generations. In their classical Western form they are also secular.

This consideration of the techniques used for managing change and transformation throws an interesting and original new light on recent developments in Europe and North America. These societies are also witnessing types of personal transformation that they find difficult to regulate. For much of the twentieth century, the most advanced industrial societies were managed by means of such ruthlessly homogenising state institutions as universal compulsory education, military service, and intervention in family or personal life by way of welfare and medical bureaucracies. Recent years, however, have seen the rise in the West of a new emphasis on personal freedom and toleration of individual choice. The latter has become permissible in a variety of matters regarding personal identity that used to be regarded as socially inadmissible or were forbidden by law, such as homosexuality. Both states and societies are becoming tolerant of such radical personal transformations as changes of sex. The prospect of people transforming from male to female, almost unthinkable in North America and Europe until quite recently, is now both relatively commonplace and increasingly accepted by mainstream opinion. The biomedical profession is taking the lead in significant forms of transformation, including through cloning, which concerns one of the most radical forms of transformation of all: the creation of life. Another extreme form of personal transformation—self-inflicted death—is increasingly countenanced by public opinion, and even by law under certain conditions, in the form of euthanasia. It is therefore unsurprising that new mechanisms for regulating personal transformations are emerging in biomedicine and genetics.

These are developments that merit further investigation in the light of relationships between transformation and governance. It could be supposed, in terms of our argument, that new forms of transformation constitute a challenge to states, which by nature crave predictability and uniformity. Accordingly, there are many conservatives who call for a more rigorous regulation of society. In the United States, Christian conservatives use religion as a means to this end. In the more secular continent of Europe, it is politicians—state managers *par excellence*—who lead the call for a return to traditional norms and values, recommending new state controls to achieve their aims. However, conservatives in North America and Europe who argue that allowing individuals the freedom to effect new forms of transformation will ultimately threaten the political order are faced by several opponents. Among those who argue to the contrary are those who deny that personal transformation has any connection to governance at all, and others who think that individual freedom is paramount. Most importantly, conservatives who fear the long-term consequences of allowing new types of personal transformation are pitted against an economic lobby. Thus, the acceptance of new areas of personal freedom is very often encouraged by commercial interests, via the media, which see prospects of increasing profits by appealing to a new class of customer.

One might argue that all this is very speculative, since instances of sex change or cloning of living matter affect only a very few people in Europe and North America, and that it is therefore unwise to use these examples as the basis for a more general argument about changing patterns of governance in Western societies. However, evidence to support our point of view concerning the relation between personal transformation and governance may be adduced from the fact that another mode of transformation has become genuinely popular in these societies since the 1960s. We refer here to the transformations that occur in individual psyches by the use of consciousness-altering drugs. It is surely one of the more significant developments of modern times that states are making major attempts to control the consumption and marketing of such drugs in the face of a massive popular demand due to what is, after all, a universal human tendency to ingest substances not on account of their nutritional value, but for their psychological effects. Why millions of people in advanced industrial and post-industrial societies should seek to transform themselves by taking drugs is a matter outside the scope of the present discussion, but it is undeniable that they do.[31] It is notable that in some of the world's poorer countries too the pattern of drug consumption is changing and escaping traditional forms of regulation. The deeper significance of these new patterns is rarely addressed in debates on drug laws.

Our line of argument attaches considerable importance to the fact that the regulation of personal transformation—present in all human life according to George Orwell, as we have noted—is central to systems of both politics and religion. In many Western countries religion has been largely displaced as a form of public regulation by the state. Elsewhere including Africa, means of regulating personal transformation continue to be socially-based, often through religion. But traditional techniques too are challenged by contemporary developments, one symptom of which is the rise of elites who are skilled in modern methods of political organisation while also professing allegiance to what purport to be tried and tested techniques of governing through religion. So, how will personal and social transformations be managed in each part of the world in years to come? It may be primarily through scientific and economic elites working via bureaucracies and media of mass communication. Or it may be through neo-traditional religious elites who evoke a mythical 'golden age'.

The profound transformations associated with religion are likely to be regarded with suspicion by secular, bureaucratic states in years to come because of the challenge they pose to the states' managerial role. The clash of secular and religious views of power raises many of the same questions wherever it occurs.

# 9

# HISTORIES

In this concluding chapter it may be useful to restate the main analytical principle used in this book: social scientists need to study the specific content of religious thought if they are to understand the political significance of religion. This proposition may be applied not only to Africa, but to any region with a widespread belief in the reality of a spirit world.

One must insist on this principle because Europe's history has given rise to particular ways of analysing the world in which perceived spiritual beings are considered only as translations, as it were, of secular forces, such as economic and political structures. As a historian of India puts it, an 'assumption running through modern European political thought and the social sciences is that the human is ontologically singular, that gods and spirits are in the end "social facts", that the social somehow exists prior to them'.[1] We do not doubt that the spiritual beings that so many people perceive to exist do indeed constitute social facts, and that these may fruitfully be studied through the social sciences. It is not our aim to establish the reality or otherwise of such perceived beings. There are many other entities that social scientists believe to exist in spite of their invisibility, such as capital, debt, and social structure, to give just a few examples.[2] The point is that we should not assume that believed spiritual beings, since they are social facts, can not also be usefully considered in other ways. There is a risk of 'oversociologising', to borrow a word, by assigning certain religious phenomena 'into familiar sociological and rational categories'.[3] Such an approach is unable to grasp some of the meanings of practices and beliefs often considered by social science to be beyond the bounds of rationality.[4] In Africa, spirit beliefs contribute substantially to shaping the realm of politics. Moreover the existence of a widespread belief in the spirit world may become a political instrument, whose nature has to be understood. Hence a priority for social science research is to develop a method of analysis that takes full account of the effective power of belief. Such a method requires putting non-Western views of reality at the centre of the analysis,

177

or in other words 'provincialising Europe',[5] rather than making these views subservient to a sociology of religion that has been shaped by the historical experience of the West.

Although our book concerns Africa, it also illuminates similar developments elsewhere. Africa is a continent conventionally described as marginal to world affairs, as it surely is when measured by the criteria of sovereignty and economic power. But when it is looked at from some other points of view, Africa proves to be integrated in global systems of governance, often via the underside of international rules and norms.[6] One authority on international relations points out that international politics are increasingly concerned not with sovereignty, but with a series of issues that 'cut across, and subvert, the boundaries of states and the role of governments. Such issues, though currently dominated by terrorism, also include international migration, global diseases, the protection of the environment', and so on, in all of which fields Africa figures mostly as a source of concern to others.[7] We would add to this that international politics is also increasingly concerned with religious movements and ideologies that traverse international frontiers. This is a domain in which Africans play a global role. With its many millions of Christians, Africa has become a leading centre of Christianity in the twenty-first century.[8] Meanwhile, about one third of Africa's inhabitants are Muslims, and, as an expert on al-Qaeda points out, 'Islamists see Black Africa as their newest theatre'.[9] Perhaps more surprisingly, some African traditional religions have taken on several characteristics of their long-term rivals and now aspire to be world religions also. Moreover, it may be expected that in years to come more Africans will adhere to Asian religions.

## Locating religious revival

Africa has a long history of dynamic religious movements, many of which have had a great impact on government. In West Africa, a series of Islamic jihads, beginning in the late seventeenth century, had a formative effect on the region's history even before the colonial period. As regards today's Christian revivalist movements, they should be considered not as novelties, but rather as the latest generation in a tradition of African-initiated churches that is well over a hundred years old. In fact, the development of new churches may be situated in a still longer history of evangelicalism that has roots in Europe and North America, including among African Americans.

Insofar as commentators have attempted to advance explanations for Africa's religious revival, they have made little allowance for this element of historical depth. This follows a period in which, according to Mary

Douglas,[10] social scientists in general, believing that modern life was fundamentally antipathetic to religion, simply failed to notice the continuing importance of religion and the manner of its insertion in changing contexts. The notion of religious revival in Africa risks gaining currency in the academic world not so much because of any true novelty of the matter under discussion, but more because of the recent discovery of religion by an academic authority. In many commentaries it is implied that the root cause of certain religious developments in Africa in recent years is economic, and that the growth of charismatic Christianity especially results from the globalisation of the world economy or from the conditions of late capitalism.[11] But neither international capitalism nor globalisation is altogether new. Financial markets were first integrated across the globe in the late nineteenth century, which, interestingly, was precisely the period when Africa was partitioned by colonial powers; it was also a time when Christian missionaries were exceptionally active. Claims that the late twentieth-century style of globalisation marks a major historical rupture do not stand up well to scrutiny.[12] Some parts of Africa were integrated into an early precursor of capitalist globalisation more than four centuries ago, with the emergence of a system in which Africans were transported to labour in mines and plantations in the Americas in order to produce goods for consumption in Europe. Less well known is that a system of commerce and slave-trading only slightly less pervasive existed in the Indian Ocean long before Europeans entered its seas at the end of the fifteenth century.[13] Religious conversions and the political use of religion in Africa have been emerging in global or globalising contexts ever since. By the same token, it is not self-evident that capitalism itself has changed so radically in recent years that it is justified to speak of an age of 'late capitalism' or 'millennial capitalism'.[14] In any case, even if the nature of contemporary capitalism were such as to produce unprecedented forms of religious expression, we would need to explain why these arise in some parts of the world only, and not in others.

It is striking that some influential analyses of the impact of new religious movements in Africa, including theories that they are motivated by consumerism, are rooted in the Marxist intellectual tradition of the 1970s and 1980s which emphasised the importance of production. To a considerable extent, the current scholarly preoccupation with consumption has replaced this older interest in production. Most of the critiques by non-Marxists of the theory that ideology is ultimately determined by modes of production could be applied with equal validity to the proposition that religious thought is determined by modes of consumption. The underlying assumption has remained the same: namely, that the real driving-force of historical change is economic, and that religious belief is a form of what Marxists used to call 'false consciousness'. A similar assumption is made by writers who describe the resurgence of religion simply as 'irrational', implying a flight from the reality of the material world.[15] This is not to deny that material conditions have an effect on spiritual ideas or that changes in international finance and investment flows are felt worldwide. Spiritual ideas and material conditions interact, including by way of the practices with which they are associated. Globalised markets and privatised political power are simply the new context for contemporary religious and political thought.

People in many historical periods and in most places, including Europe and North America, have perceived there to be a connection between religion and economic fortunes. Specifically in regard to Africa, the idea that prosperity has a mystical aspect, and that its roots are in the spirit world, predates the continent's current economic problems by hundreds of years, at least as far as historical records allow us to judge. Techniques for communicating with a spirit world have changed constantly during that time, although the basic idea of using spiritual resources to sustain material life has remained. In that sense the 'prosperity gospel', or radical forms of Islam, or even rumours about human body-parts being used to acquire wealth and power, are simply recent or not-so-recent adaptations of much older beliefs that have often assimilated ideas from outside. Thus, the globalisation of ideas, like that of finance, needs to be placed in a historical context. While the transmission of ideas by global media increased enormously in speed and reach in the late twentieth century, Africa has been gradually integrating into global systems of advanced communication for many decades. Even before they had access to radios—popularised by the introduction of the transistor in the mid-twentieth century—Africans were already assimilating new ideas based on external sources of information. They have also been exporting ideas for centuries, notably to the Americas. Whether the enhanced speed of communication affects the way people apprehend ideas and how their mode of apprehension may change over time, including in regard to religious ideas, are matters in dire need of further research. One cannot begin with the assumption that late-twentieth century globalisation has made previous history irrelevant.

The significance of religious revival in Africa and elsewhere can hardly be grasped without considering the historical trajectories of religion in particular contexts. This raises a question regarding how to identify such trajectories and how to think about them. They are best defined not by an absence—in other words by reference to what Africa does not generally have, such as strong and efficient states—but by what it has indeed had over a long period. It no longer makes much sense to take a view of history, whether applied to Africa or anywhere else, that draws its terms of reference from conventional readings of the European and North American past. Specific events that occur in Africa, others have warned, cannot automatically be assimilated into 'categories of analysis' that are 'drawn from Europe', including the construction of European-style states, the disenchantment of the world, or even the growth of capitalism.[16] However, the opposite is no better, in the sense of trying to identify an allegedly authentic Africa, as this risks reproducing romantic notions of a pure or timeless Africa that were characteristic of colonial thinking and that, more damagingly, are still attached to African nationalism and pan-Africanism. It is therefore accurate to describe the method required for understanding new formations of religion and politics in Africa as one that will situate these in the passage of time, taking full account of the continent's evolving insertion in the world, but without seeking to place historical facts in a sequence that has been anticipated in the past of Europe.

This apparent conundrum is not insoluble. Those who have puzzled over the terms in which postcolonial histories may be written have pointed out that many categories used by social scientists, and borrowed by historians, may have their genealogical origins in Europe, but that they have become common property since their export around the globe.[17] No longer can they be regarded as the exclusive property of Europeans. These same categories need to be tested and reviewed in the light of a range of historical experiences from all parts of the world.[18] It is for this reason that we chose to work with a definition of religion that appears appropriate to the data we have identified, rather than setting out with one that reflects a sociological notion of religion that is difficult to detach from a Western history in which the religious and the secular have been pervasively separated.

In principle, theories of postcolonialism[19] open the way to assessing how elements of indigenous African pasts (such as certain religious beliefs) may coexist with other features introduced during colonial times (such as secular bureaucratic states) in modern societies. Postcolonial studies often take a lively interest in representations of the past, which they see as contributing to discourses of power. They can, however, be notably evasive when it comes to the relationship between such representations and chronology.[20] History, after all, is not only a discourse: it is also a record of things that actually happened. It is also relevant to note in this context that perceptions of novelty may to some degree be a consequence of changes

in the way the academic world is organised and financed. Academia itself
is becoming a consumer industry, which places a high premium on theories that have an appearance of originality, that are marketable, and that
are destined to be replaced by other theories.[21] This is perhaps one reason
why studies that pay close attention to empirical data may lose prestige in
the academy. As one African scholar has noted in a penetrating essay, turning everything into a commodity is a central feature of our cultural lives
today. 'To sell oneself and one's products as art in the marketplace, one
must, above all, clear a space in which one is distinguished from other pro-
ducers and products—and one does this by the construction and the
marking of differences'.[22] This observation is paraphrased by another scholar in a statement that 'the "post" in both postmodernism and postcolonialism works primarily as a means, in a highly commodified age, of clearing
space to market cultural products wrapped in ever gaudier colours of new-
ness'.[23] It is a cruel thought that this may apply to academic production.

## Reconnecting the past

The world into which Africa is inserted still retains the institutional architecture created after the end of the Second World War. Since 1945 the
world's most powerful governments have developed an infrastructure designed to provide the outline of a world system of governance based on
national sovereignty. Vast territories in Asia and Africa were deemed to be
sovereign states, sometimes in places where no comparable entity had
existed before colonial times. The dismantling of the European colonial
empires has led to an increase in the number of United Nations member-
states from 51 in 1945 to over 190 today. Decolonisation represented not
only a major political change but, above all perhaps, a revolution in international law. Henceforth, recognition of sovereignty depended not on the
prior existence of a state, but on the right of national self-determination.[24]
Newly independent territories in Africa had juridical statehood more than
they had substantive states.[25] Each state had the right—the duty, even—to
designate a government and to maintain a host of other institutions, usually including armed forces and a central bank. In the name of development, the richer countries made transfers of technology and money to the
poorer ones. In regard to most of Africa and Asia, this political decolonisation occurred during the longest and most widespread economic boom
the world has ever seen, lasting until the oil crises of the 1970s. This was
also a period of astonishing demographic change. United Nations and
World Bank figures suggest that the population of the whole continent—

including North Africa—was around 250 million in 1950 and had almost doubled by 1980. Today it is somewhere close to 800 million. The urban population of sub-Saharan Africa is now about 35 per cent, and of Africa as a whole, probably about 38 per cent.[26]

The populations of newly-independent countries in Africa experienced the first years of their sovereign status as a time of unprecedented change. People whose ancestors had always lived in small communities with access to a restricted and only slowly changing range of consumer goods and technology were moving to cities. Their children were going to schools, and even stood a chance of getting salaried employment. The creation of juridical independence in itself created national economic booms as the new apparatuses recruited thousands of officials, leading to spectacular economic growth rates at a time when commodity prices were reaching sustained highs. Such developments, occurring throughout what was first dubbed the third world in 1954, brought with them 'the disintegration of an entire universe of social relations'.[27] Planners and other theoreticians intended to replace this disintegrating universe with a new one, fashioned according to models from the industrialised world.

One of the achievements of the golden age of African independence and modernisation, in the third quarter of the twentieth century, seemed to be the insertion of Africa, through its states and other bureaucratic institutions of management, into the rhythm of a world marching to the beat of a single drum. A French historian at that time, distinguishing between the past as a social memory of bygone times, and the discipline of history based on rigorous chronology as it has emerged in the industrialised world, noted that colonialism had torn Africans from their previous sense of the past. Since African intellectuals were now creating for themselves a history in the conventional modern mode, he noted, then 'it is a sign that they aspire to play by the rules of the world, which were to a large extent written in the West'.[28]

Quoting this view prompts one to realise just how much has changed in the last few decades. Even before the end of the cold war, many people were already rejecting the idea that the former colonial world ought to play by such rules at all. In the case of Africa, many people are now living at a tempo different from that of the rich world. The decline in the power and bureaucratic efficiency of many African states since the 1970s has been accompanied by a decline in the knowledge of history (in its narrowest, academic sense) in African societies.[29] In many parts of the continent there has been a decrease in the use of official archives, and sometimes even a wholesale destruction of such records in deliberate acts of vandalism, as in Monrovia, Freetown and Brazzaville. Systems of formal education have such massive problems that they are tending to produce new generations with little knowledge of history text-books. Even those with a high standard of formal education pay less heed than before to formal history. The continent's professional historians struggle with material conditions that make it supremely difficult for them to diffuse their work, hence the academic writing of Africa's history is dominated by Western scholars and propagated in channels that barely touch Africa.

These observations should not be taken to imply that memories of times past have diminished in their power and importance, for memories, whether or not based on fact, are not the same as history in its academic sense. It is quite likely that in many African countries today people view their past much as the ancient Greeks did.[30] That is, when they think deliberately about the past, they divide it into a recent time that may be rigorously and critically examined through discussion with people who remember it, preceded by a period of myth or social memory whose accuracy is untestable. It is possible that most Africans have always thought of the past in this way, but until recently they were governed by elites that had themselves been exposed to formal, written histories, and by institutions with a bureaucratic memory, relayed by archives. Today, in a substantial number of countries, bureaucratic, record-keeping institutions have eroded or are unable to govern the whole country, while in some cases the people in power have no interest in bureaucratic rule of this type.

Archives, in the sense of public records stored in the form of documents, are only one of the repositories of information by which the past weighs on living generations. Knowledge of the past becomes operational by informing repertoires of action that may be accompanied by a conscious recall of memory but that also may be an unconscious legacy of the past. Such repertoires of action are not arbitrary in their relationship to the past; they are comparable to the grammatical rules that people use to govern the way in which they speak. In other words, Africans, like other people, act on the basis of repertoires transmitted from the past not only in the form of states or other bureaucratic institutions, but also rituals, language, social structures and so on. Religion, including in its ritual practice, is a key method by which people gain access to memories transmitted in such ways.[31] In the many parts of Africa where bureaucratic memory and formal histories have declined, religion tends to take on an enhanced social function as a means of both remembering and forgetting the past in ways that are conducive to present needs.

History, however, does more than offer information that may guide or inspire present action. As Michel de Certeau points out, it is also a way of 'calming the dead who still haunt the present, and offering them tombs in written form'.[32] Where people believe in the reality of the spirit world, recollection of the past may fulfil the role of calming the spirits of the dead explicitly, through exorcism. The function of both history, in its formal, modern, sense of an objectified record of the past, and memory recalled through ritual or some other form of practice, is similar in this respect. In theory, a society or community could compensate for a loss of historical recall by using religious or other techniques for retrieving the past.

In some parts of Africa, though, religion is nowadays unable to exorcise the spirits of the dead, for reasons that we have discussed.[33] We may cite as an example the Democratic Republic of Congo, where a bloody colonial history has left particularly acute traumas, by many accounts. Congolese who are troubled by spirits traditionally seek a cure from healers, but the healers' work has often become less effective than it was in the past, as we have seen, and this is one reason why Congo has so many stories of zombies and spirits of the dead returning to torment the living.[34] Furthermore, Congo is one of several places where there is no consensus regarding the history of the country or of specific communities. Like Angola,[35] it has been riven by conflict for decades, to the extent that different groups of people have such divergent versions of their history that they seem to be hardly talking about the same place. When people in these circumstances recall the past deliberately, they are obliged to do so in their own ways, including through theatre, painting and songs, and also by analogy with religious myths. Myths, although not identical to history, may indeed allow 'access to the processes which constitute history at the level of the here-and-the-now'.[36] But versions of the past brought to mind through religion are not organised in precise chronological terms in the same way as versions produced by bureaucracies with archives or by academic historians. When religion measures time, it does not do so by reference to homogeneous units, but rather by providing the passage of time with a rhythm.[37] According to one African intellectual, Africans tend to consider time as 'an event and not something that is pursued like setting a time for a board meeting, where every member is guarded by the company laws'.[38] Leading African philosophers agree that there is a widespread tendency in African societies to organise time by reference to events, rather than in terms of even and precisely measured units, and that historical memory is structured in this way.[39]

The lack of national historical canons makes it difficult for people to create theories of change in secular form. With few exceptions, including the handful of professional historians working in the continent, many

Africans struggle to find ways of apprehending the massive historical forces that they feel bearing upon their lives. They see that the formal institutions deemed to govern them are largely devoid of power, which, instead, is located in informal circuits. The difficulty in locating power contributes greatly to the existence of pervasive conspiracy theories that blame everything on forces beyond their control. Conspiracy theories often assume religious features inasmuch as they suppose the exercise of a mystical power. Rumours that vast networks of satanists are working to spread AIDS and cause harm are one example of this.[40] This tendency to identify grand sources of intrigue in the world is all the more redoubtable in that it also draws on nationalist political ideologies that often, the world over, tend to convey a notion of authentic nations that exist outside time. Many nationalist movements were formed in the nineteenth century amid an international order that was already dominated by existing great powers, namely Britain and France. In Germany, Russia and elsewhere, nationalism was conceived as the expression of a political community aspiring to take its rightful place in a world from which it was being excluded by existing powers jealous of new rivals. A similar sense of mixed right and resentment animated African nationalist movements.[41] 'Seek ye first the political kingdom', Ghana's President Kwame Nkrumah was fond of urging his fellow-Africans, believing that the continent would thereby take its proper place in the world.

They did indeed seek the political kingdom, but now, forty or fifty years later, few African states have maintained a stable position in an international order that is itself looking distinctly fragile. International bankers and diplomats today regard only a couple of states south of the Sahara—Mauritius and Botswana—as properly functioning, without reservation. South Africa, the continent's number one industrial power, is often viewed with a certain ambivalence because of doubt about its longer-term future. At the other end of the range of bureaucratic governability is Somalia, the one state in Africa that is usually seen as having effectively disappeared in just about everything except international law. Nearly all the sub-Saharan countries in between these extremes are conventionally regarded by international observers and officials, with varying degrees of emphasis, as being on the path to full international respectability through reforms managed by the World Bank, or, less optimistically, as doing just enough to retain their place in the official ranks of the world's states while muddling through. Africans' frustration at the failure of modern states to deliver what they promised—a place at the table where the rich and powerful of this world are seated—is shared in some other parts of the former third world. In Africa and elsewhere—notably in the Middle East—this sense of frustration further encourages people to believe that their continent is being excluded from its rightful place by the machinations of great powers. It is of course true that major powers pursue their own interests in the first instance, and that Africa often suffers from this, but the incorporation of these facts into vast and elaborate conspiracy theories becomes an impediment to political thought. Consequently, creating a workable theory of change by which living generations can take control of their lives appears to be a vital task. Many Africans engage in this task by means of religion, a unique form of 'self-fashioning' that governs people's relations with the world at large.

Finally, it is worth noting that, just as recent developments have led to a marked change in the way Africans view their relationship to the past, so, too, have they affected the world-views of Europeans and North Americans.[42] In the late twentieth century, Western countries abandoned many of their earlier aspirations to transform their own societies *en masse* through social engineering by the state. Since there is less ambition to transform society in the future, there is correspondingly less curiosity about how this was done in the past.[43] Some observers thus detect a decline in the importance of history as a tool of governing elites,[44] even though universities continue to employ professional historians and Western publics maintain a lively interest in reading certain types of history and watching historical documentaries.

## *A new historical age*

When Europeans began to penetrate other parts of the world in early modern times, doing business there on an ever-increasing scale, they encountered societies with novel ways of managing their affairs. They eventually came to be considered by Europeans either as incapable of making history, or at least as having lost the knack of doing so. At one extreme of a precolonial gamut were societies, including in parts of Africa, that Westerners regarded as having no real history[45] because they lacked the type of state that was gradually being thought of as the main vehicle of historical change. At the other extreme were places like Moghul India or imperial China that had hierarchical and even bureaucratic systems of administration of great antiquity, but which, by the nineteenth century, appeared to Europeans to have ossified. This particular view of history was part of the West's distinctive world-view that developed in tandem with its formidable drive to power.

A distinctive view of history as a story of an evolution developed after the Reformation and Europe's more or less contemporaneous encounter with other continents. Sustained and substantial contact with previously unknown societies prompted Europeans to reflect on a world that was not commensurate with Christianity,[46] in the course of which they came to think of religion—both their own and others'—in a new light. They applied their new insights to societies that did not always have a comparable concept of religion, and quite often not even a ready translation for the word. The colonising process consisted in a reorganisation of power, including into separate components considered by Europeans as politics and religion. What these non-Europeans almost always did have, however, was a range of ideas and practices concerning a perceived invisible world. From the great variety of encounters entailed by the expansion of Europe and the mutual, uneven assimilation that followed, today's world was formed.

The various forms of religious revival that are today so noteworthy may usefully be considered in light of the long, historic engagement of the West and the rest. The first, heady, years of African independence in the 1960s seemed to many commentators at that time as the start of a new and hopeful era, but it soon became commonplace to note just how much the new African states owed to their colonial forebears. With every year that passes, it becomes increasingly evident how great was the continuity between the Africa of the late colonial period, after 1945, and the first years of independence. By the same token, the last quarter of the twentieth century begins to look increasingly as though it marks the closing of that particular chapter, and the start of another.[47] Moreover, it is not just Africa which underwent important historical changes in the last quarter of the twentieth century—particularly since the oil crises of the 1970s[48]—but the whole of an increasingly interconnected world.

In many parts of the former third world, the modernisation that brought such massive changes, and that appealed to so many intellectuals and power-brokers, has lost its former lustre. It is useful to consider the worldwide revival of religion in this light. Religion is now providing a way of reconnecting to older pasts: sometimes assumed deliberately, but perhaps less self-consciously by many millions of people. 'How to reconcile membership in vivacious primary communities with the imperatives of an emerging cosmopolitanism is, perhaps, the most urgent issue of our time', according to a leading world historian,[49] who notes that a prime way of achieving this in antiquity was by way of religion. Today's religious revivals could, then, be described as reconfigurations of available resources for a successful life today. But the enhanced public and political importance of religion in a new historical age in which some of the less pleasing consequences of modernisation have become apparent, is not to be confused with a return to the past, nor considered as an anachronism, not even when it takes forms that have historical roots extending to precolonial times. It is no longer satisfactory to make stark distinctions between tradition and modernity and to suggest that the former always precedes the latter; the two coexist, and it is this very co-presence that results in change and progress.[50] Hence, revivals of traditional religion should not be taken for a sign that Africa is peeling off several layers of development, as Western newspapers' addiction to 'Heart of Darkness' headlines[51] implies. No more than anyone else do Africa and Africans have an authentic, unchanging, culture that is transmitted from one generation to another, or ought to be. What they do have, instead, are histories that are culturally transmitted. All of the practices that these entail are 'constitutive of the present'.[52]

Sceptical readers of this book may accept this last point, but nevertheless question whether some of the practices and beliefs that we have described are properly regarded as religion or politics at all. There are analysts who regard witchcraft beliefs and accusations, for example, as falling outside the sphere of religion, and others who consider ritual healing to be apolitical.[53] Some readers may prefer to consider such practices simply in terms of discourses that imply power. However, the currently fashionable approach of regarding all social interaction in terms of discourses of power easily becomes bland: if power is everywhere, then it is undifferentiated. Just as colonisation involved a redefinition of the legal relations between different parts of the world, it also imposed the separation of religion from power that had become conventional in Europe.[54] It is because contemporary religious revivals mark a reordering of religion and politics, sometimes recalling older, indigenous patterns, that it is so important to insist on paying due regard to religion in its own right, and not merely as a discourse.

Anyone who wishes to make sense of the revival of religion in the world must think of spiritual power as real power. Religion is itself a major historical vector, which links today's practices with the many systems of governance in precolonial Africa in which religious specialists or elders with spiritual authority formed a counter-balance to rulers. Before African societies became subject to organisation by bureaucratic institutions, and subsequently acquired written constitutions, their religious specialists functioned as checks and balances in systems of governance. They mediated the rights and claims of various groups, ensuring that power was not abused in whatever terms it was understood locally. Of course, they were not always effective in this regard, so that precolonial Africa had its share of usurpers and tyrants. However, the governmental or political function of religion was changed by colonisers who sought to separate religion from power, and church from state, in a process that has shaped religion and politics in their contemporary African form. European scholars and administrators, operating with Western precepts of order and governance, sought to confine religion to a private sphere or within the ambit of cultures that colonial officials tended to regard as discrete systems. Even the chiefs who implemented indirect rule were often expected to make their religious duties subservient to the needs of bureaucratic administration.

The separation of the secular and religious realms in many former colonies, or in pursuit of a vision of modernisation, was most successful in the institutional field. This formal separation did not eradicate older beliefs concerning the relationship between the material and the invisible worlds, or ideas about the spiritual basis of prosperity. This observation throws an interesting light on the history of the nationalist movements in the mid-twentieth century, which promised a liberation that had religious and even millenarian overtones. Rulers who, notwithstanding their formal status as heads of secular states, were perceived partly in religious terms, often adopted extravagant personality cults that were reflections of a power presumed to have its ultimate origin in the spirit world. More recently, a decline in the effectiveness of state institutions has led to a great deal of political and economic activity taking place outside the formal sphere. A juridical statehood enjoying international recognition coexists with an effective lack of many of the structures and services that states are supposed to deliver. Power is located other than where the law proclaims it to be, and it is this odd situation that defines the real space of politics in much of Africa. It also forms an economic sphere in which a few people are able to make a lot of money while most live in poverty. For everyone living in Africa, rich or poor, African or foreign, the environment has become very unpredictable, a circumstance that has had a major influence on people's ideas about chance, probability or providence in general, as well as about time and about the nature of power. Politicians in search of a political legitimacy that has been lost may have recourse to religion to fill the gap. Thus, the great variety of religious systems and practices existing in Africa has invaded modern politics.

The contemporary African spirit world is chaotic. Traditional spiritual experts have often lost their influence, as we have seen,[55] while the field is wide open to entrepreneurs of every type. Traditional or quasi-traditional cults and the new religious movements that have entered public space tend to operate without any sense of moderation or checks and balances, 'because the modern space is supposed to be an unlimited and unbounded space'.[56] The current religious renewal in Africa may be read in part as an effort to end this spiritual confusion by creating new patterns of stability. Such endeavours include attempts to recreate the form and content of village-style or neighbourhood communities in modern towns, implying a more or less self-conscious return to traditional ideas. In other cases new religious allegiances can be seen as a deliberate break with the past, attempts to create new practices that are thought to offer a better hope of stability and prosperity in today's world. Charismatic Christianity, strongest in Africa's cities, is often associated with moral appeals to break with village customs, including traditional rituals and polygamy, and to build individual responsibility. Everywhere that religion is emerging in public space, the remaking of public institutions and their moral standing are at stake. What seems to be required for a greater sense of stability and order, therefore, is a higher degree of consensus than exists at present on the nature of the spirit world and on legitimate ways of access to it. This implies the development of institutions that govern the relationship between the spirit and the material worlds.

It may be that, as the colonial era fades into history, a growing number of countries will adopt institutions and legal systems that have roots in their own precolonial history. There is a debate in several African countries as to whether 'witchcraft' is to be made a criminal offence. Another pertinent example is the reintroduction of shari'a into the criminal code in much of northern Nigeria. Such developments cannot be considered as a simple boon. They may cause concern on various grounds, including their implications for human rights, as we have discussed in regard to witchcraft.[57] On the other hand, the rulers of a country must take account of popular views on such matters. For example, if a majority of people in northern Nigeria, or any other part of the world, prefers a shari'a system of law to a colonial system of justice that has become increasingly unworkable and no longer guarantees physical security, their right to self-determination should not simply be ignored. This may not be an easy matter for anyone interested in international justice or equity to countenance. Yet, nor is it impossible, in principle at least, that shari'a law could be made compatible with international views of human rights.[58] To continue with an example from Nigeria, the same principle could apply to the proper regulation of the vigilante groups that have become common throughout the south of the country, which often seek the support of local deities and which are associated with traditional patterns of attributing young people to age-sets.[59] Another example of how ingrained spiritual values might contribute to new forms of governance is the effort being made in South Africa to examine the philosophical concept of *ubuntu* and develop it into a basis for government and business management.[60] However, this and similar ideas are at permanent risk of being hijacked by political and intellectual opportunists in search of patronage, and of going the same way as earlier ideas about African socialism, African humanism and such like, discredited in the process of political cooptation.

## *Knowledge universal and local*

In this book we have taken pains not to represent religion as either a positive or a negative force. Rather, we have looked at it in terms of ideas that can be used for different purposes and that may be subject to various moral judgements according to context. Religion can be as easily used to support thoroughly unpleasant regimes, as we have seen,[61] as it can to maintain social harmony. The re-creation of the political and religious fields can as easily lead to such aberrations as Mobutu-like personality cults or the sinister use of human body-parts to acquire power as it can to a proper sense of order. The key point at issue, then, is not that religion is a force for good, but that ideas about the moral nature of power in Africa are rooted in a religious world-view. Consequently, shifts in this world-view will be crucial for the development of new institutions as well as new ways of thinking about the power that has been so abused. This is not at all unique to Africa, but applies to contemporary religious change in many parts of the world. In earlier European history, too, shifts in religious thought played a major role in the formation of those institutions that we have come to think of as quintessentially modern. This is not to say that Africa must repeat the same journey by following the same footsteps, but it suggests that the idea of religious thought opening the way to economic and political progress is neither absurd nor unprecedented.

What has happened in Africa over the last two or three decades calls into question assumptions that have been made about the role of Africa in the world system of governance as it has evolved over a much longer period.[62] The relative weakness of law-based institutions in Africa is not only of concern to Africans themselves. Foreign diplomats need such institutions to secure African participation for regulating matters such as terrorism, migration and a great range of other issues concerning international governance. Even in a free-market economy, states and legal institutions are central mechanisms for creating and investing capital, making the rule of law an essential condition for full participation in international life. (The 'rule of law' refers to a type of government that is effected by reference to written codes; it does not necessarily imply a low level of crime). However, the development of institutions that are bound by rules, but that also reflect in formal terms the way people actually do things, is not something that Africans can easily create on their own. Such an evolution will depend on interaction between the three parties, broadly defined, that have been instrumental in Africa's history over a very long period: foreign actors, African elites, and the broad mass of the continent's people. It must be said that there are serious obstacles to any such positive development. Africa's current political elites and their foreign partners are able to exploit to their advantage the differences between how things are done in theory and how they are done in practice, or the gap between the formal and informal. Therefore, they have little incentive for changing things.[63] Many ordinary Africans—those who are not part of any elite—show deep ambivalence about how they are governed, engaging enthusiastically in clientelist politics when it suits them and lamenting its failures at other times. Pretty much the same can be said of foreign donor governments too over the years.

Moreover, Western governments will increasingly find that the performance of institutions of governance in Africa has a relationship to their own domestic affairs. For Africans are set to migrate in even greater numbers than at present. Some parts of Africa have a long tradition of migration in search of greater prosperity or for self-improvement, and, these days, the most attractive destinations for migration are in the rich world. Remittances to Africa sent by diaspora communities overseas exceed by far foreign direct investment and can compare with the levels of foreign aid and export receipts.[64] Falling birth-rates in Europe and Japan, especially, suggest that rich countries will also exercise a considerable 'pull' factor, needing large numbers of immigrants to take up employment. The growing presence of Africans overseas means that public officials in the European Union and North America will need to develop a serious interest in the religious world-views of the increasing proportion of their populations that is of non-Western origin. Analysts have to refine their understanding of religion both as a system of belief and in its effects on people's actions. Adopting such an attitude towards religion may pose difficulties for people in Western countries where the separation of church and state has been an achievement gained at considerable cost. Our argument, however, is not that this separation should be abandoned, but that the precise nature of the relationship between religion and politics needs to be reconsidered in the light of current developments.

It is clear that the late twentieth-century style of globalisation is not a purely homogenising force, but is also combined with myriad creations of local difference. The end of formal colonial rule, the loss of confidence in the ability of social science to enunciate universal laws, and the revival of religious ideologies, have combined to open up a vital space of intellectual and political contention throughout the world. This process has turned culture into a buzz-word of our times, much debated by academics and often used by politicians.[65] A vital question concerns the development of effective understandings about which cultural attributes are of a universal nature, and which ones apply only to certain groups, and who decides on these matters. Thus, there are politicians and academics who claim that certain types of belief and behaviour are proper to particular cultures only. Some claim, by this token, that the world consists of major cultural blocs that would be well advised to keep their distance from each other.[66] On the same grounds, there are governments that claim exemption from criticism of their human rights records on the grounds that their policies are based on distinctive cultural values.

It is instructive in this regard to compare current debates about culture with the field of natural science.[67] In the biotechnology industries, the search for universally valid theories and models has led to an interest in what is known as 'indigenous knowledge'. This refers to knowledge of the natural world that is possessed by people in the non-Western world but that is not directly accessible to international scientists, since it is not contained in books or on internet sites but only in the memories of people living in often geographically remote areas. This concerns notably knowledge of plants and herbal medicines, considered as a potential boon to the whole of humanity.[68] If knowledge of a herbal medicine held by people living in a rain forest is found by qualified specialists in California or Switzerland to be scientifically exact and commercially useful, leading to the eventual manufacture of a patented drug, it ceases to be considered as indigenous knowledge and is reclassified as scientific knowledge. It is then deemed to be of universal value, and becomes universally sellable, thanks to intellectual property regimes. Indigenous knowledge, it could be said, is that which is awaiting discovery by scientific and business elites.

The idea that all human knowledge can be examined by qualified specialists with a view to testing its universal validity is witness to the continuing confidence of scientists in their ability to develop sound models of the natural world, as we argued at the beginning of this book. How, then, it may be asked, does this apply to religious knowledge? And what may social science have to say on the matter? Natural scientists are generally uninterested in spiritual knowledge since it is not seen as being directly related to the natural world, but to invisible beings whose existence can be neither proved nor disproved. Social scientists, whose province this is, are less sure than they were even forty years ago how to consider religious belief. Few sociologists or anthropologists nowadays would state baldly that people who believe in spirits are simply misinformed about the way the world really works. Nor would they be as sure as they once were that cases of spirit possession, for example, could be analysed by a foolproof method to reveal what was 'really' happening. These days, they would be more likely to consider a belief in spirits as having a meaning valid only in its own context, or in other words as a form of indigenous knowledge belonging to a particular culture. But, unlike indigenous knowledge having a material application, indigenous spiritual knowledge is not considered as having much potential to become internationally validated or be universally applied.

Interestingly, Africans are in increasing numbers adhering to religions that claim to articulate a type of cultural knowledge that is of universal value. They even organise missionary activity outside their continent in a reversal of old patterns of Christian evangelisation,[69] at a time when many Europeans (but not Americans) have abandoned the field of religion altogether. African Muslims too are actively spreading a religious message they claim to have universal validity. In this respect, Africans as well as others from the former third world are in the forefront of efforts to create global networks. In this situation, Europeans, especially, tend to take a defensive position, suggesting that spiritual knowledge is best confined to private space or is applicable to specific cultures only. Belief in democracy and markets, meanwhile—neither of them any more visible than spirits— they claim to be of universal application. The United States is in a more complex position, since it has traditions of both religious belief and religious pluralism that show no sign of flagging. Furthermore, some Christian groups in the United States, influential in politics, are actively seeking to spread their particular form of belief worldwide. Clearly, the world is engaged in a massively important debate about what types of knowledge are appropriate and applicable for whom.

Religious allegiance is likely to be of growing importance in strategic and diplomatic calculations in years to come. While Islamic revivalist movements in the Middle East, North Africa and Asia are not the only examples of religious revival in the world, they are the ones that have effectively brought religion into the heart of the political debate. Hence, what is happening in Africa is not an isolated case of religion occupying modern political space, but part of a wider trend. It is of considerable historical importance in that it signifies a reaction to (and not a comprehensive rejection of) the Western model of modernisation that was so influential in the mid-twentieth century. It is a way of being a part of the modern world at the same time as it marks an aspiration to connect with local traditions.

# NOTES

*Introduction*

1. Gerrie ter Haar, *Halfway to Paradise: African Christians in Europe*, Cardiff Academic Press, 1998.
2. Following the *Oxford English Dictionary*, we take the notion of public as 'existing, done or made in public', or 'open to general observation'.
3. Elom Dovlo, 'The Church in Africa and religious pluralism: the challenges of new religious movements and charismatic churches', *Exchange*, 27, 1 (1998), pp. 52–69.
4. See chapter one, note 6. Other scholarly definitions of religion, notably derived from classical sociologists such as Durkheim and Weber, are popular in some branches of the social sciences, but we do not find them conducive to understanding the relation of religion and politics in Africa. See also chapter one.
5. Stephen Ellis and Gerrie ter Haar, 'Religion and politics in sub-Saharan Africa', *Journal of Modern African Studies*, 36, 2 (1998), pp. 175–201.
6. Michael G. Schatzberg, *Political Legitimacy in Middle Africa: Father, family, food*, Bloomington, IN: Indiana University Press, 2001, p. 74. Schatzberg uses the phrase 'middle Africa' to designate the majority of people, by analogy with 'middle America'.
7. The phrase 'politics from below' is associated with the work of the French political scientist Jean-François Bayart: cf. 'Le politique par le bas en Afrique noire: questions de méthode', *Politique africaine*, 1 (1981), pp. 53–82.
8. Calculated by the historian David Fieldhouse, quoted in Ania Loomba, *Colonialism/Postcolonialism*, London: Routledge, 1998, p. xiii.
9. Éloi Messi Metogo, *Dieu peut-il mourir en Afrique? Essai sur l'indifférence religieuse et l'incroyance en Afrique noire*, Paris/Yaounde: Karthala/UCAC, 1997; Aylward Shorter and Edwin Onyancha, *Secularism in Africa. A Case Study: Nairobi City*, Nairobi: Paulines Publications Africa, 1997.
10. Ambrose Moyo, 'Religion in Africa', in April A. Gordon and Donald L. Gordon (eds), *Understanding Contemporary Africa*, 3rd edn, Boulder, CO: Lynne Rienner, 2001, p. 299.

*Chapter 1*  Ideas

1. Martin Sommer, 'Het gerucht van Abbeville', *De Volkskrant* [Amsterdam], 3 May 2001, summarising similar articles from the French press.

2. Jean-Noël Kapferer, *Rumeurs, le plus vieux média du monde*, Paris: Edns. du Seuil, 1987, p. 49. An English version, translated by B. Fink, was published under the title *Rumors: Uses, interpretations and images*, New Brunswick: Transaction Publishers, 1990.

3. Edgar Morin, *La rumeur d'Orléans*, Paris: Edns. du Seuil, 1969.

4. Jan-Bart Gewald, 'El Negro, El Niño, witchcraft and the absence of rain in Botswana', *African Affairs*, 100, 401 (2001), pp. 555–80.

5. For the problems in defining religion, see Jan G. Platvoet and Arie L. Molendijk (eds), *The Pragmatics of Defining Religion: Contexts, concepts and contests*, Leiden: E. J. Brill, 1999.

6. E. B. Tylor, *Religion in Primitive Culture*, New York: Harper Torchbooks, 1958, p. 8. This was first published in 1871 under the title *Primitive Culture*.

7. For further discussion of this point, see chapter three, note 4.

8. Cf. Jan Platvoet, 'To define or not to define: the problem of the definition of religion', in *The Pragmatics of Defining Religion*, esp. pp. 260–1.

9. For further discussion of this point, see p. 16.

10. For a discussion of the role of religion in African philosophy, see e.g. Kwame Anthony Appiah, *In My Father's House: Africa in the philosophy of culture*, Oxford University Press, 1992, p. 135.

11. Martin Nkafu Nkemnkia uses the term 'vitalogy' to refer to this: *African Vitalogy: A step forward in African thinking*, Nairobi: Paulines Publications, 1999, p. 11.

12. Ernest Gellner, *Thought and Change*, London: Weidenfeld & Nicolson, 1964, p. 103.

13. Harold D. Lasswell, *Politics: Who gets what, when, how*, New York: Smith, 1936.

14. Cf. Bernard Crick and Tom Crick, *What is Politics?*, London: Edward Arnold, 1987, p. 1.

15. '...une fonction de signification': Ruth Marshall-Fratani and Didier Péclard, 'La religion du sujet en Afrique', *Politique africaine*, 87 (2002), p. 8.

16. Ibid., pp. 7–8. The article as a whole contains an incisive critique of recent anthropological work on religion in Africa.

17. Edward Luttwak, 'The missing dimension', in Douglas Johnston and Cynthia Sampson (eds), *Religion, the Missing Dimension of Statecraft*, Oxford University Press, 1994, pp. 8–19.

18. Jack Goody, 'Bitter icons', *New Left Review*, second series, 7 (2001), p. 15.

19. Cf. Colin Leys, *The Rise and Fall of Development Theory*, London: James Currey, 1996.

20. Achille Mbembe, *On the Postcolony*, Berkeley: University of California Press, 2001, p. 7.

21. A francophone school of political science, strongly influenced by a wider literature of philosophy, history and anthropology, has succeeded rather better than the anglophone tradition of political science in incorporating religion in its frame of analysis. See e.g. Jean-François Bayart (ed), *Religion et modernité politique en Afrique noire*, Paris: Karthala, 1993, esp. the conclusion.

22. Robin Horton, *Patterns of Thought in Africa and the West: Essays on magic, religion and science*, Cambridge University Press, 1997, p. 306.

23. Deepak Lal, 'Asia and Western dominance: retrospect and prospect', International Institute of Asian Studies Annual Lecture, Leiden, 27 October 2000, summarised in *IIAS Newsletter*, 24 (February 2001), p. 3. This is explored at full length in D. Lal, *Unintended Consequences: The impact of factor endowments, culture and politics on long-run economic performance*, Cambridge, MA: MIT Press, 1998.

24. John Lonsdale, 'States and social processes in Africa: a historiographical survey', *African Studies Review*, 24, 2–3 (1981), p. 139. We return to aspects of this in chapter eight.

25. See notably Jeff Haynes, *Religion and Politics in Africa*, London: Zed Books, 1996.

26. E.g. Paul Gifford (ed), *The Christian Churches and the Democratisation of Africa*, Leiden: E. J. Brill, 1995; Laurenti Magesa and Zablon Nthamburi (eds), *Democracy and Reconciliation: A challenge for African Christianity*, Nairobi: Acton Publishers, 1999.

27. E.g. on Christianity see Paul Gifford (ed), *New Dimensions in African Christianity*, Nairobi: All Africa Conference of Churches, 1992; on Islam, René Otayek (ed), *Le radicalisme islamique au sud du Sahara: da'wa, arabisation et critique de l'Occident*, Paris: Karthala, 1993; on revivals of African traditional religion, Rosalind Hackett, 'Revitalization in African Traditional Religion', in Jacob K. Olupona (ed), *African Traditional Religions in Contemporary Society*, New York: Paragon House, 1991, pp. 135–48.

28. E.g. Simeon O. Ilesanmi, 'The myth of a secular state: a study of religious politics with historical illustrations', *Islam and Christian-Muslim Relations*, 6, 1 (1995), pp. 105–17.

29. For a critique of the notion of fundamentalism, see Gerrie ter Haar, 'Religious fundamentalism and social change: a comparative inquiry', in Gerrie ter Haar and James J. Busuttil (eds), *The Freedom to do God's Will: Religious fundamentalism and social change*, London: Routledge, 2002, pp. 1–24. We will follow some scholars of Islam in labelling modern exponents of political Islam as Islamists.

30. See note 27.

31. Among exceptions to this is e.g. Matthew Schoffeleers (ed), *Guardians of the Land: Essays on central African territorial cults*, Gwelo: Mambo Press, 1978.

32. Etienne de Flacourt (ed. Claude Allibert), *Histoire de la Grande Isle, Madagascar*, Paris: Karthala, 1995, p. 153.

33. The concept of the West is in many respects a political one, grouping together a number of otherwise disparate countries in Western Europe and North America, but also Japan and Australia, for example. We use it here primarily to designate countries whose intellectual life has been decisively affected by the eighteenth-century Enlightenment, which in some ways makes it a more exclusive category. Ashis Nandy considers that 'The West is now everywhere, within the West and outside; in structures and in minds': *The Intimate Enemy:*

*Loss and recovery of self under colonialism*, New Delhi: Oxford University Press, 1988, xi.

34. See T. O. Ranger, 'African Traditional Religion', in Stewart Sutherland and Peter Clarke (eds), *The Study of Religion, Traditional and New Religion*, London: Routledge, 1991, pp. 106–14, esp. pp. 109–12. Our summary closely follows Gerrie ter Haar, *World Religions and Community Religions: Where does Africa fit in?*, University of Copenhagen, 2000, pp. 5–12.

35. 'L'imaginaire, ce n'est pas l'irréel, mais l'indiscernabilité du réel et de l'irréel': Gilles Deleuze, *Pourparlers 1972–90*, Paris: Edns. de Minuit, 1990, p. 93.

36. Ibid.

37. See chapter six.

38. Anthony Giddens, *Modernity and Self-Identity: Self and society in the late modern age*, Cambridge: Polity Press, 1991, pp. 32–4.

39. For further discussion on this point, see chapter eight.

40. Horton, *Patterns of Thought in Africa and the West*, p. 306.

41. E.g. Véronique Campion-Vincent and Jean-Bruno Renard, *Légendes urbaines: rumeurs d'aujourd'hui*, Payot, Paris, 1992.

42. Cf. Johannes Fabian, *Moments of Freedom: Anthropology and popular culture*, Charlottesville: University of Virginia Press, 1998, pp. 1–3.

## *Chapter 2*  Words

1. Interview in *L'Autre Afrique*, 60, 23 Sept. 1998, p. 52.

2. *En attendant le vote des bêtes sauvages*, Paris: Edns. du Seuil, 1998.

3. '...la vie des chasseurs, leur lutte magique contre les animaux et les fauves, supposés posséder de la magie. La chasse est donc une lutte entre des magiciens': 'Entretien avec Ahmadou Kourouma', *Politique africaine*, 75 (1999), p. 178.

4. S. T. Kgatla, 'Containment of witchcraft accusations in South Africa: a search for a transformational approach to curb the problem', in Gerrie ter Haar (ed), *Imagining Evil: Witchcraft beliefs and accusations in contemporary Africa*, Trenton, NJ: Africa World Press (forthcoming).

5. See notes 16 and 17.

6. Duasenge Ndundu Ekambo, *Radio-trottoir: une alternative de communication en Afrique contemporaine*, Louvain-la-Neuve: Cabay, 1985.

7. Cf. Sabakinu Kivilu, 'Le radio-trottoir dans l'exercice du pouvoir politique au Zaïre', in B. Jewsiewicki et H. Moniot (eds), *Dialoguer avec le léopard?*, Paris: L'Harmattan, 1988, pp. 179–93; on *radio trottoir* in general, Stephen Ellis, 'Tuning in to pavement radio', *African Affairs*, 88, 352 (1989), pp. 321–30; Cf. David Hecht and Maliqalim Simone, *Invisible Governance: The art of African micropolitics*, Brooklyn, NY: Autonomedia, 1994.

8. Ekambo, *Radio-trottoir*, p. 15.

9. Stories of penis-thieves occasionally surface in West African newspapers. Searching the internet with the words 'penis thieves Ghana' produces dozens of references.

10. Luise White, 'The traffic in heads: bodies, borders, and the articulation of regional histories', *Journal of Southern African Studies*, 23, 2 (1997), pp. 325–82.

11. Luise White, *Speaking with Vampires: Rumor and history in colonial Africa*, Berkeley: California Press, 2000, esp. pp. 3–86.

12. Françoise Raison-Jourde, *Bible et pouvoir à Madagascar*, Paris: Karthala, 1991, pp. 775–86; Lucy A. Jarosz, 'Agents of power, landscapes of fear: the vampires and heart thieves of Madagascar', *Environment and Planning D: Society and Space*, 12, 4 (1994), pp. 421–36.

13. Léopold Sédar Senghor, 'Eléments constructifs d'une civilisation d'inspiration négro-africaine', *Présence africaine*, 24–5 (1959), p. 278: '... mais de toutes les manifestations culturelles négro-africaines, l'oralité est l'un de leurs caractères communs.'

14. Ibid: 'l'oralité n'est pas que des langues'.

15. Georges Lefebvre, *La grande peur de 1789*, Paris: Armand Colin, 1970.

16. UNESCO, *Rapport mondial sur la culture*, 2000, Paris: UNESCO, 2000, p. 311. The same source has information on the availability of books, libraries, etc.

17. World Bank, *African Development Indicators 2003*, Washington, DC: World Bank, 2003, p. 249.

18. *Cameroon Tribune*, no. 3080, 21 September 1984.

19. Jean-Claude Gakosso, *La nouvelle presse congolaise: du goulag à l'agora*, Paris: L'Harmattan, 1997, p. 60; on obscenity in *radio trottoir*, Mbembe, *On the Post-colony*, esp. pp. 102–41.

20. Ellis, 'Tuning in to pavement radio'.

21. Amadu Wurie Khan, 'Journalism and armed conflict in Africa: the civil war in Sierra Leone', *Review of African Political Economy*, 78 (1998), pp. 594–5.

22. Cornelis Nlandu-Tsasa, *La rumeur au Zaïre de Mobutu: radio-trottoir à Kinshasa*, Paris: L'Harmattan, 1997, pp. 75–7.

23. Stephen Ellis, 'Reporting Africa', *Current History*, 99, 637 (2000), pp. 221–6.

24. Tom Rosentiel, in the *Washington Post*, 2 March 1999.

25. Robert Darnton, 'Journalism: all the news that fits we print', in *The Kiss of Lamourette: Reflections in cultural history*, New York: Norton, 1990, pp. 60–93.

26. Edward L. Bernays, *Propaganda*, New York: Horace Liveright, 1928, p. 9.

27. Walter Lippmann, *Public Opinion*, London: Geo. Allen & Unwin, 1922, p. 15.

28. Claude Ake, 'What is the problem of ethnicity in Africa?', *Transformation*, 22 (1993), p. 7.

29. Anand A. Yang, 'A conversation of rumours: the language of popular *mentalités* in late nineteenth-century colonial India', *Journal of Social History*, 20 (1986–7), p. 485.

30. *Africa Confidential*, one of the few journals that takes *radio trottoir* seriously as a source of political analysis, reports the Ghanaian episode in 'Ghana: Rolling with the punches', 37, 2 (19 January 1996), p. 3. The source for the Togolese example is…*radio trottoir*, rumours heard by one of the authors during visits to Togo.

31. Such as Samuel Doe, president of Liberia in the 1980s: Bill Frank Enoanyi, *Behold Uncle Sam's Step-Child*, Sacramento, CA: SanMar Publications, 1991, p. 36.
32. A good eye-witness description is Henrique F. Tokpa, 'Cuttington University College during the Liberian civil war: an administrator's experience', *Liberian Studies Journal*, XVI, 1 (1991), p. 87.
33. The following is drawn notably from Kapferer, *Rumeurs*.
34. Chapter one, p. 12.
35. Kapferer, *Rumeurs*, p. 93: 'sa force tient à son effet structurant sur notre perception…Elle fournit ainsi un système explicatif cohérent à un grand nombre de faits épars'.
36. Theodore R. Sarbin, 'Believed-in imaginings: a narrative approach', in Joseph De Rivera and Theodore R. Sarbin (eds), *Believed-In Imaginings: The narrative construction of reality*, Washington, DC: American Psychological Association, 1998, pp. 15–30.
37. Ibid., pp. 15–30, 194. See also Campion-Vincent and Renard, *Légendes urbaines*.
38. A seminal text, and a good statement of the postmodern approach to the study of discourse, is Michel Foucault, *L'Ordre du discours*, Paris: Gallimard, 1971.
39. Cf. Marshall Sahlins, *Culture in Practice: Selected essays*, New York: Zone Books, 2000, pp. 9–32.
40. Kapferer, *Rumeurs*, p. 88.
41. Robert Darnton, 'Paris: the early internet', *New York Review of Books*, XLVII, 11 (29 June 2000), pp. 42–7.
42. An interesting exposition on the issue can be found in Kwesi Yankah, *Free Speech in Traditional Society: The cultural foundations of communication in contemporary Ghana*, Accra: Ghana University Press, 1998, originally delivered as a lecture at his inauguration as professor of linguistics at the University of Ghana (20 November 1997).
43. Cf. J. L. Austin, *How to Do Things with Words*, Oxford: Clarendon Press, 1975.
44. Cf. Bernhard Udelhoven, 'Missionary curses on the Luapula', unpublished paper, 2002.
45. See e.g. Modupe Oduyoye, 'Potent speech', in E. A. Ade Adegbola (ed), *Traditional Religion in West Africa*, Ibadan: Daystar Press, 1983, pp. 203–32.
46. Yankah, *Free Speech*, pp. 15–16.
47. Cf. Elizabeth Tonkin, 'Investigating oral tradition', *Journal of African History*, 27, 2 (1986), pp. 203–13.
48. Robert B. Shoemaker, 'The decline of public insult in London, 1660–1800', *Past and Present*, 169 (2000), p. 129.
49. Emmanuel Obiechina, *Literature for the Masses: An analytical study of popular pamphleteering in Nigeria*, Enugu: Nwamife Books, 1971.
50. Adewale Maja-Pearce, 'Onitsha home movies', *London Review of Books*, 23, 9 (10 May 2001), pp. 24–6.

51. Amos Tutuola, *My Life in the Bush of Ghosts*, London: Faber & Faber, 1954; Ben Okri, *The Famished Road*, London: Jonathan Cape, 1991; Kourouma, *En attendant le vote des bêtes sauvages*.

52. On this point, in a discussion of intercultural philosophy, see Heinz Kimmerle, *Mazungumzo: Dialogen tussen Afrikaanse en westerse filosofieën*, Amsterdam: Boom, 1995, pp. 41–2. Cf. Appiah, *In My Father's House*, pp. 98–100, 118.

53. Even the excellent African Books Collective, the concern based in Oxford, England, which distributes books outside Africa on behalf of some fifty leading African publishers, rarely handles the type of literature to which we refer in subsequent footnotes.

54. For example, D. D. Kaniaki and Evangelist Mukendi, *Snatched from Satan's Claws: An amazing deliverance by Christ*, Nairobi: Enkei Media Services, 1994, is published in both English and Kiswahili editions. This text will be discussed in more detail below, on pages 49–51.

55. The pioneer in scholarship in this field is Paul Gifford, some of whose writings are listed in the bibliography. A number of African scholars have also written on this subject but have attracted less international attention. See e.g. Matthews Ojo, 'The growth of campus Christianity and charismatic movements in western Nigeria', PhD thesis, Univ. of London, 1986; idem, 'Deeper Life Christian Ministry: a case study of the charismatic movements in western Nigeria', *Journal of Religion in Africa*, 18 (1988), pp. 141–62; idem, 'The contextual significance of the charismatic movements in independent Nigeria', *Africa*, 58 (1987), pp. 175–92; E. Kingsley Larbi, *Pentecostalism: The eddies of Ghanaian Christianity*, Accra: Centre for Pentecostal and Charismatic Studies (CPCS), 2001.

56. '...dans la mesure où le désir de changement politique, économique et social se traduit par la constitution d'une nouvelle existence éthique et spirituelle, autrement dit par le changement de soi': Marshall-Fratani and Péclard, 'La religion du sujet en Afrique', p. 12.

57. See chapter five.

58. A number of such works are listed in a separate section in the bibliography.

59. Gerrie ter Haar, 'A wondrous God: miracles in contemporary Africa', *African Affairs*, 102, 408, (2003), p. 417.

60. Lindsey Hilsum, 'Mary who "met Jesus" invokes Second Coming in Kenya slum', *Guardian* [London], 23 June 1988.

61. Jack Nandi, 'The Jerusalem Church of Christ: A historical and theological analysis', MA thesis, University of Nairobi, Department of Religion, 1993. Gerrie ter Haar saw Mary Akatsa in action in 1995.

62. Personal communication to Gerrie ter Haar. See further E. Jensen Krige and J. D. Krige, *The Realm of a Rain-Queen: A study of the pattern of Lovedu society*, London: Oxford University Press for the International African Institute, 1943.

63. Kofi Akosah-Sarpong, 'Voodoo rule in Africa', part 5, *Expo Times*, http://www.expotimes.net/issue000913/renaissance.htm

64. Marie-Louise Martin, *Kimbangu: An African prophet and his church*, Oxford: Basil Blackwell, 1975, originally published in German as *Kirche ohne Weisse* in 1971.

65. Karin Barber, 'Popular reactions to the petro-naira', *Journal of Modern African Studies*, 20, 3 (1982), pp. 431–50.

66. Ed Hooper, *The River: A journey back to the source of HIV and AIDS*, London: Allen Lane, 1999.

67. Nlandu-Tsasa, *La rumeur au Zaire*, p. 130.

68. C. Bawa Yamba, 'Cosmologies in turmoil: witchfinding and AIDS in Chiawa, Zambia', *Africa*, 67, 2 (1997), pp. 200–23.

69. Mary Myers, 'Community radio and development: issues and examples from francophone West Africa', in Richard Fardon and Graham Furniss (eds), *African Broadcast Cultures: Radio in transition*, Oxford: James Currey, 2000, p. 97, note 6.

70. Personal communication by Hugo Hinfelaar, a Dutch White Father in Zambia and former secretary to Archbishop Emmanuel Milingo, former archbishop of Lusaka.

71. Matthew Schoffeleers, 'The AIDS pandemic, the prophet Billy Chisupe, and the democratization process in Malawi', *Journal of Religion in Africa*, XXXIX, 4 (1999), pp. 412–4.

72. For a polemic on this subject, Paul R. Gross and Norman Levitt, *Higher Superstition: The academic left and its quarrels with science*, Baltimore, MD: Johns Hopkins University Press, 1994, esp. pp. 45–70.

73. Cf. Steven Lukes, 'On the social determination of truth', in Robin Horton and Ruth Finnegan (eds), *Modes of Thought: Essays on thinking in western and non-western societies*, London: Faber & Faber, 1973, pp. 230–48.

74. Susan D. Moeller, *Compassion Fatigue: How the media sell disease, famine, war and death*, New York and London: Routledge, 1999, pp. 64–5.

75. For an elaboration of the notion of 'mental constructs', see Jan Platvoet, 'Contexts, concepts and contests: towards a pragmatics of defining religion', in Platvoet and Molendijk, *The Pragmatics of Defining Religion*, p. 505, n. 177.

*Chapter 3*  Spirits

1. The word 'witch' is often used in and outside Africa in a loose sense to indicate any person believed to have the ability to manipulate mystical forces of any type. This is different from the more precise meaning we discuss in chapter seven, where the term 'witchcraft' is used to refer exclusively to the manipulation of evil forces.

2. Kaniaki and Mukendi, *Snatched from Satan's Claws*. The quotations are from pages 38–42 of the English version.

3. Ibid., p. 42.

4. Clifford Geertz, 'Religion as a cultural system', in Michael Banton (ed), *Anthropological Approaches to the Study of Religion*, London: Tavistock Publications, 1966, p. 42.

5. See e.g. Abdou Touré and Yacouba Konaté, *Sacrifices dans la ville: le citadin chez le divin en Côte d'Ivoire*, Abidjan: Douga, 1990.

6. See chapter five.

7. E.g. Wyatt MacGaffey, *Modern Kongo Prophets: Religion in a plural society*, Bloomington: Indiana University Press, 1983, pp. 126–7.

8. E.g. Kathleen O'Brien Wicker, 'Mami Water in African religion and spirituality', in Jacob K. Olupona (ed), *African Spirituality: Forms, meanings and expressions*, New York: Crossroad Publishing, 2000, pp. 198–222. A pamphlet on the same subject is Victoria Eto, *Exposition on Water Spirits*, Warri, Nigeria: Shallom Christian Mission International, 1983.

9. Cf. Gerrie ter Haar, 'African Independent Churches: the ideological implications of continuity and change', in Anton Houtepen (ed), *The Living Tradition: Towards an ecumenical hermeneutics of the Christian tradition*, Zoetermeer: Meinema, 1995, pp. 159–170.

10. See Cephas Narh Omenyo, *Pentecost outside Pentecostalism: A study of the development of Charismatic Renewal in the mainline churches in Ghana*, Zoetermeer: Boekencentrum, 2002.

11. Gerrie ter Haar, *Spirit of Africa: The healing ministry of Archbishop Milingo of Zambia*. London: Hurst & Co, 1992.

12. Cf. e.g. John S. Mbiti, *African Religions and Philosophy*, Oxford: Heinemann, 1990, p. 78.

13. Cf. Laurenti Magesa, *African Religion: The moral traditions of an abundant life*, Maryknoll, NY: Orbis Books,1997, p. 56.

14. Emmanuel Milingo, *Plunging into Darkness*, Broadford, Victoria: Scripture Keys Ministries Australia, 1993.

15. Ibid., p. v.

16. Chapter one, p. 23.

17. Such as the novelists referred to on p. 40. A great number of theologians and scholars of religion make it plain that many people share such views: see e.g. Olupona, *African Traditional Religions in Contemporary Society*; Simon Bockie, *Death and the Invisible Powers: The world of Kongo belief*, Bloomington: Indiana University Press, 1993; Magesa, *African Religion*. Many other references could be added.

18. Cf. E. Bọ́lájí Ìdòwú, *Olaḍùmarè: God in Yorùbá belief*. New York: Wazobia, 1994, pp. 77–80, 171–85.

19. Donald T. Regan, *For the Record: From Wall Street to Washington*, San Diego: Harcourt Brace Jovanovich, 1988, pp. 73–4.

20. D. W. Winnicott, 'Transitional objects and transitional phenomena', in *Collected Papers: Through paediatrics to psycho-analysis*, London: Tavistock Publications, 1958, p. 240.

21. Misty L. Bastian, 'Married in the water: spirit kin and other afflictions of modernity in southeastern Nigeria', *Journal of Religion in Africa*, 27, 2 (1997), p. 117.

22. On the healing dimension of trance, see A. M. Ludwig, 'Altered states of con-
    sciousness', in R. Prince (ed), *Trance and Possession States*, Montreal: R. M. Buckle
    Memorial Society, 1968, pp. 69–95. For an illustrative example from Africa,
    see Edith Turner with William Blodgett, Singleton Kahona, and Fideli Benwa,
    *Experiencing Ritual: A new interpretation of African healing*, Philadelphia: University
    of Pennsylvania Press, 1992.

23. See Gerrie ter Haar and Jan Platvoet, 'Bezetenheid en christendom',
    *Nederlands Theologisch Tijdschrift*, 43, 3 (1989), pp. 176–191.

24. Felicitas Goodman, *How About Demons? Possession and exorcism in the modern world*,
    Bloomington: Indiana University Press, 1988, p. 2.

25. Ludwig, 'Altered states of consciousness'; see also Barbara Lex, 'The neuro-
    biology of ritual trance', in E.G. d'Aquili, Ch.D. Laughlin and J. McManus
    (eds), *The Spectrum of Ritual: A biogenetic structural analysis*, New York: Columbia
    University Press, 1979, pp. 117–51.

26. The factor of cultural expectation, dependent on a specific social context,
    tends to be overlooked by neurobiologists, but is present or implicit in the
    works of anthropologists writing on the subject. Cf. I. M. Lewis, *Ecstatic Reli-
    gion: A study of shamanism and spirit possession*, London: Routledge, 1989 (first
    published 1971); Erika Bourguignon (ed), *Religion, Altered States of Consciousness
    and Social Change*, Columbus: Ohio University Press, 1973; and Felicitas
    D. Goodman, *Ecstasy, Ritual and Alternate Reality: Religion in a pluralistic world*,
    Bloomington: Indiana University Press, 1992.

27. Erika Bourguignon, 'Introduction: a framework for the comparative study of
    altered states of consciousness', in *Religion, Altered States of Consciousness and
    Social Change*, pp. 3–35, notably pp. 9–11.

28. Ibid., p. 18.

29. Cf. T. M. Luhrmann, *Of Two Minds: The growing disorder in American psychiatry*,
    New York: Knopf, 2000.

30. See David Martin, *Pentecostalism: The world their parish*, Oxford: Blackwell, 2001;
    Paul Freston, *Evangelicals and Politics in Asia, Africa and Latin America*, Cambridge
    University Press, 2001.

31. See also chapter eight.

32. According to David Barrett, generally considered the most authoritative
    source of statistics on global Christianity, the twentieth-century spiritual re-
    newal movement as a whole makes up at least 21 per cent of organised glo-
    bal Christianity: 'A survey of the twentieth-century pentecostal/charismatic
    renewal in the Holy Spirit, with its goal of world evangelization', in S. M.
    Burgess, G. B. McGee & P. H. Alexander (eds), *Dictionary of Pentecostal and
    Charismatic Movements*, Grand Rapids, MI: Zondervan Publishing House,
    1988, pp. 810–30. See also David B. Barrett and Todd M. Johnson, 'Annual
    statistical table on global mission: 2002', *International Bulletin of Missionary
    Research*, 26, 1 (2002), pp. 22–3, in which they claim a number of some 544
    million adherents of Christian pentecostal/charismatics worldwide.

33. For a fascinating account of the use of such techniques by US intelligence officers, see David Morehouse, *Psychic Warrior*, London: Penguin, 1997.

34. Ludwig, 'Altered states of consciousness'.

35. Two classic studies are Gérard Althabe, *Oppression et libération dans l'imaginaire: les communautés villageoises de la côte orientale de Madagascar*, Paris: Maspéro, 1969, and David Lan, *Guns and Rain: Guerrillas and spirit mediums in Zimbabwe*, London: James Currey, 1985.

36. Adeline Masquelier, *Prayer Has Spoiled Everything: Possession, power, and identity in an Islamic town of Niger*, Durham, NC: Duke University Press, 2001, pp. 11–15.

37. Lewis, *Ecstatic Religion*.

38. See note 26.

39. Janice Boddy, *Wombs and Alien Spirits: Women, men and the zar cult in northern Sudan*, Madison: University of Wisconsin Press, 1989, pp. 139–40.

40. E.g. Heike Behrend and Ute Luig (eds), *Spirit Possession: Modernity and power in Africa*, Oxford: James Currey, 1999; Masquelier, *Prayer Has Spoiled Everything*, esp. p. 14.

41. Lewis, *Ecstatic Religion*, notably pp. 27–9, 114–33.

42. Ibid., p. 69; also I. M. Lewis, *Religion in Context: Cults and charisma*, Cambridge University Press, 1986, p. 35.

43. Lewis, *Ecstatic Religion*, pp. 125–7.

44. Bourguignon, *Religion, Altered States of Consciousness and Social Change*, pp. 29–31.

45. Chapter two, p. 33.

46. Aldous Huxley, *The Doors of Perception*, London: Chatto & Windus, 1954.

47. Chapter seven.

48. See further in chapter five.

49. Jean S. La Fontaine, *Speak of the Devil: Tales of satanic abuse in contemporary England*, Cambridge University Press, 1998.

50. Grace Nyatugah Wamue, 'Revisiting our indigenous shrines through *Mungiki*', *African Affairs*, 100, 400 (2001), pp. 453–67.

51. Lan, *Guns and Rain*.

52. James Astill, '"Meditation is the path to peace"', *Weekly Mail and Guardian*, 28 Sept.–4 Oct. 2001, p. 30.

53. Alison Des Forges, *"Leave None to Tell the Story": Genocide in Rwanda*, New York: Human Rights Watch, 1999, pp. 43–4.

54. Donal B. Cruise O'Brien, *The Mourides of Senegal: The political and economic organization of an Islamic brotherhood*, Oxford: Clarendon Press, 1971.

55. For an overview of press reactions, see Ineke Vegter, 'Waar olifanten vechten, groeit het gras niet. Apartheid en de Zion Christian Church', MA thesis, Free University of Amsterdam, 1988.

56. Other parties were also represented, including in the persons of Democratic Party leader Zach de Beer, PAC leader Clarence Makwetu and others. See the page-long report in *Trouw*, one of the leading Dutch dailies, on 12 April 1994 by Eric Brassem ('Pasen in Zuid-Afrika').

57. This was noted before independence by Georges Balandier, 'Messianism and nationalism in Black Africa', in Pierre L. van den Berghe (ed), *Africa: Social problems of change and conflict*, San Francisco: Chandler Publishing, 1965, pp. 443–60, a translation of a text first published in 1953. Recent studies include e.g. Abel Kouvouama, 'Imaginaire religieux et logiques symboliques dans le champ politique', *Rupture*, nouvelle série, 1, Paris: Karthala, 1999, pp. 76–92.

58. Joseph Mampouya, *Une histoire de rat: contribution à la critique du messianisme politique au Congo Brazzaville*, Paris: Encre noire, 1999, esp. pp. 49–56.

*Chapter 4* Secrets

1. Andrew Roberts, *A History of Zambia*, London: Heinemann, 1981, p. 221, puts the number at over 700 dead.

2. Beatwell S. Chisala, *The Downfall of President Kaunda*, Lusaka: private publication, 1994, pp. 45–6.

3. According to the dust-jacket of M. A. Ranganathan, *The Political Philosophy of President Kaunda of Zambia*, Edinburgh: Holmes McDougall, 1985.

4. Described by Ranganathan in an interview with Shikha Trivedy in the *Illustrated Weekly of India*, 23 August 1987.

5. Chisala, *The Downfall of President Kaunda*, pp. 45–51.

6. Ibid., p. 47.

7. Meinrad P. Hebga, 'Interpellation des mouvements mystiques', *Cahiers des religions africaines* (special number: 'L'Afrique et ses formes de vie spirituelle'), 24, 47 (1990), p. 74: '…beaucoup de révolutionnaires tonitruants, d'intellectuels férus de rationalisme et de cartésianisme, sont en même temps assujettis à touts sortes de griots, de marabouts, de féticheurs, de devins; pratiquent des sacrifices humains rituels pour conserver le pouvoir…'.

8. See note 42.

9. Jonathan Bloch and Patrick Fitzgerald, *British Intelligence and Covert Action*, Dingle, Ireland: Brandon, 1983, p. 48.

10. Chisala, *The Downfall of President Kaunda*, pp. 50–1.

11. Mbembe, *On the Postcolony*, pp. 102–41.

12. Cf. Philip Bobbit, *The Shield of Achilles: War, peace and the course of history*, London: Allen Lane, 2002, pp. 783–5.

13. Chapter two.

14. Georg Simmel *The Sociology of Georg Simmel*, New York: The Free Press, 1964, p. 330.

15. Stephen Knight, *The Brotherhood: The secret world of the Freemasons*, London: Granada, 1984.

16. Commissione Parlamentare d'Inchiesta sulla Loggia Massonica P2, *Allegati alla Relazione, serie II*, multi-volume publication, Rome: Stabilimenti Tipografici Carlo Colombo, 1984.

17. Jean-François Mayer, University of Fribourg, personal communication.

18. '…beaucoup d'intéllectuels, d'hommes politiques et d'hommes d'affaires': Hebga, 'Interpellation des mouvements mystiques', p. 71.

19. 'Anglican denies knowledge of Ige's cult membership', *This Day* [Lagos], 30 January 2002.
20. 'AMORC offers free membership to Anglican priests', *This Day*, 4 March 2002.
21. According to the report of a French judge. *Le Monde*, 17 August 2000, p. 7.
22. We are indebted to Jean-François Mayer, who was an expert witness in the judicial investigation. Personal communication.
23. Philippe Broussard, 'Les millions africains d'un ancien grand maître', *Le Monde*, 24 December 1999, p. 8.
24. François Gaulme, *Le Gabon et son ombre*, Paris: Karthala, 1988, p. 135; a formal ethnographic description of Bwiti is James W. Fernandez, *Bwiti: An ethnography of the religious imagination in Africa*, Princeton University Press, 1982. This 731-page work apparently makes no mention of President Bongo, whose name is not listed in the index. There is a passage on the role of Bwiti in the political career of his predecessor, President Léon Mba, on pp. 350–3.
25. Pierre Péan, *Affaires africaines*, Paris: Fayard, 1983, pp. 32–5.
26. Ibid. Elf—now merged into a larger consortium—was associated with a string of financial and political scandals and known for the lack of transparency of its affairs.
27. United States Senate, *Private Banking and Money Laundering: A case study of opportunities and vulnerabilities*, hearings before the Permanent Subcommittee on Investigations, 9–10 November 1999, Washington, DC: US Government Printing Office, 2000, pp. 13–18.
28. Freemasonry was also strong among the coastal elites of English-speaking West Africa, but has declined since the 1979 and 1980 coups in Ghana and Liberia respectively, both of which resulted in mob attacks on masonic lodges.
29. The term 'secret societies' was originally used by Europeans to designate initiation societies they found to be present in many parts of West and central Africa especially. We may note that many such secret societies in fact incorporate most adult members of a community, making the notion of secrecy rather problematic, but since the expression has gained such general currency we will continue to use it here.
30. Among many works on Poro, see e.g. Beryl Bellman, *The Language of Secrecy: Symbols and metaphors in Poro ritual*, New Brunswick NJ: Rutgers University Press, 1984; on Sande, Caroline H. Bledsoe, 'The political use of Sande ideology and symbolism', *American Ethnologist*, 11 (1984), pp. 455–72.
31. Cf. Stephen Ellis, *The Mask of Anarchy: The destruction of Liberia and the religious dimension of an African civil war*, London: Hurst & Co., 1999, esp. pp. 220–80.
32. Chapter one, pp. 21–4.
33. Ayodeji Olukoju, 'Christianity and the development of the Nigerian state', in Akinjide Osuntokun and Ayodeji Olukoju (eds), *Nigerian Peoples and Cultures*, Ibadan: Davidson Press, 1997, p. 140.
34. Reginald B. Goodridge (ed), *Presidential Papers: A premiere edition*, vol. I, Monrovia: publisher unknown, 1999, p. 268. Goodridge was President Taylor's press secretary.

35. In the possession of the authors.

36. Ellis, *The Mask of Anarchy*, p. 264.

37. Despatch by Sierra Leone News Agency, Freetown, 11 December 2000.

38. Denis Sassou N'Guesso, *Le manguier, le fleuve et la souris*, Paris: J.-C. Lattès, 1997, p. 114.

39. 'Raelity', *Africa Confidential*, 43, 1 (11 January 2002), p. 8.

40. Comi M. Toulabor, *Le Togo sous Eyadéma*, Paris: Karthala, 1986, pp. 105–31.

41. Jacques Baulin, *La politique intérieure d'Houphouët-Boigny*, Paris: Eurafor-press, 1982, pp. 116–18.

42. Comi Toulabor, 'Sacrifices humains et politique: quelques exemples contemporains en Afrique', in Piet Konings, Wim van Binsbergen and Gerti Hesseling (eds), *Trajectoires de libération en Afrique contemporaine*, Paris: Karthala, 2000, pp. 213–14.

43. Samba Diarra, *Les faux complots d'Houphouët-Boigny*, Paris: Karthala, 1997, pp. 223–43.

44. Alpha-Abdoulaye Diallo, *La vérité du ministre: dix ans dans les geôles de Sékou Touré*, Paris: Calmann-Lévy, 1985, p. 131: 'Les voyants avaient convaincu Sékou Touré qu'en sacrifiant autant de cadres que ce dernier [Houphouët-Boigny] avait d'années d'age, le jour anniversaire de sa naissance, cela entraînerait irrémédiablement sa chute….'

45. Toulabor', 'Sacrifices humains', pp. 216–17; Ellis, *The Mask of Anarchy*, p. 264.

46. Chapter two, pp. 36–7.

47. Some such rumours are reported in Toulabor, 'Sacrifices humains', pp. 207–8; White, 'The traffic in heads'; Elom Dovlo, 'Religion and the politics of Fourth Republican elections in Ghana', unpublished paper.

48. Personal communication by Umar Danfulani of the University of Jos, Nigeria. Charles S. Johnson, an African American official of the League of Nations, reported after a stay in Liberia in 1930 that there were people who not only consumed human flesh, but also 'on occasion, had brought human flesh to the market for sale'. *Bitter Canaan: The story of the Negro Republic*, New Brunswick, NJ: Transaction Books, 1989, p. 169.

49. 'Special Assignment', broadcast on South African Broadcasting Corporation, 7 May 2002. We are grateful to Steven Robins of the University of Western Cape for this reference.

50. 'Entretien avec Ahmadou Kourouma', *Politique africaine*, pp. 178–83: 'J'écris des vérités, comme je les ressens, sans prendre parti. J'écris les choses commes elles sont' [p. 178]. 'Les comportements des dictateurs africains sont tels que les gens ne les croient pas; ils pensent que c'est de la fiction. Leurs comportements dépassent en effet souvent l'imagination. Les dictateurs africains se comportent dans la réalité comme dans mon roman. Nombre de faits et d'événements que je rapporte sont vrais. Mais ils sont tellement impensables que les lecteurs les prennent pour des inventions romanesques. C'est terrible!' [p. 179]. 'En Afrique, il n'y a pas un seul dirigeant qui n'ait son magicien ou

son marabout; magie et pouvoir (politique) sont des entités presque identiques' [p. 179].

51. Biko Agozino & Unyierie Idem, *Nigeria: Democratising a militarised civil society*, Occasional Paper no. 5, London: Centre for Democracy and Development, 2001, pp. 30–2.

52. A. O. Nkwoka, 'Acts 19$^{18-19}$: the Ephesian cultists and the Nigerian campus secret cults: a study of the spiritual and social side of cultism', *African Journal of Biblical Studies*, XV, 1 (2000), pp. 148–63; see also Ogbu U. Kalu, *The Scourge of the Vandals: Nature and control of cults in Nigerian university system*, Enugu: Joen Publishers, 2001.

53. J. H. P. Serfontein, *Brotherhood of Power: An exposé of the secret Afrikaner Broederbond*, London: Rex Collings, 1979. The organisation has now been renamed the Afrikaner Bond and admits both men and women of all races.

54. Frank Welsh, *Dangerous Deceits: Julian Askin and the Tollgate scandal*, London: HarperCollins, 1999.

55. The SACP succeeded the Communist Party of South Africa, founded in 1921 and disbanded after being declared illegal in 1950.

56. Vladimir Shubin, *ANC: A view from Moscow*, Bellville: Mayibuye Books, 1999, p. 244.

57. Yohannes Petros, 'A survey of political parties in Ethiopia', *Northeast African Studies*, 43, 2–3 (1991), p. 160.

58. Dan Connell, 'Inside the EPLF: the origins of the "People's Party" and its role in the liberation of Eritrea', *Review of African Political Economy*, 28, 89 (2001), pp. 345–64.

59. List of members of the 1001 Club in the possession of the authors; see also Stephen Ellis, 'Of elephants and men: politics and nature conservation in South Africa', *Journal of Southern African Studies*, 20, 1 (1994), pp. 53–69.

60. For a critical study of gender in Africa, see Ife Amadiume, *Male Daughters, Female Husbands: Gender and sex in an African society*, London: Zed Books, 1987.

61. Max Weber (ed Max Rheinstein), *Max Weber on Law in Economy and Society*, Cambridge, MA: Harvard University Press, 1954, p. 334.

62. The authors have heard this allegation in Ghana on several occasions.

63. The same has been reported for previous elections. Cf. Elom Dovlo, 'Religion and the politics of Fourth Republican elections in Ghana'.

64. Ellis, *The Mask of Anarchy*, pp. 10–11.

65. Dominique Malaquais, *Architecture, pouvoir et dissidence au Cameroun*, Paris/Yaounde: Karthala/UCAC, 2002, p. 19.

66. On the coup, see Julius O. Ihonvbere, 'The failed 1990 coup in Nigeria', *Journal of Modern African Studies*, 29, 4 (1991), pp. 601–26.

67. Karl Maier, *This House Has Fallen: Nigeria in crisis*, London: Allen Lane, 2001, pp. 16–19.

68. Quoted in *Africa Confidential*, 42, 12 (15 June 2001), p. 1.

69. Personal communication by a former cabinet minister in Mali.

70. Maurice Chabi, *Banqueroute, mode d'emploi: un marabout dans les griffes de la maffia béninoise*, Porto Novo: Editions Gazette Livres, no date.

71. Emmanuelle Kadya Tall, 'De la démocratie et des cultes voduns au Bénin', *Cahiers d'études africaines*, 137, XXXV, 1 (1995), pp. 199–200.

72. Camilla Strandsbjerg, 'Kérékou, God and the ancestors: religion and the conception of political power in Benin', *African Affairs*, 99, 396 (2000), pp. 395–414.

73. Robert B. Charlick, *Niger: Personal rule and survival in the Sahel*, Boulder, CO: Westview Press, 1991, pp. 69–70.

74. On the Belgian Congo, see Martin, *Kimbangu*; on colonial Northern Rhodesia, Karen E. Fields, *Revival and Rebellion in Colonial Central Africa*, Princeton University Press, 1985.

75. David Palmer, 'Falun Gong: la tentation du politique', *Critique internationale*, 11 (2001), pp. 36–43.

*Chapter 5* Power

1. M. N. Tetteh, *Anatomy of Rumour Mongering in Ghana*, Accra: Ghana Publicity Ltd., 1976, p. 38.

2. Ivor Wilks, 'Space, time and "human sacrifice"', in *Forests of Gold: Essays on the Akan and the Kingdom of Asante*, Athens, OH: Ohio University Press, 1993, pp. 215–40; Emmanuel Terray, 'Le pouvoir, le sang et la mort dans le royaume asante au XIXe siècle', *Cahiers d'études africaines*, XXXIV, 4 (1994), pp. 549–61.

3. Richard Rathbone, *Murder and Politics in Colonial Ghana*, New Haven, CT: Yale University Press, 1993.

4. John S. Pobee, *Kwame Nkrumah and the Church in Ghana, 1949–1966*, Accra: Asempa Publishers, 1988, pp. 45–6, 140–51.

5. Toulabor, 'Sacrifices humains et politique', p. 211.

6. Personal communication by Cephas Omenyo, University of Ghana.

7. Nlandu-Tsasa, *La rumeur au Zaïre*, p. 130. See also above, chapter two, p. 45.

8. Toulabor, 'Sacrifices humains et politique', p. 216. The film is 'Mobutu, roi du Zaïre' by Thierry Michel.

9. Schatzberg, *Political Legitimacy in Middle Africa*, p. 133.

10. Mukendi, *Snatched from Satan's Claws*, p. 42.

11. Patrice Yengo, 'Guerre des légitimités et démocide convenu: la restauration autoritaire au Congo-B', *Ruptures*, 'Les Congos dans la tourmente', nouvelle série, 2, Paris: Karthala, 2000, p. 91.

12. James Thomas-Queh, 'La politique de contrôle social dans un pays en voie de développement: analyse des lois, des institutions judiciaires et de l'application de la justice pénale au Liberia', thèse de 3e cycle, Sorbonne-II, Paris, 1985, pp. 411–47.

13. Enoanyi, *Behold Uncle Sam's Step-Child*, p. 36.

14. The following examples are drawn from a range of popular pamphlets, such as those listed in the bibliography by Mmasi, Kaniaki and Mukendi, and Hassim. We know of no extensive bibliography of such publications, but some are analysed in Ellis and Ter Haar, 'Religion and politics'.

15. Chapter three, p. 54.

16. For the opinions of fighters in Sierra Leone on these matters, see Mariane Ferme and Daniel Hoffman, 'Combattants irréguliers et discours international des droits de l'homme dans les guerres civiles africaines: le cas des "chasseurs" sierra-léonais', *Politique africaine*, 88 (2002), pp. 27–48.

17. E.g. Jean and John L. Comaroff (eds), *Modernity and its Malcontents: Ritual and power in postcolonial Africa*, University of Chicago Press, 1993; Peter Geschiere, *The Modernity of Witchcraft: Politics and the occult in postcolonial Africa*, Charlottesville, VA: University Press of Virginia, 1997.

18. E.g. Birgit Meyer, *Translating the Devil: Religion and modernity among the Ewe in Ghana*, Edinburgh University Press, 1999.

19. See chapter two, note 55.

20. The expression 'life-force' is notably connected with Placide Tempels, whose 1945 work *La philosophie bantoue* uses the phrase in the English translation published in 1959, but earlier accounts can be found. See also Nkemnkia, *African Vitalogy*, notably ch. six.

21. Filip De Boeck, 'Le "Deuxième monde" et les enfants-sorciers en République démocratique du Congo', *Politique africaine*, 80 (2000), pp. 32–57.

22. Among European press reports, see e.g. Hermine Bokhorst, 'Sexe payant et prison vaudoue', *Le Soir* [Brussels], 1 December 2001. Some humanitarian organisations in Europe have investigated the issue, such as Terre des Hommes in the Netherlands, which in 1999 published a report, 'Handel in Nigeriaanse meisjes naar Nederland'. For a general analysis, see Peter O. Ebigbo, 'Child trafficking in Nigeria: the state of the art', Geneva: International Labour Organisation, 2000.

23. Schatzberg, *Political Legitimacy in Middle Africa*, pp. 121–9. Among many newspaper articles, see e.g. one about the African Cup of Nations: Jonathan Wilson, 'Magic of the Cup: muti, marabouts, and witch doctors—all bad for game's image', *Observer* [London], 10 February 2002.

24. G. L. Chavunduka, *The Zimbabwe National Traditional Healers Association*, Harare: no publisher given, 1984, p. 38.

25. G. L. Chavunduka, *Traditional Healers and the Shona Patient*, Gwelo: Mambo Press, 1978, pp. 27–8.

26. 'Treatment Charge Sheet for Dr R. Vongo Traditional Healer', Lusaka, Zambia. Authors' own collection.

27. Allan Anderson, 'Pentecostal pneumatology and African power concepts: continuity or change?', *Missionalia*, 1 (1991), p. 69.

28. Ter Haar, *Halfway to Paradise*, p. 53.

29. Cf. Magesa, *African Religion*; Ogbu U. Kalu, *Power, Poverty and Prayer: The challenges of poverty and pluralism in Africa, 1960–1996*, Frankfurt/M: Peter Lang, 2000.

30. Anderson, 'Pentecostal pneumatology and African power concepts', p. 67.

31. Schatzberg, *Political Legitimacy in Middle Africa*, pp. 38–40. See also below, chapter eight.

32. Cf. Ursula King, *Women and Spirituality: Voices of protest and promise*, London: Macmillan, 1989, notably ch. four.

33. See e.g. R. S. Rattray, *Ashanti*, Oxford University Press, 1923, ch. 16.

34. Christian Coulon and Odile Reveyrand, *L'Islam au féminin: Sokhna Magat Diop, cheikh de la confrérie mouride (Sénégal)*, Talence: Centre d'étude d'Afrique noire, 1990.

35. Abamfo O. Atiemo, 'Zetaheal Mission in Ghana: Christians and Muslims worshipping together?', *Exchange*, 32, 1 (2003), pp. 15–36.

36. Lewis, *Ecstatic Religion*, pp. 66–71. *Zar* and *sar* are alternative spellings.

37. Heike Behrend, *Alice Lakwena and the Holy Spirits: War in northern Uganda, 1986–97*, Oxford: James Currey, 1999.

38. Chapter two, pp. 43–4.

39. Kalu, *Power, Poverty and Prayer*, pp. 93–102.

40. Cf. Hackett, 'Revitalization in African Traditional Religion'.

41. Max Weber, *The Sociology of Religion*, Boston, MA: Beacon Press, 1964.

42. Dovlo, 'Religion and the politics of Fourth Republican elections in Ghana'.

43. Osofo Okomfo Damuah, *Miracle at the Shrine: Religious and revolutionary miracle in Ghana*, Accra: no publisher or date [1994], p. 99.

44. Ibid., p. 54.

45. Moyo, 'Religion in Africa', p. 317.

46. Warren L. D'Azevedo, 'Tribe and chiefdom on the Windward Coast', *Liberian Studies Journal*, XIV, 2 (1989), p. 102.

47. '…un être hors nature': Luc de Heusch, *Ecrits sur la royauté sacrée*, Edns. de l'Université de Bruxelles, 1987, p. 292.

48. Ibid., p. 290.

49. Joseph Tonda, 'La guerre dans le "Camp Nord" au Congo-Brazzaville: ethnicité et ethos de la consommation/consumation', *Politique africaine*, 72 (1998), pp. 54–6.

50. Stephen Ellis, 'Rumour and power in Togo', *Africa*, 63, 4 (1993), pp. 462–76.

51. Thomas Hobbes (ed. C. B. Macpherson), *Leviathan*, Harmondsworth: Penguin, 1968, p. 150.

52. Cf. Liisa H. Malkki, *Purity and Exile: Violence, memory, and national cosmology among Hutu refugees in Tanzania*, University of Chicago Press, 1995; Jean-François Bayart, Peter Geschiere and Francis Nyamnjoh, 'Autochtonie, démocratie et citoyenneté en Afrique', *Critique internationale*, 10 (2001), pp. 177–94.

53. Metena M'Nteba, 'Les Conférences Nationales africaines et la figure politique de l'évêque-président', *Zaïre-Afrique*, 276 (1993), pp. 361–72.

54. Personal communication by Hugo Hinfelaar, a White Father in Zambia.

55. Paul Gifford, *African Christianity: Its public role*, London: Hurst & Co., 1998.

56. Notably by Gifford, *The Christian Churches and the Democratisation of Africa*, esp. pp. 1–7.

57. Matthew Schoffeleers, 'Ritual healing and political acquiescence: the case of the Zionist churches in southern Africa', *Africa*, 61, 1 (1991), pp. 1–25.

58. Yvan Droz, 'Si Dieu veut…ou suppôts de Satan? Incertitudes, millénarisme et sorcellerie chez les migrants kikuyu', *Cahiers d'études africaines*, 145, XXXVII, 1 (1997), pp. 85–117.

59. Ter Haar, *Spirit of Africa*, p. 145.

60. Chapter four, pp. 81–2.

61. Cf. Mariane Ferme, 'La figure du chasseur et les chasseurs-miliciens dans le conflit sierra-léonais', *Politique africaine*, 82 (2001), pp. 119–32.

62. Ernest Pianim, *Ghana in Prophecy*, Kumasi: no publisher given, 1995.

63. Christopher Hill, *The English Bible and the Seventeenth-Century Revolution*, London: Allen Lane, 1993.

64. Max Weber, *The Protestant Ethic and the Spirit of Capitalism*, London: Routledge, 1992; R. H. Tawney, *Religion and the Rise of Capitalism: A historical study*, London: Penguin, 1975.

## *Chapter 6*   Wealth

1. Iyke Nathan Uzorma, *Occult Grand Master Now in Christ*, Benin City: private publication, 1994, pp. 96–7.

2. Ibid, pp. 126–7 and back cover. Interestingly, Lakshmi is the Hindu god of wealth. Cf. n. 27.

3. J. K. Galbraith, *Money: Whence it came, where it went*, Harmondsworth: Penguin Books, 1976, pp. 14–15.

4. Ibid., p. 15.

5. Joseph Schumpeter, *A History of Economic Analysis*, London: Routledge, 1986, pp. 317–22.

6. Hernando de Soto, *The Mystery of Capital: Why capitalism triumphs in the West and fails everywhere else*, New York: Basic Books, 2000, p. 43.

7. Ibid., p. 41.

8. Philippe Le Billon, 'The political economy of resource wars', in Jakkie Cilliers and Christian Dietrich (eds), *Angola's War Economy: The role of oil and diamonds*, Pretoria: Institute for Security Studies, 2000, p. 26.

9. Adam Smith (ed. Kathryn Sutherland), *The Wealth of Nations: A selected edition*, Oxford University Press, 1993.

10. James Buchan, *Frozen Desire: The meaning of money*, New York: Farrar, Straus and Giroux, 1997, p. 31.

11. Ibid.

12. *Timon of Athens*, act 4, scene 3, lines 28–38.

13. Karl Marx and Friedrich Engels, 'Manifesto of the Communist Party', in Lewis S. Feuer (ed), *Marx and Engels: Basic writings on politics and philosophy*, New York: Fontana, 1969, p. 52.

14. Buchan, *Frozen Desire*, p. 31.

15. Joseph Tonda, 'Capital sorcier et travail de Dieu', *Politique africaine*, 79 (2000), p. 56.

16. Quoted in Buchan, *Frozen Desire*, p. 32.

17. Mark Juergensmeyer, *Terror in the Mind of God: The global rise of religious violence*, Berkeley: University of California Press, 2000, p. 34.

18. Hugh Brody, *The Other Side of Eden: Hunter-gatherers, farmers and the shaping of the world*, London: Faber & Faber, 2001, p. 132.

19. Filip De Boeck, 'Domesticating diamonds and dollars: identity, expenditure and sharing in southwestern Zaire (1984–1997), *Development and Change*, 29, 4 (1998), pp. 777–810.

20. Ian Smillie, Lansana Gberie and Ralph Hazleton, 'The Heart of the Matter: Sierra Leone, diamonds and human security', Partnership Africa Canada, 2000: http://action.web.ca/home/pac/attach/Heart%20the%20Matter%20 complete.rtf

21. J. Richardson, *A New Malagasy-English Dictionary*, Farnborough: Gregg Int. Publishers, 1967, entry *vola*.

22. Quoted in Sharon E. Hutchinson, *Nuer Dilemmas: Coping with money, war and the state*, Berkeley: University of California Press, 1996, p. 56.

23. Ralph Austen, 'The moral economy of witchcraft: an essay in comparative history', in J. and J. Comaroff, *Modernity and its Malcontents*, pp. 92–5.

24. Igor Kopytoff, *The African Frontier: The reproduction of traditional African societies*, Bloomington: Indiana University Press, 1987, p. 46.

25. Cf. Joseph C. Miller, *Way of Death: Merchant capitalism and the Angolan slave trade, 1730–1830*, Madison: University of Wisconsin Press, 1988, esp. pp. 40–70.

26. Raombana (ed. Simon Ayache), *Histoires*, vol. I, Fianarantsoa: Ambozontany, 1980, p. 245; cf. Alan Rice, '"Who's eating whom?" The discourse of cannibalism in the literature of the Black Atlantic from Equiano's Travels to Toni Morrison's Beloved', *Research in African Literatures*, 29, 4 (1998), pp. 107–19.

27. Mammy Wata has also clearly acquired some attributes of Asian deities: see H. J. Drewal, 'Mami Wata shrines: exotica and the constitution of self', in M. J. Arnoldi, C. M. Geary and K. L. Hardin (eds), *African Material Culture*, Bloomington: Indiana University Press, 1996, pp. 308–33.

28. Daniel A. Offiong, *Witchcraft, Sorcery, Magic and Social Order among the Ibibio of Nigeria*, Enugu: Fourth Dimension, 1991, pp. 90–1. Cf. above chapter three, p. 52.

29. Florence Bernault and Joseph Tonda, 'Dynamiques de l'invisible en Afrique', *Politique africaine*, 79 (2000), p. 10.

30. 'Comme on le voit, dans le monde visible et invisible, la loi du travail et de la rétribution, est une réalité vivante': Bruno Hassim, *Les plus étonnantes révélations du monde des esprits malins*, Brazzaville: Edns. Ferlo, 1994, p. 16.

31. Cf. Jean and John L. Comaroff, 'Alien-nation: zombies, immigrants, and millennial capitalism', *CODESRIA Bulletin*, 3–4 (1999), pp. 17–28.

32. Jonathan Stadler, 'Witches and witch-hunters: witchcraft, generational relations and the life cycle in a Lowveld village', *African Studies*, 55, 1 (1996), p. 92; cf. Isak Niehaus, 'Witches of the Transvaal Lowveld and their familiars: conceptions of duality, power and desire', *Cahiers d'études africaines*, XXXV, 138–9,

(1995), pp. 533–4, and note 18. On whites as witches, see the quotations from Kaniaki and Mukendi in chapter three, p. 50.

33. Neil Whitehead and Sylvia Vidal (eds), *In Darkness and Secrecy: The anthropology of assault sorcery and witchcraft in Amazonia*, Durham, NC: Duke University Press, 2003.

34. Some examples are provided by Toulabor, 'Sacrifices humains'.

35. Campion-Vincent and Renard, *Légendes urbaines*, pp. 101–2.

36. T. David Williams, *Malawi: The politics of despair*, Ithaca, NY: Cornell University Press, 1978, pp. 252–3.

37. Reuters despatch, in the *Otago Daily Times* [Dunedin, New Zealand], 26 December 2002.

38. Cf. Ekpenyong E. Okon, 'The association of bloodmen (in old Calabar): a reinterpretation', *Africana Marburgensia*, 21, 2 (1988), pp. 51–62; Tekena Tamuno and Robin Horton, 'The changing position of secret societies and cults in modern Nigeria', *African Notes*, 5, 2 (1969), pp. 36–62.

39. Toyin Falola, 'Money and informal credit institutions in colonial Western Nigeria', in Jane Guyer (ed), *Money Matters: Instability, values and social payments in the modern history of West African communities*, London: James Currey, 1995, pp. 165–6.

40. Cf. Karin Barber, 'Money, self-realization and the person in Yorùbá texts', in Guyer (ed), *Money Matters*, pp. 205–24.

41. E.g. George Shepperson and Thomas Price, *Independent African: John Chilembe and the origins, setting and significance of the Nyasaland native rising of 1915*, Edinburgh University Press, 1958, pp. 9–10; Rosalind Shaw, 'The production of witchcraft/witchcraft as production: memory, modernity, and the slave trade in Sierra Leone', *American Ethnologist*, 24, 4 (1997), pp. 856–76; Peter Geschiere, 'Sorcellerie et modernité: retour sur une étrange complicité', *Politique africaine*, 79 (2000), pp. 21–6.

42. This was most quickly and acutely identified by novelists. Chinua Achebe, author of a string of novels containing a sharp critique of political corruption, also wrote a remarkable political pamphlet, *The Trouble with Nigeria*, Enugu: Fourth Dimension, 1983.

43. A formula attributed to General Ishiola Williams, chairman of Transparency International's Nigerian chapter.

44. Barber, 'Popular reactions', p. 438.

45. Andrew Apter, 'Atinga revisited: Yoruba witchcraft and the cocoa economy, 1950–1951', in J and J. Comaroff, *Modernity and Its Malcontents*, p. 119.

46. Offiong, *Witchcraft, Sorcery, Magic and Social Order among the Ibibio of Nigeria*, p. 52; see also J. Lorand Matory, 'Government by seduction: history and the tropes of "mounting" in Oyo-Yoruba religion', in J. and J. Comaroff, *Modernity and Its Malcontents*, p. 81.

47. Agwuncha Arthur Nwankwo, *Nigeria: The stolen billions*, Enugu: Fourth Dimension, 1999.

48. Penny Green, *Drug Couriers*, London: Howard League for Penal Reform, 1991, p. 5.

49. Observatoire géopolitique des drogues, *Les drogues en Afrique subsaharienne*, Paris: Karthala, 1998, p. 243.

50. 'Nigeria—the 419 Coalition Website', http://home.rica.net/alphae/419 coal/scamstat.htm. One of the few books on the subject is Charles Tive, *419 Scam: Exploits of the Nigerian con man*, Lagos: Chicha Favours, 2001.

51. Christopher Elliott, 'Nigerian scam cheats Britain out of billions', *Guardian Weekly*, 15 February 1998.

52. Sam Olukoya, 'Nigeria grapples with e-mail scams', BBC news, 23 April 2002: http://news.bbc.co.uk/hi/english/world/africa/newsid_1944000/1944801.stm

53. Achille Mbembe, 'An essay on the political imagination in wartime', *CODESRIA Bulletin*, 2–4 (2000), pp. 7–8 and 19, note 9; Rémy Bazenguissa-Ganga, 'The spread of political violence in Congo-Brazzaville', *African Affairs*, 98, 390 (1999), esp. p. 50.

54. Céline Moyroud and John Katunga, 'Coltan exploitation in the eastern Democratic Republic of Congo', in Jeremy Lind and Kathryn Sturman (eds), *Scarcity and Surfeit: The ecology of Africa's conflicts*, Pretoria: Institute for Security Studies, 2002, pp. 159–85.

55. The figure is taken from *West Africa* magazine, 12 August 2002, quoted in Douglas Rimmer, 'Learning about economic development from Africa', *African Affairs*, 102, 408 (2003), p. 488.

56. Georges Duby, *L'Europe au Moyen-Age*, Paris: Flammarion, 1984, p. 107.

57. Comi Toulabor, 'Bellissima basilica yamoussoukroensis: l'entéléchie du "miracle ivoirien"', *L'Année africaine* (1990–1), Talence: Centre d'étude d'Afrique noire, 1991, pp. 191–213.

58. A. G. Hopkins, *An Economic History of West Africa*, London: Longman, 1973.

59. Tanella Boni, 'La dictature de l'argent', *Sentiers* [Abidjan], 3 (2000), pp. 9–11; bargaining is analysed by Georg Simmel, *The Philosophy of Money*, London: Routledge, 1990, pp. 94–101.

60. Béatrice Hibou (ed), *La privatisation des Etats*, Paris: Karthala, 1999.

61. Cf. Weber's classic, *The Protestant Ethic and the Spirit of Capitalism*.

62. Buchan, *Frozen Desire*, pp. 138–9.

63. Jean-François Bayart (ed), *La réinvention du capitalisme*, Paris: Karthala, 1994.

64. Michael Rowlands, 'Accumulation and the cultural politics of identity in the Grassfields', in Peter Geschiere and Piet Konings (eds), *Itinéraires d'accumulation au Cameroun*, Paris: Karthala, 1993, pp. 71–97.

65. Buchan, *Frozen Desire*, p. 114.

66. Ibid, p. 112.

67. Ibid, p. 61.

68. Ibid, p. 113.

69. Jean-François Bayart, Stephen Ellis and Béatrice Hibou, *The Criminalisation of the State in Africa*, Oxford: James Currey, 1999.

70. Chester Crocker, quoted in Constance J. Freeman, 'The three economies of Africa', *African Security Review*, 9, 4 (2000), p. 76.

71. Reported in the *New York Times*, 14 June 2002, quoted in Crawford Young, 'The end of the post-colonial state in Africa? Reflections on changing African political dynamics', *African Affairs*, 103, 410 (2004), p. 40.

72. Quoted in Rimmer, 'Learning about economic development', p. 491.

73. '[ils] considèrent les jeux comme des "tontines" auxquelles chacun participe pour avoir accès à ce que l'on pourrait qualifier de "ticket d'attente à la chance"', Oumarou Diembeydou, director of the Nigerien national lottery, quoted in 'Loto, PMU, millionaire....qui gagne?', *L'Autre Afrique*, 38, 18 Feb. 1998, p. 13.

74. Buchan, *Frozen Desire*, p. 113.

75. On deception and forgery in African economies, see Béatrice Hibou, 'The "social capital" of the state as an agent of deception, or the ruses of economic intelligence', in Bayart, Ellis and Hibou, *The Criminalisation of the State in Africa*, esp. pp. 102–13.

76. On the *sapeurs*, Justin-Daniel Gandoulou, *Au coeur de la Sape: moeurs et aventures des Congolais à Paris*, Paris: L'Harmattan, 1984; on the beaux, Buchan, *Frozen Desire*, pp. 116–9.

77. Dominique Malaquais, 'Arts de feyre au Cameroun', *Politique africaine*, 82 (2001), pp. 101–18.

78. Jean-Pierre Tuquoi, 'L'affaire des faux dinars de Bahreïn', *Le Monde*, 23 June 1999, p. 16.

79. Graham Furniss, 'The Hausa contractor: the image of an entrepreneur', in Stephen Ellis and Yves-A. Fauré (eds), *Entreprises et entrepreneurs africains*, Paris: Karthala, 1995, pp. 229–38.

80. Peter Truell and Larry Gurwin, *False Profits: The inside story of BCCI, the world's most corrupt financial empire*, Boston: Houghton Mifflin, 1992; on BCCI frauds in Africa, see *The BCCI Affair: A report to the Committee on Foreign Relations, United States Senate, by Senator John Kerry and Senator Hank Brown*, Washington, DC: US Government Printing Office, 1993, pp. 93–122.

81. Hibou, 'The "social capital" of the state as an agent of deception', pp. 104–5.

82. Ineke van Kessel, personal communication.

83. Cheikh Anta Babou, 'Brotherhood solidarity, education and migration: the role of the *Dahiras* among the Murid muslim community of New York', *African Affairs*, 101, 403 (2002), pp. 151–70.

84. http://www.winners-chapel.com

85. 'Nigeria: beware false profits', *Africa Confidential*, 43, 14 (12 July 2002), pp. 1–3.

86. Ruth Marshall-Fratani, 'Prospérité miraculeuse: les pasteurs pentecôtistes et l'argent de Dieu au Nigéria', *Politique africaine*, 82 (2001), pp. 24–7.

87. Joseph Tonda, 'Capital sorcier et travail de Dieu', p. 57.

88. Larbi, *Pentecostalism*, p. 313. The author is an ordained minister of the International Central Gospel Church (ICGC), one of the largest charismatic churches in Ghana. He is vice-chancellor of Central University College and

executive director of the Centre for Pentecostal and Charismatic Studies, both of which are initiatives of the ICGC.

89. Ibid.; see also Kalu, *Power, Poverty and Prayer.*

90. E.g. Birgit Meyer, 'Commodities and the power of prayer: pentecostalist attitudes towards consumption in contemporary Ghana', *Development and Change*, 29, 4 (1998), pp. 751–66.

91. The starting-point for much recent literature on these lines is Michael Taussig, *The Devil and Commodity Fetishism in South America*, Chapel Hill, NC: University of North Carolina Press, 1980, reflecting a Marxist interpretation in which religion is considered a form of false consciousness. Taussig writes on page ix: 'The devil is a stunningly apt symbol of the alienation experienced by peasants as they enter the ranks of the proletariat, and it is largely in terms of that experience that I have cast my interpretation'. In African studies, a basic reference for theorists of this school is J. and J. Comaroff, *Modernity and its Malcontents.*

92. Marshall-Fratani, 'Prospérité miraculeuse', pp. 41–4; Tonda, 'Capital sorcier et travail de Dieu', pp. 48–65.

93. Jean and John L. Comaroff, 'Privatizing the millenium: new protestant ethics and the spirits of capitalism in Africa, and elsewhere', *Afrika Spectrum*, 35, 3 (2000), pp. 297 and 304. On the notion of 'occult economies' see J. and J. Comaroff, 'Occult economies and the violence of abstraction: notes from the South African postcolony', *American Ethnologist*, 26, 2 (1999), pp. 279–303.

94. Jean and John L. Comaroff (eds), *Millennial Capitalism and the Culture of Neoliberalism*, Durham, NC: Duke University Press, 2001, p. 23.

*Chapter 7*   Morality

1. BBC World Service, 10 December 1998.

2. Chapter five, pp. 103–4.

3. One of many relevant works by African theologians is J. N. K. Mugambi and A. Nasimiyu-Wasike (eds), *Moral and Ethical Issues in African Christianity: Exploratory essays in moral theology*, Nairobi: Acton Publishers, 1999.

4. Kwasi Wiredu, 'Custom and morality: a comparative analysis of some African and Western conceptions of morals', in Albert G. Mosley (ed), *African Philosophy: Selected readings*, Englewood Cliffs, NJ: Prentice-Hall Inc., 1995, pp. 403–4.

5. Kwasi Wiredu, 'Modes of thought in African philosophy', in John Middleton (ed-in-chief), *Encyclopedia of Africa South of the Sahara*, New York: Charles Scribner's Sons, 1997, vol. 3, p. 171.

6. Polycarp Ikuenobe, 'Moral thought in African cultures? A metaphilosophical question', *African Philosophy*, 12, 2 (1999), p. 110.

7. Walter Bagehot, 'The danger of lending to semi-civilised countries', in Norman St John Stevas (ed), *The Collected Works of Walter Bagehot*, vol. 10, London: The Economist, 1978, p. 419.

8. Ibid., p. 421.

9. Cf. Peter Cain and A. G. Hopkins, *British Imperialism: Innovation and expansion, 1688–1914*, London: Longman, 1993, pp. 351–96.

10. Bayart et al., *The Criminalisation of the State in Africa*, pp. 19–25.

11. These remarks are based on, among others, Eric Wolf, *Europe and the People without History*, Berkeley, CA: University of California Press, 1982; Sally Falk Moore, 'Certainties undone: Fifty turbulent years of legal anthropology, 1949–1999', *Journal of the Royal Anthropological Institute*, 7 (2001), pp. 95–116, and esp. p. 98; and Barbara Oomen, *Chiefs in South Africa*, Oxford: James Currey (forthcoming). H. F. Morris and James S. Read, *Indirect Rule and the Search for Justice: Essays in East African legal history*, Oxford University Press, 1972, pp. 167–212, emphasise rather more the flexibility of customary law in colonial times.

12. Cf. chapter one.

13. An expression borrowed from Oomen, *Chiefs in South Africa*.

14. E.g. Basil Davidson, *Black Man's Burden: The curse of the nation-state in Africa*, London: James Currey, 1992.

15. Cf. V. Y. Mudimbe, *The Invention of Africa: Gnosis, philosophy, and the order of knowledge*, Bloomington: Indiana University Press, 1988.

16. Mahmood Mamdani, *Citizen and Subject: Contemporary Africa and the legacy of late colonialism*, Princeton University Press, 1996.

17. Jean-François Bayart, *The State in Africa: The politics of the belly*, London: Longman, 1993, pp. 150–79.

18. Cf. Joshua N. Kudadjie, *Moral Renewal in Ghana: Ideals, realities and possibilities*, Accra: Asempa Publishers, 1995.

19. Philip Ostien, 'Ten good things about the implementation of Shari'a in some states of northern Nigeria', *Swedish Missiological Themes*, 90, 2 (2002), pp. 163–74.

20. Cf. Wyatt MacGaffey, preface to Geschiere, *The Modernity of Witchcraft*.

21. E. E. Evans-Pritchard, *Witchcraft, Oracles and Magic among the Azande*, Oxford: Clarendon Press, 1937, pp. 9–10.

22. S. T. Kgatla et al., *Crossing Witchcraft Barriers in South Africa. Exploring Witchcraft Accusations: Causes and solutions*, Utrecht University, 2003, p. 5.

23. Notably J. and J. Comaroff, *Modernity and its Malcontents*; and Geschiere, *The Modernity of Witchcraft*.

24. Cyprian Fisiy, 'Containing occult practices: witchcraft trials in Cameroon', *African Studies Review*, 41, 3 (1998), pp. 143–63.

25. La Fontaine, *Speak of the Devil*, p. 14.

26. J. Arch Getty and Oleg V. Naumov, *The Road to Terror: Stalin and the self-destruction of the Bolsheviks, 1932–1939*, New Haven, CT: Yale University Press, 1999, p. 7.

27. La Fontaine, *Speak of the Devil*.

28. *Algemeen Dagblad*, 23 June 2001.

29. Willy De Craemer, Jan Vansina and Renée Fox, 'Religious movements in central Africa: a theoretical study,' *Comparative Studies in Society and History*, 18, 4 (1976), pp. 458–75.

30. Cf. Stephen Ellis, 'Witch-hunting in central Madagascar, 1828–1861', *Past and Present*, 175 (2002), pp. 90–123.

31. The following is based largely on Kgatla et al, *Crossing Witchcraft Barriers*. See also especially Isak Niehaus, with Eliazaar Mohlala and Kally Shokane, *Witchcraft, Power and Politics: Exploring the occult in the South African Lowveld*, London: Pluto Press, 2001.

32. Fisiy, 'Containing occult practices'.

33. Robin Briggs, *Witches and Neighbours: The social and cultural context of European witchcraft*, London: Fontana, 1996, p. 8. Brian P. Levack, *The Witch-Hunt in Early Modern Europe*, London: Longman, 1995, pp. 21–6, gives a slightly higher estimate of numbers executed.

34. Kgatla et al., *Crossing Witchcraft Barriers*, p. 28; Fisiy, 'Containing occult practices'.

35. This is argued, for example, by John Hund in 'African witchcraft and Western law', *African Legal Studies*, II (2001), pp. 22–60. This is a special issue, entitled *Witchcraft Violence and the Law*, which discusses the situation in South Africa, including the findings and recommendations of the Ralushai Commission (1995), whose members take a similar culturalist position. For a critical overview in the same issue, see Isak Niehaus, 'Witchcraft in the new South Africa', pp. 116–48.

36. Kgatla et al., *Crossing Witchcraft Barriers*, p. 23. See also W. E. A. van Beek, 'A model of escalation of witchcraft accusations', in Ter Haar, *Imagining Evil.*

37. Frederick C. Schaffer, *Democracy in Translation: Understanding politics in an unfamiliar culture*, Ithaca, NY: Cornell University Press, 1998, p. 23; Anastase Nzeza Bilakila, 'The Kinshasa "bargain"', in Theodore Trefon (ed), *Political Constraints and Social Invention in Kinshasa* (forthcoming).

38. Yengo, 'Guerre des légitimités et démocide convenu', p. 91.

39. Cf. Alan Bullock and Oliver Stallybrass (eds), *The Fontana Dictionary of Modern Thought*, London: Fontana, 1977, p. 490.

40. F. Nietzsche, *The Will to Power*, quoted in *The Penguin Dictionary of Political Quotations*, Harmondsworth: Penguin, 1986, p. 122.

41. K. Moses Nagbe, 'Liberia: a land of the magic God', *Daily Observer* [Monrovia], 10, 76 (12 June 1990).

42. Kayode Soyinka, *Diplomatic Baggage. MOSSAD and Nigeria: The Dikko story*, Lagos: Newswatch Books, 1994, p. 241.

43. Ken Flower, *Serving Secretly: An intelligence chief on record. Rhodesia into Zimbabwe, 1964–1981*, London: John Murray, 1987, p. 156.

44. Hassim, *Les plus étonnantes révélations du monde des esprits malins*, p. 34. 'L'Univers comporte plusieurs esprits de degré et de catégorie différents. Il existe donc des esprits supérieurs infernaux, qui gouvernent le monde des esprits, depuis les espaces inter-sidéraux. Parmi ces grands esprits, on peut citer l'empereur Lucifer, le prince des ténèbres Asmode…et un secrétaire-général Lucifuge Rofocale'.

45. S. N. I. Okeke, *Satanic Ministers: The ministries of Lucifer*, Isolo, Lagos: Emabal Company, 1991, p. 4.

46. Interview by Stephen Ellis, Cotonou, August 1993.
47. The following is from Arthur F. Kulah, *Theological Education in Liberia: Problems and opportunities*, Lithonia, GA: SCP/Third World Literature Publishing House, 1994, pp. 76–7.
48. Ibid., p. 77.
49. Emmanuel Dolo, *Democracy Versus Dictatorship: The quest for freedom and justice in Africa's oldest republic, Liberia*, Lanham, MD: University Press of America, 1996, p. 12.
50. The following argument is derived from John Lonsdale in his essay 'The moral economy of Mau Mau: wealth, poverty and civic virtue in Kikuyu political thought', in Bruce Berman and John Lonsdale, *Unhappy Valley: Conflict in Kenya and Africa*, London: James Currey, 1992, vol. 2, pp. 315–504. A summary of his arguments can be found in John Lonsdale, 'Ethnicité morale et tribalisme politique', *Politique africaine*, 69 (1996), pp. 98–115.
51. Centre for Law and Research International (CLARION), 'The anatomy of corruption: legal, political and socio-economic perspectives', Nairobi: Clarion research monograph no. 7, 1994, esp. p. 233.
52. Schatzberg, *Political Legitimacy in Middle Africa*, esp. pp. 145–73.
53. The following paragraph partly draws on papers and discussions at the Association pour le développement (APAD) conference held in Leiden, May 2002, devoted to the study of corruption.
54. E.g. Magesa, *African Religion*; Kudadjie, *Moral Renewal in Ghana*; Kwame Gyekye, *Political Corruption: A philosophical inquiry into a moral problem*, Accra: Sankofa Publishing, 1997.
55. Gerrie ter Haar, *Rats, Cockroaches and People Like Us: Views of humanity and human rights*, The Hague: Institute of Social Studies, 2000, p. 13.
56. Bayart, Geschiere and Nyamnjoh, 'Autochtonie, démocratie et citoyenneté en Afrique'.

*Chapter 8*  Transformations

1. 'The lion and the unicorn: socialism and the English genius', in Sonia Orwell and Ian Angus (eds), *The Collected Essays, Journalism and Letters of George Orwell*, Harmondsworth: Penguin, 1970, vol. 2, p. 76.
2. John Ralston Saul, *The Unconscious Civilization*, New York: The Free Press, 1997, esp. p. 98.
3. The phrase 'government of the soul' was coined by Pope Gregory the Great, reflecting one of the central preoccupations of an earlier period of European history. Peter Brown, *The Rise of Western Christendom: Triumph and diversity AD 200–1000*, Oxford: Blackwell, 1996, p. 139.
4. See chapter one, p. 21–4.
5. See above, chapter three, but also e.g. pp. 116–7.
6. Karl Popper, *The Poverty of Historicism*, London and New York: Ark Paperbacks, 1986, p. 33.

7. '...permettent à des individus d'effectuer, par eux-mêmes, un certain nombre d'opérations sur leur corps, leur âme, leur pensée, leurs conduites, et ce de manière à produire en eux une transformation, une modification et atteindre un certain état de perfection, de bonheur, de pureté, de pouvoir surnaturel'. Quoted in Joseph Tonda, 'Economie des miracles et dynamiques de "subjectivation/civilisation" en Afrique centrale', *Politique africaine*, 87 (2002), p. 22.

8. Cf. Robert P. Weller, 'Living at the edge: religion, capitalism, and the end of the nation-state in Taiwan', in J. and J. Comaroff, *Millennial Capitalism*, esp. pp. 220–32.

9. Behrend, *Alice Lakwena and the Holy Spirits*. Cf. also above chapter five, p. 99.

10. Chapter six, esp. pp. 116–17.

11. See Popper, *The Poverty of Historicism*, pp. 42–5.

12. Rita Abrahamsen, 'African studies and the postcolonial challenge', *African Affairs*, 102, 407 (2003), p. 199, summarising the work of Michel Foucault and others.

13. See note 7.

14. Michel Foucault, *Dits et écrits, 1954–1988*, Paris: Gallimard, 1994, vol. 4, p. 785.

15. Loïc Wacquant, 'From slavery to mass incarceration: rethinking the "race question" in the US', *New Left Review*, second series, 13 (2002), pp. 41–60.

16. Karl Polanyi, *The Great Transformation*, New York: Octagon Books, 1975.

17. Bernard Crick, *In Defence of Politics*, Harmondsworth: Penguin, 1964, p. 19.

18. Charlotte Beradt, *The Third Reich of Dreams: The nightmares of a nation, 1933–1939*, Wellingborough: Aquarian Press, 1985.

19. Chapter two, p. 33.

20. Zbigniew Brzezinski, *Out of Control: Global turmoil on the eve of the twenty-first century*, New York: Charles Scribner's Sons, 1993, p. 17.

21. Michael Burleigh, *The Third Reich: A new history*, New York: Hill and Wang, 2000, pp. 6–14. Emilio Gentile, *The Sacralization of Politics in Fascist Italy*, Cambridge, MA: Harvard University Press, 1996, notes how many nationalist movements have co-opted religious ideas and symbols.

22. Cf. Claude Ake, *Democracy and Development in Africa*, Washington, DC: Brookings Institution Press, 1996.

23. Ter Haar and Busuttil, *The Freedom to do God's Will*.

24. See e.g. chapter five, pp. 95–9., and chapter six, pp. 123–8.

25. Cf. Jean-François Bayart, 'Finishing with the idea of the Third World: the concept of the political trajectory', in James Manor (ed), *Rethinking Third World Politics*, London: Longman, 1991, pp. 51–71.

26. The classic source on this is Arnold van Gennep, *The Rites of Passage*, University of Chicago Press, 1975 (first published in French in 1908). The concept of liminality is from Victor Turner, *The Ritual Process: Structure and anti-structure*, Harmondsworth: Penguin, 1969.

27. Mary Moran, 'Warriors or soldiers? Masculinity and ritual transvestism in the Liberian civil war', in Constance R. Sutton (ed), *Feminism, Nationalism and Mili-*

*tarism*, Arlington, VA: Association for Feminist Anthropology/American Anthropological Association, 1995, pp. 73–88.

28. It is interesting to note that *persona* is the Latin name for the mask used by actors in the Roman theatre.

29. The following is drawn from Elias Canetti, *Crowds and Power*, Harmoundsworth: Penguin, 1987, pp. 440–2.

30. Ibid., pp. 442–3. Italics are in the original.

31. See chapter three, p. 59.

*Chapter 9*　Histories

1. Dipesh Chakrabarty, *Provincializing Europe: Postcolonial thought and historical difference*, Princeton University Press, 2000, p. 16.

2. Cf. chapter six, pp. 115–6.

3. Bruce Kapferer, 'Introduction: outside all reason—magic, sorcery and epistemology in anthropology', *Social Analysis*, 46, 3 (2002), p. 20.

4. Ibid., pp. 1–30.

5. Chakrabarty, *Provincializing Europe*.

6. Jean-François Bayart, 'Africa in the world: a history of extraversion', *African Affairs*, 99, 395 (2000), pp. 217–67.

7. Christopher Clapham, 'Afrique dans les relations internationales: quelles évolutions depuis la guerre froide?', *Marchés tropicaux et méditerranéens*, 3000, 9 May 2003, p. 950. The quotation is taken from the original paper in English, kindly supplied by the author.

8. See Kwame Bediako, *Christianity in Africa: The renewal of a non-Western religion*, Edinburgh University Press, 1995, esp. pp. 252–67, and also the foreword by Andrew Walls.

9. Rohan Gunaratna, *Inside Al Qaeda: Global network of terror*, London: Hurst & Co., 2002, p. 151.

10. Mary Douglas, 'The effects of modernization on religious change', *Daedalus*, 111, (1982), pp. 1–21.

11. See e.g. references in chapter six, pp. 138–9.

12. Frederick Cooper, 'What is the concept of globalization good for? An African historian's perspective', *African Affairs*, 100, 399 (2001), pp. 189–213.

13. K. N. Chaudhuri, *Trade and Civilisation in the Indian Ocean: An economic history from the rise of Islam to 1750*, Cambridge University Press, 1985.

14. Concepts applied to Africa notably in recent works by Jean and John Comaroff: see e.g. *Millennial Capitalism and the Culture of Neoliberalism*.

15. Patrick Chabal and Jean-Pascal Daloz, *Africa Works: Disorder as a political instrument*, Oxford: James Currey, 1999, esp. p. 63.

16. Steven Feierman, 'African histories and the dissolution of world history', in R. H. Bates, V. Y. Mudimbe and Jean O'Barr (eds), *Africa and the Disciplines: The contributions of research in Africa to the social sciences and humanities*, University of Chicago Press, 1993, pp. 178–9.

17. Cf. Chakrabarty, *Provincializing Europe*, esp. the introduction.

18. Cf. Fred W. Riggs, 'Indigenous concepts: a problem for social and information science', *International Social Science Journal*, 114 (1987), pp. 607–17.

19. For a discussion of postcolonial theory with particular bearing on Africa, see Abrahamsen, 'African studies and the postcolonial challenge'.

20. E.g. Richard Werbner, 'Introduction: multiple identities, plural arenas', in Richard Werbner and Terence Ranger (eds), *Postcolonial Identities in Africa*, London: Zed Books, 1996, esp. pp. 4–5.

21. See e.g. the remarks by Tony Judt, 'America and the world', *New York Review of Books*, L, 6 (10 April 2003), p. 28; and Chakrabarty, *Provincializing Europe*, p. 7.

22. Kwame Anthony Appiah, 'Is the post- in postmodernism the post- in postcolonial?', in Padmini Mongia (ed), *Contemporary Postcolonial Theory: A reader*, London: Edward Arnold, 1996, p. 59.

23. Paul Tiyambe Zeleza, 'Fictions of the postcolonial: a review article', *CODESRIA Bulletin*, 2 (1997), p. 17.

24. Gerard Kreijen, 'The transformation of sovereignty and African independence: no shortcuts to statehood', in Gerard Kreijen et al. (eds), *State, Sovereignty and International Governance*, Oxford University Press, 2002, pp. 45–107.

25. Robert H. Jackson, *Quasi-states: Sovereignty, international relations and the third world*, Cambridge University Press, 1991.

26. Figures taken from *UN Statistical Yearbook*, 45th edition, New York, 2001, p. 12; *African Development Indicators 2003*, p. 312.

27. The phrase is by Pierre Bourdieu, quoted in Juergensmeyer, *Terror in the Mind of God*, p. 225.

28. '...c'est signe qu'ils veulent entrer dans le jeu du Monde, qui est en grande partie le jeu de l'Occident'. Henri Brunschwig, 'Histoire, passé et frustration en Afrique noire', *Annales*, 17, 5 (1962), p. 875.

29. The following is based on Stephen Ellis, 'Writing histories of contemporary Africa', *Journal of African History*, 43 (2002), pp. 24–6.

30. Cf. R. G. Collingwood, *The Idea of History*, Oxford: Clarendon Press, 1993, pp. 24–5.

31. For a survey of relevant literature, see Rosalind Shaw, *Memories of the Slave Trade: Ritual and the historical imagination in Sierra Leone*, University of Chicago Press, 2002, pp. 1–24.

32. '...de calmer les morts qui hantent encore le présent, et à leur offrir des tombeaux scriptuaires': quoted in Filip De Boeck, 'Zombificatie en de postkolonie: een opstel over geschiedschrijving, herinnering en dood in Congo-Kinshasa', Académie des sciences d'outremer, *Bulletin des séances* [Brussels], 44, 3 (1998), p. 287.

33. Chapter five.

34. De Boeck, 'Zombificatie en de postkolonie', pp. 285–304.

35. Sousa Jamba, 'The idea of Angola', *Times Literary Supplement*, 8 June 2001, p. 12.

36. Nandy, *The Intimate Enemy*, p. 59.

37. H. Hubert and M. Mauss, 'Etude sommaire de la représentation du temps dans la religion et la magie', in *Mélanges d'histoire des religions*, Paris: Félix Alcan, 1929, esp. pp. 195–7.

38. Jacob Olupona, 'Introduction', in *African Spirituality*, pp. xvii–xviii.

39. Kimmerle, *Mazungumzo*, pp. 80–4.

40. See chapters two, pp. 42, 45–7, and five, pp. 105, 109, 112. The notion of the world as a vast conspiracy is also commented on by Achille Mbembe in 'A propos des écritures africaines de soi', *Politique africaine*, 77 (2000), pp. 25–6. The same author has written other interesting essays on historiography and related matters. See e.g. 'At the edge of the world: boundaries, territoriality and sovereignty in Africa', *Public Culture*, 12, 1 (2000), pp. 259–84.

41. Daniel Chirot, *Modern Tyrants: The power and prevalence of evil in our age*, New York: The Free Press, 1994, p. 411.

42. Cf. Appiah, 'Is the post- in postmodernism the post- in postcolonial?'

43. Frank Furedi, 'History has not yet begun', *Spiked Politics* (15 May 2002), http://www.spiked-online.com/Articles/00000006D8EE.htm

44. E.g. Bobbitt, *The Sword of Achilles*, p. 10, who notes a tendency towards 'presentism' in government.

45. Cf. Wolf, *Europe and the People Without History*.

46. Talal Asad, *Genealogies of Religion: Discipline and reasons of power in Christianity and Islam*, Baltimore, MD: Johns Hopkins University Press, 1993, introduction and esp. pp. 18–21.

47. Ellis, 'Writing histories of contemporary Africa'.

48. Cf. Eric Hobsbawm, *Age of Extremes: The short twentieth century, 1914–1991*, London: Michael Joseph, 1994, p. 6.

49. William H. McNeill, 'The changing shape of world history', in Philip Pomper, Richard H. Elphick and Richard T. Vann (eds), *World History: Ideologies, structures and identities*, Oxford: Blackwell, 1998, p. 39.

50. Fabian, *Moments of Freedom*, p. 73.

51. Larry Minear, Colin Scott and Thomas Weiss, *The News Media, Civil War, and Humanitarian Action*, Boulder, CO: Lynne Rienner, 1996, esp. pp. 47–50.

52. Chakrabarty, *Provincializing Europe*, p. 251.

53. Chapter five, p. 108.

54. Asad, *Genealogies of Religion*, pp. 27–54.

55. Chapter five, p. 94.

56. Ogbu Kalu, 'Harsh flutes: the religious dimension of the legitimacy crisis in Nigeria, 1993–1998', in Toyin Falola (ed), *Nigeria in the Twentieth Century*, Durham, NC: Carolina Academic Press, 2002, pp. 667–85.

57. Chapter seven, pp. 152–4.

58. The Sudanese Muslim scholar and human rights activist Abdullahi Ahmed An-Na'im is a leading proponent of the view that there is no inherent incompatibility between Islam and universal human rights. Cf. 'Islamic fundamentalism and social change: neither the "end of history" nor a "clash of civilizations"', in Ter Haar and Busuttil, *The Freedom to do God's Will*, pp. 25–48.

59. Charles Gore and David Pratten, 'The politics of plunder: the rhetorics of order and disorder in southern Nigeria', *African Affairs*, 102, 407 (2003), pp. 211–40. The revival of secret societies in a non-traditional setting in Nigeria was noted as long ago as 1969 by Tamuno and Horton, 'The changing position of secret societies'. On the use of secret society traditions in forming modern militias in Sierra Leone, see Ferme, 'La figure du chasseur et les chasseurs-miliciens'.

60. E.g. Piet Human, *Yenza: A blueprint for transformation*, Cape Town: Oxford University Press, 1998.

61. Chapters three and four.

62. Cf. Robert Cooper, 'The post-modern state', in Mark Leonard (ed), *Re-Ordering the World: The long-term implications of 11 September*, London: Foreign Policy Centre, 2002, pp. 11–20.

63. For specific examples, see Hibou, 'The "social capital" of the state', pp. 69–113.

64. Some figures and observations on this are provided by Rimmer, 'Learning about economic development from Africa', pp. 487–8.

65. For a widely-accepted definition of culture, see Clifford Geertz, *The Interpretation of Cultures: Selected essays*, New York: Basic Books, 1973, p. 89.

66. Samuel Huntington, *The Clash of Civilizations and the Remaking of the World Order*, New York: Simon & Schuster, 1996.

67. The following two paragraphs closely resemble Stephen Ellis, 'Violence and history: a response to Thandika Mkandawire', *Journal of Modern African Studies*, 41, 3 (2003), p. 471.

68. On the search for new genetic material, see Calestous Juma, *The Gene Hunters: Biotechnology and the scramble for seeds*, London: Zed Books, 1989. We are indebted to Arie Rip for insights derived from his paper 'Indigenous knowledge and Western science—in practice', presented at the Demarcation Socialized conference, Cardiff, 2000.

69. Ter Haar, *Halfway to Paradise*, pp. 1–3.

# BIBLIOGRAPHY

In addition to listing works cited in the footnotes to the text, this bibliography includes a section entitled 'Religious Tracts and Pamphlets' listing some works not cited in the footnotes, but which have been useful sources for this book. They are recommended for any reader wanting to know more about popular views of religion.

## BOOKS AND ARTICLES

Abrahamsen, Rita, 'African studies and the postcolonial challenge', *African Affairs*, 102, 407 (2003), pp. 189–210.

Achebe, Chinua, *The Trouble with Nigeria*. Enugu: Fourth Dimension, 1983.

Agozino, Biko, and Unyierie Idem, *Nigeria: Democratising a militarised civil society*. Occasional Paper no. 5, London: Centre for Democracy and Development, 2001.

Ake, Claude, 'What is the problem of ethnicity in Africa?', *Transformation*, 22 (1993), pp. 1–14.

———, *Democracy and Development in Africa*. Washington, DC: Brookings Institution Press, 1996.

Althabe, Gérard, *Oppression et libération dans l'imaginaire: les communautés villageoises de la côte orientale de Madagascar*. Paris: Maspero, 1969.

Amadiume, Ife, *Male Daughters, Female Husbands: Gender and sex in an African society*. London: Zed Press, 1987.

An-Na'im, Abdullahi Ahmed, 'Islamic fundamentalism and social change: neither the "end of history" nor a "clash of civilizations"', in Ter Haar and Busuttil, *The Freedom to do God's Will*, pp. 25–48.

Anderson, Allan, 'Pentecostal pneumatology and African power concepts: continuity or change?', *Missionalia*, 1 (1991), pp. 65–74.

Appiah, Kwame Anthony, *In My Father's House: Africa in the philosophy of culture*. New York: Oxford University Press, 1992.

———, 'Is the post- in postmodernism the post- in postcolonial?', in Padmini Mongia (ed), *Contemporary Postcolonial Theory: A reader*, London: Edward Arnold, 1996, pp. 55–71 (essay originally published 1991).

Apter, Andrew, 'Atinga revisited: Yoruba witchcraft and the cocoa economy, 1950–1951', in J. and J. Comaroff, *Modernity and its Malcontents*, pp. 111–28.

Asad, Talal, *Genealogies of Religion: Discipline and reasons of power in Christianity and Islam*. Baltimore, MD: Johns Hopkins University Press, 1993.

Astill, James, '"Meditation is the path to peace"', *Weekly Mail and Guardian*, 28 Sept.–4 Oct. 2001, p. 30.

Atiemo, Abamfo O., 'Zetaheal Mission in Ghana: Christians and Muslims worshipping together?', *Exchange*, 32, 1 (2003), pp. 15–36.

Austen, Ralph, 'The moral economy of witchcraft: an essay in comparative history', in J. and J. Comaroff, *Modernity and its Malcontents*, pp. 89–110.

Austin, J. L., *How to Do Things with Words*. Oxford: Clarendon Press, 1976 (first published 1962).

Babou, Cheikh Anta, 'Brotherhood solidarity, education and migration: the role of the *Dahiras* among the Murid Muslim community of New York', *African Affairs*, 101, 403 (2002), pp. 151–70.

Bagehot, Walter, 'The danger of lending to semi-civilized countries', in Norman St John Stevas (ed), *The Collected Works of Walter Bagehot*, vol. 10, London: The Economist, 1978 (original essay dated 23 Nov. 1867).

Balandier, Georges, 'Messianism and nationalism in Black Africa', in Pierre L. van den Berghe (ed), *Africa: Social problems of change and conflict*, San Francisco: Chandler Publishing, 1965, pp. 443–60 (first published in French 1953).

Barber, Karin, 'Popular reactions to the petro-naira', *Journal of Modern African Studies*, 20, 3 (1982), pp. 431–50.

———, 'Money, self-realization and the person in Yorùbá texts', in Jane Guyer, *Money Matters*, pp. 205–24.

Barrett, David B., 'A survey of the twentieth-century pentecostal/charismatic renewal in the Holy Spirit, with its goal of world evangelization', in S. M. Burgess, G. B. McGee & P. H. Alexander (eds), *Dictionary of Pentecostal and Charismatic Movements*, Grand Rapids, MI: Zondervan Publishing House, 1988, pp. 810–30.

———, and Todd M. Johnson, 'Annual statistical table on global mission: 2002', *International Bulletin of Missionary Research*, 26, 1 (2002), pp. 22–3.

Bastian, Misty L., 'Married in the water: spirit kin and other afflictions of modernity in southeastern Nigeria', *Journal of Religion in Africa*, 27, 2 (1997), pp. 116–34.

Baulin, Jacques, *La politique intérieure d'Houphouët-Boigny*. Paris: Eurafor-press, 1982.

Bayart, Jean-François, 'Le politique par le bas en Afrique noire: questions de méthode', *Politique africaine*, 1 (1981), pp. 53–82.

———, 'Finishing with the idea of the Third World: the concept of the political trajectory', in James Manor (ed), *Rethinking Third World Politics*, London: Longman, 1991, pp. 51–71.

——— (trans. Mary Harper et al.), *The State in Africa: The politics of the belly*. London: Longman, 1993 (first published in French 1989).

——— (ed), *Religion et modernité politique en Afrique noire*. Paris: Karthala, 1993.

——— (ed), *La réinvention du capitalisme*. Paris: Karthala, 1994.

————, 'Africa in the world: a history of extraversion', *African Affairs*, 99, 395 (2000), pp. 217–67.

————, Stephen Ellis and Béatrice Hibou, *The Criminalisation of the State in Africa*. Oxford: James Currey, 1999 (first published in French 1997).

————, Peter Geschiere and Francis Nyamnjoh, 'Autochtonie, démocratie et citoyenneté en Afrique', *Critique internationale*, 10 (2001), pp. 177–94.

Bazenguissa-Ganga, Rémy, 'The spread of political violence in Congo-Brazzaville', *African Affairs*, 98, 390 (1999), pp. 37–54.

Bediako, Kwame, *Christianity in Africa: The renewal of a non-Western religion*. Edinburgh University Press, 1995.

Behrend, Heike (trans. Mick Cohen), *Alice Lakwena and the Holy Spirits: War in northern Uganda, 1986–97*. Oxford: James Currey, 1999 (first published in German 1993).

———— and Ute Luig (eds), *Spirit Possession: Modernity and power in Africa*. Oxford: James Currey, 1999.

Bellman, Beryl, *The Language of Secrecy: Symbols and metaphors in Poro ritual*. New Brunswick, NJ: Rutgers University Press, 1984.

Beradt, Charlotte (trans. Adriane Gottwald), *The Third Reich of Dreams: The nightmares of a nation, 1933–1939*. Wellingborough: Aquarian Press, 1985 (first published in German 1966).

Bernault, Florence, and Joseph Tonda, 'Dynamiques de l'invisible en Afrique', *Politique africaine*, 79 (2000), pp. 5–16.

Bernays, Edward L., *Propaganda*. New York: Horace Liveright, 1928.

Bilakila, Anastase Nzeza, 'The Kinshasa "Bargain"', in Theodore Trefon (ed), *Political Constraints and Social Invention in Kinshasa* (forthcoming).

Bledsoe, Caroline H., 'The political use of Sande ideology and symbolism', *American Ethnologist*, 11 (1984), pp. 455–72.

Bloch, Jonathan, and Patrick Fitzgerald, *British Intelligence and Covert Action*. Dingle, Co. Kerry: Brandon Books, 1983.

Bobbit, Philip, *The Shield of Achilles: War, peace, and the course of history*. London: Allen Lane, 2002.

Bockie, Simon, *Death and the Invisible Powers: The world of Kongo belief*. Bloomington: Indiana University Press, 1993.

Boddy, Janice, *Wombs and Alien Spirits: Women, men and the zar cult in northen Sudan*. Madison: University of Wisconsin Press, 1989.

Boni, Tanella, 'La dictature de l'argent', *Sentiers* [Abidjan], 3, 2000, pp. 9–11.

Bourguignon, Erika (ed), *Religion, Altered States of Consciousness and Social Change*. Columbus: Ohio University Press, 1973.

————, 'Introduction: a framework for the comparative study of altered states of consciousness', in idem, *Religion, Altered States of Consciousness and Social Change*, pp. 3–35.

Briggs, Robin, *Witches and Neighbours: The social and cultural context of European witch-craft*. London: Fontana, 1996.

Brody, Hugh, *The Other Side of Eden: Hunter-gatherers, farmers and the shaping of the world*. London: Faber & Faber, 2001.

Broussard, Philippe, 'Les millions africains d'un ancien grand maître', *Le Monde*, 24 December 1999, p. 8.

Brown, Peter, *The Rise of Western Christendom: Triumph and diversity, AD 200–1000*. Oxford: Blackwell, 1996.

Brunschwig, Henri, 'Histoire, passé et frustration en Afrique noire', *Annales*, 17, 5 (1962), pp. 873–84.

Brzezinski, Zbigniew, *Out of Control: Global turmoil on the eve of the twenty-first century*. New York: Charles Scribner's Sons, 1993.

Buchan, James, *Frozen Desire: The meaning of money*. New York: Farrar, Straus and Giroux, 1997.

Bullock, Alan, and Oliver Stallybrass (eds), *The Fontana Dictionary of Modern Thought*. London: Fontana, 1977.

Burleigh, Michael, *The Third Reich: A new history*. New York: Hill and Wang, 2000.

Cain, Peter, and A. G. Hopkins, *British Imperialism: Innovation and expansion, 1688–1914*. Harlow: Longman, 1993.

Campion-Vincent, Véronique, and Jean-Bruno Renard, *Légendes urbaines: rumeurs d'aujourd'hui*. Paris: Payot, 1992.

Canetti, Elias, *Crowds and Power*. Harmondsworth: Penguin, 1987 (first published in German 1960).

Chabal, Patrick, and Jean-Pascal Daloz, *Africa Works: Disorder as a political instrument*. Oxford: James Currey, 1999.

Chabi, Maurice, *Banqueroute, mode d'emploi: un marabout dans les griffes de la maffia béninoise*. Porto Novo: Gazette Livres, no date.

Chakrabarty, Dipesh, *Provincializing Europe: Postcolonial thought and historical difference*. Princeton University Press, 2000.

Charlick, Robert B., *Niger: Personal rule and survival in the Sahel*. Boulder, CO: Westview Press, 1991.

Chaudhuri, K. N., *Trade and Civilisation in the Indian Ocean: An economic history from the rise of Islam to 1750*. Cambridge University Press, 1985.

Chavunduka, G. L., *Traditional Healers and the Shona Patient*. Gwelo: Mambo Press, 1978.

———, *The Zimbabwe National Traditional Healers' Association*. Harare: no publisher given, 1984.

Chirot, Daniel, *Modern Tyrants: The power and prevalence of evil in our age*. New York: The Free Press, 1994.

Chisala, Beatwell, S., *The Downfall of President Kaunda*. Lusaka: private publication, 1994.

Clapham, Christopher, 'L'Afrique dans les relations internationales: quelles évolutions depuis la guerre froide?', *Marchés tropicaux et méditerranéens*, 3000, 9 May 2003, pp. 949–50.

Collingwood, R. G. (ed. Jan van der Dussen), *The Idea of History*. Oxford: Clarendon Press, 1993 (first published 1946).

Comaroff, Jean, and John L. Comaroff (eds), *Modernity and its Malcontents: Ritual and power in postcolonial Africa*. University of Chicago Press, 1993.

———, 'Alien-nation: zombies, immigrants, and millennial capitalism', *CODESRIA Bulletin*, 3–4 (1999), pp. 17–28.

———, 'Occult economies and the violence of abstraction: notes from the South African postcolony', *American Ethnologist*, 26, 2 (1999), pp. 279–303.

———, 'Privatizing the millenium: new protestant ethics and the spirits of capitalism in Africa, and elsewhere', *Afrika Spectrum*, 35, 3 (2000), pp. 293–312.

——— (eds), *Millennial Capitalism and the Culture of Neoliberalism*, Durham, NC: Duke University Press, 2001.

———, 'Millennial capitalism: first thoughts on a second coming', in idem, *Millennial Capitalism and the Culture of Neoliberalism*, pp. 1–56.

Commissione Parlamentare d'Inchiesta sulla Loggia Massonica P2, *Allegati alla Relazione, serie II*. Rome: Stabilimenti Tipografici Carol Colombo, 1984.

Connell, Dan, 'Inside the EPLF: the origins of the "People's Party" and its role in the liberation of Eritrea', *Review of African Political Economy*, 28, 89 (2001), pp. 345–64.

Cooper, Frederick, 'What is the concept of globalization good for? An African historian's perspective', *African Affairs*, 100, 399 (2001), pp. 189–213.

Cooper, Robert, 'The post-modern state', in Mark Leonard (ed), *Re-Ordering the World: The long-term implications of 11 September*, London: The Foreign Policy Centre, 2002, pp. 11–20.

Coulon, Christian, and Odile Reveyrand, *L'Islam au féminin: Sokhna Magat Diop, cheikh de la confrérie mouride (Sénégal)*. Talence: Centre d'étude d'Afrique noire, 1990.

Crick, Bernard, *In Defence of Politics*. Harmondsworth: Penguin, 1964 (first published 1962).

———, and Tom Crick, *What is Politics?* London: Edward Arnold, 1987.

Crick, Malcolm, *Explorations in Language and Meaning: Towards a semantic anthropology*. London: Malaby Press, 1976.

Cruise O'Brien, Donal B., *The Mourides of Senegal: The political and economic organization of an Islamic brotherhood*. Oxford: Clarendon Press, 1971.

D'Azevedo, Warren L., 'Tribe and chiefdom on the Windward Coast', *Liberian Studies Journal*, XIV, 2 (1989), pp. 90–116.

Darnton, Robert, 'Journalism: all the news that fits we print', in idem, *The Kiss of Lamourette: Reflections in cultural history*, New York: Norton, 1990, pp. 60–93.

———, 'Paris: the early internet', *New York Review of Books*, XLVII, 11 (29 June 2000), pp. 42–7.

Davidson, Basil, *Black Man's Burden: The curse of the nation-state in Africa*. London: James Currey, 1992.

De Boeck, Filip, 'Domesticating diamonds and dollars: identity, expenditure and sharing in southwestern Zaire (1984–1997)', *Development and Change*, 29, 4 (1998), pp. 777–810.

———, 'Zombificatie en de postkolonie: een opstel over geschiedschrijving, herinnering en dood in Congo-Kinshasa', Académie des sciences d'outre-mer, *Bulletin des séances* [Brussels], 44, 3 (1998), pp. 285–304.

———, 'Le "Deuxième monde" et les enfants-sorciers en République démocratique du Congo', *Politique africaine*, 80 (2000), pp. 32–57.

De Craemer, Willy, Jan Vansina and Renée Fox, 'Religious movements in central Africa: a theoretical study,' *Comparative Studies in Society and History*, 18, 4 (1976), pp. 458–75.

De Flacourt, Etienne (ed. Claude Allibert), *Histoire de la Grande Isle, Madagascar*. Paris: Karthala, 1995 (first published 1658.)

De Heusch, Luc, *Ecrits sur la royauté sacrée*. Editions de l'Université de Bruxelles, 1987.

De Rivera, Joseph, and Theodore R. Sarbin (eds), *Believed-In Imaginings: The narrative construction of reality*. Washington, DC: American Psychological Association, 1998.

De Soto, Hernando, *The Mystery of Capital: Why capitalism triumphs in the West and fails everywhere else*. New York: Basic Books, 2000.

Deleuze, Gilles, *Pourparlers 1972–90*. Paris: Edns. de Minuit, 1990.

Des Forges, Alison, *"Leave None to Tell the Story"*: *Genocide in Rwanda*. New York: Human Rights Watch, 1999.

Diallo, Alpha-Abdoulaye, *La vérité du ministre. Dix ans dans les geôles de Sékou Touré*. Calmann-Lévy, Paris, 1985.

Diarra, Samba, *Les faux complots d'Houphouët-Boigny*. Paris: Karthala, 1997.

Dolo, Emmanuel, *Democracy Versus Dictatorship: The quest for freedom and justice in Africa's oldest republic, Liberia*. Lanham, MD: University Press of America, 1996.

Douglas, Mary, 'The effects of modernization on religious change', *Daedalus*, 111, 1 (1982), pp. 1–21.

Dovlo, Elom, 'The Church in Africa and religious pluralism: the challenges of new religious movements and charismatic churches', *Exchange*, 27, 1 (1998), pp. 52–69.

Drewal, H. J., 'Mami Wata shrines: exotica and the constitution of self', in M. J. Arnoldi, C. M. Geary and K. L. Hardin (eds), *African Material Culture*, Bloomington: Indiana University Press, 1996, pp. 308–33.

Droz, Yvan, 'Si Dieu veut...ou suppôts de Satan? Incertitudes, millénarisme et sorcellerie chez les migrants kikuyu', *Cahiers d'études africaines*, 145, XXXVII, 1 (1997), pp. 85–117.

Duby, Georges, *L'Europe au Moyen-Age*. Paris: Flammarion, 1984 (first published 1981).

Ekambo, Duasenge Ndundu, *Radio-trottoir: une alternative de communication en Afrique contemporaine*. Louvain-la-Neuve: Cabay, 1985.

Ellis, Stephen, 'Tuning in to pavement radio', *African Affairs*, 88, 352 (1989), pp. 321–30.

———, 'Rumour and power in Togo', *Africa*, 63, 4 (1993), p. 462–76.

———, 'Of elephants and men: politics and nature conservation in South Africa', *Journal of Southern African Studies*, 20, 1 (1994), pp. 53–69.

———, *The Mask of Anarchy: The destruction of Liberia and the religious dimension of an African civil war.* London: Hurst & Co., 1999.

———, 'Reporting Africa', *Current History*, 99, 637 (2000), pp. 221–6.

———, 'Writing histories of contemporary Africa', *Journal of African History*, 43 (2002), pp. 1–26.

———, 'Witch-hunting in central Madagascar, 1828–1861', *Past and Present*, 175 (2002), pp. 90–123.

———, 'Violence and history: a response to Thandika Mkandawire', *Journal of Modern African Studies*, 41, 3 (2003), pp. 457–75.

——— and Gerrie ter Haar, 'Religion and politics in sub-Saharan Africa', *Journal of Modern African Studies*, 36, 2 (1998), pp. 175–201.

Enoanyi, Bill Frank, *Behold Uncle Sam's Step-Child*. Sacramento, CA: SanMar Publications, 1991.

Evans-Pritchard, E. E., *Witchcraft, Oracles and Magic among the Azande*. Oxford: Clarendon Press, 1937.

Fabian, Johannes, *Moments of Freedom: Anthropology and popular culture*. Charlottesville: University of Virginia Press, 1998.

Falk Moore, Sally, 'Certainties undone: fifty turbulent years of legal anthropology, 1949–1999', *Journal of the Royal Anthropological Institute*, 7 (2001), pp. 95–116.

Falola, Toyin, 'Money and informal credit institutions in colonial Western Nigeria', in Jane Guyer, *Money Matters*, pp. 162–87.

Feierman, Steven, 'African histories and the dissolution of world history', in R. H. Bates, V. Y. Mudimbe and Jean O'Barr (eds), *Africa and the Disciplines: The contributions of research in Africa to the social sciences and humanities*, University of Chicago Press, 1993, pp. 167–212.

Ferme, Mariane C., 'La figure du chasseur et les chasseurs-miliciens dans le conflit sierra-léonais', *Politique africaine*, 82 (2001), pp. 119–32.

———, and Daniel Hoffman, 'Combattants irréguliers et discours international des droits de l'homme dans les guerres civiles africaines: le cas des "chasseurs" sierra-léonais', *Politique africaine*, 88 (2002), pp. 27–48.

Fernandez, James W., *Bwiti: An ethnography of the religious imagination in Africa*. Princeton University Press, 1982.

Fields, Karen E., *Revival and Rebellion in Colonial Central Africa*. Princeton University Press, 1985.

Fisiy, Cyprian, 'Containing occult practices: witchcraft trials in Cameroon', *African Studies Review*, 41, 3 (1998), pp. 143–63.

Flower, Ken, *Serving Secretly: An intelligence chief on record. Rhodesia into Zimbabwe, 1964–1981*. London: John Murray, 1987.

Foucault, Michel, *L'Ordre du discours*. Paris: Gallimard, 1971.

———, *Dits et écrits*. 4 vols, Paris: Gallimard, 1994.

Freeman, Constance J., 'The three economies of Africa', *African Security Review*, 9, 4 (2000), pp. 66–81.

Freston, Paul, *Evangelicals and Politics in Asia, Africa and Latin America*. Cambridge University Press, 2001.

Furniss, Graham, 'The Hausa Contractor: the image of an entrepreneur', in Stephen Ellis and Yves-André Fauré (eds), *Entreprises et entrepreneurs africains*, Paris: Karthala, 1995, pp. 229–38.

Gakosso, Jean-Claude, *La nouvelle presse congolaise: du goulag à l'agora*. Paris: L'Harmattan, 1997.

Galbraith, J. K., *Money: Whence it came, where it went*. Harmondsworth: Penguin, 1976.

Gandoulou, Justin-Daniel, *Au coeur de la Sape: moeurs et aventures des Congolais à Paris*. Paris: L'Harmattan, 1984.

Gaulme, François, *Le Gabon et son ombre*. Paris: Karthala, 1988.

Geertz, Clifford, 'Religion as a cultural system', in Michael Banton (ed), *Anthropological Approaches to the Study of Religion*, London: Tavistock Publications, 1966, pp. 1–46.

———, *The Interpretation of Cultures: Selected essays*. New York: Basic Books, 1973.

Gellner, Ernest, *Thought and Change*. London: Weidenfeld & Nicolson, 1964.

Gentile, Emilio (trans. Keith Botsford), *The Sacralization of Politics in Fascist Italy*. Cambridge, MA: Harvard University Press, 1996 (first published in Italian 1993).

Geschiere, Peter, *The Modernity of Witchcraft: Politics and the occult in postcolonial Africa*. Charlottesville, VA: University Press of Virginia (first published in French 1995.)

———, 'Sorcellerie et modernité: retour sur une étrange complicité', *Politique africaine*, 79 (2000), pp. 17–32.

Getty, J. Arch, and Oleg V. Naumov, *The Road to Terror: Stalin and the self-destruction of the Bolsheviks, 1932–1939*. New Haven, CT: Yale University Press, 1999.

Gewald, Jan-Bart, 'El Negro, El Niño: Witchcraft and the absence of rain in Botswana', *African Affairs*, 100, 401 (2001), pp. 555–80.

Giddens, Anthony, *Modernity and Self-Identity: Self and society in the late modern age.* Cambridge: Polity Press, 1991.

Gifford, Paul (ed), *New Dimensions in African Christianity.* Nairobi: All Africa Conference of Churches, 1992.

———, (ed), *The Christian Churches and the Democratisation of Africa*, Leiden: E. J. Brill, 1995.

———, *African Christianity: Its public role.* London: Hurst & Co, 1998.

Goodman, Felicitas D., *How About Demons? Possession and exorcism in the modern world.* Bloomington, IN: Indiana University Press, 1988.

———, *Ecstasy, Ritual and Alternate Reality: Religion in a pluralistic world.* Bloomington, IN: Indiana University Press, 1992.

Goodridge, Reginald B. (ed), *Presidential Papers: A premiere edition*, Monrovia: no publisher given,1999.

Goody, Jack, 'Bitter icons', *New Left Review*, second series, 7 (2001), pp. 5–15.

Gore, Charles, and David Pratten, 'The politics of plunder: the rhetorics of order and disorder in southern Nigeria', *African Affairs*, 102, 407 (2003), pp. 211–40.

Green, Penny, *Drug Couriers.* London: Howard League for Penal Reform, 1991.

Gross, Paul R., and Norman Levitt, *Higher Superstitition: The academic left and its quarrels with science.* Baltimore, MD: Johns Hopkins University Press, 1994.

Gunaratna, Rohan, *Inside Al Qaeda: Global network of terror.* London: Hurst & Co., 2002.

Guyer, Jane (ed), *Money Matters: Instability, values and social payments in the modern history of West African communities.* London: James Currey, 1995.

Gyekye, Kwame, *Political Corruption: A philosophical inquiry into a moral problem.* Accra: Sankofa Publishing, 1997.

Hackett, Rosalind, 'Revitalization in African Traditional Religion', in Olupona, *African Traditional Religions in Contemporary Society*, pp. 135–48.

Haynes, Jeff, *Religion and Politics in Africa.* London: Zed Books, 1996.

Hebga, Meinrad P., 'Interpellation des mouvements mystiques', *Cahiers des Religions Africaines* (special number: 'L'Afrique et ses formes de vie spirituelle'), 24, 47 (1990), pp. 69–81.

Hecht, David, and Maliqalim Simone, *Invisible Governance: The art of African micropolitics.* Brooklyn, NY: Autonomedia, 1994.

Hibou, Béatrice, 'The "social capital" of the state as an agent of deception, or the ruses of economic intelligence', in Bayart, Ellis and Hibou, *The Criminalisation of the State in Africa*, pp. 69–113.

——— (ed), *La privatisation des Etats*, Paris: Karthala, 1999 (English translation by Hurst & Co., forthcoming).

Hill, Christopher, *The English Bible and the Seventeenth-Century Revolution.* London: Allen Lane, 1993.

Hilsum, Lindsey, 'Mary who "met Jesus" invokes Second Coming in Kenya slum', *Guardian* [London], 23 June 1988.

Hobbes, Thomas (ed C.B. Macpherson), *Leviathan*. Harmondsworth: Penguin, 1968 (first published 1651.)

Hobsbawm, Eric, *Age of Extremes: The short twentieth century, 1914–1991*. London: Michael Joseph, 1994.

Hooper, Ed, *The River: A journey back to the source of HIV and AIDS*. London: Allen Lane, 1999.

Hopkins, A. G., *An Economic History of West Africa*. London: Longman, 1973.

Horton, Robin, *Patterns of Thought in Africa and the West: Essays on magic, religion and science*. Cambridge University Press, 1997.

Hubert, H., and M. Mauss, 'Etude sommaire de la représentation du temps dans la religion et la magie', in idem, *Mélanges d'histoire des religions*, 2nd edn, Paris: Félix Alcan, 1929, pp. 189–229 (first published 1909).

Human, Piet, *Yenza: A blueprint for transformation*. Cape Town: Oxford University Press, 1998.

Hund, John, 'African witchcraft and Western law', *African Legal Studies*, II (2001), pp. 22–60.

Huntington, Samuel, *The Clash of Civilizations and the Remaking of the World Order*. New York: Simon & Schuster, 1996.

Hutchinson, Sharon E., *Nuer Dilemmas: Coping with money, war and the state*. Berkeley: University of California Press, 1996.

Huxley, Aldous, *The Doors of Perception*. London: Chatto and Windus, 1954.

Idòwú, E. Bọ́lájì, *Oládùmarè: God in Yorùbá belief.* New York: Wazobia, 1994 (first published 1962).

Ihonvbere, Julius O., 'The failed 1990 coup in Nigeria', *Journal of Modern African Studies*, 29, 4 (1991), pp. 601–26.

Ikuenobe, Polycarp, 'Moral thought in African cultures? A metaphilosophical question', *African Philosophy*, 12, 2 (1999), pp. 105–23.

Ilesanmi, Simeon O., 'The myth of a secular state: a study of religious politics with historical illustrations', *Islam and Christian-Muslim Relations*, 6, 1 (1995), pp. 105–17.

Jackson, Robert H., *Quasi-states: Sovereignty, international relations and the third world*. Cambridge University Press, 1991.

Jamba, Sousa, 'The idea of Angola', *Times Literary Supplement*, 8 June 2001, p. 12.

Jarosz, Lucy A., 'Agents of power, landscapes of fear: the vampires and heart thieves of Madagascar', *Environment and Planning D: Society and Space*, 12, 4 (1994), pp. 421–36.

Johnson, Charles S., *Bitter Canaan: The story of the Negro Republic*. New Brunswick, NJ: Transaction Books, 1989.

Judt, Tony, 'America and the world', *New York Review of Books*, L, 6 (10 April 2003), pp. 28–31.

Juergensmeyer, Mark, *Terror in the Mind of God: The global rise of religious violence.* Berkeley: University of California Press, 2000.

Juma, Calestous, *The Gene Hunters: Biotechnology and the scramble for seeds.* London: Zed Books, 1989.

Kalu, Ogbu U., *Power, Poverty and Prayer: The challenges of poverty and pluralism in Africa, 1960–1996.* Frankfurt/M: Peter Lang, 2000.

———, *The Scourge of the Vandals: Nature and control of cults in Nigerian university system.* Enugu: Joen Publishers (publication of the Committee on Eradication of Cultism, University of Nigeria, Nsukka), 2001.

———, 'Harsh flutes: the religious dimension of the legitimacy crisis in Nigeria, 1993–1998', in Toyin Falola (ed), *Nigeria in the Twentieth Century,* Durham, NC: Carolina Academic Press, 2002, pp. 667–85.

Kapferer, Bruce, 'Introduction: outside all reason—magic, sorcery and epistemology in anthropology', *Social Analysis,* 46, 3 (2002), pp. 1–30.

Kapferer, Jean-Noël, *Rumeurs, le plus vieux média du monde.* Paris: Edns. du Seuil, 1987.

Kgatla, S. T., 'Containment of witchcraft accusations in South Africa: a search for a transformational approach to curb the problem', in Ter Haar, *Imagining Evil.*

———, G. ter Haar, W. E. A. van Beek and J. J. de Wolf, *Crossing Witchcraft Barriers in South Africa. Exploring witchcraft accusations: Causes and solutions.* Utrecht University, 2003.

Khan, Amadu Wurie, 'Journalism and armed conflict in Africa: the civil war in Sierra Leone', *Review of African Political Economy,* 78 (1998), pp. 585–97.

Kimmerle, Heinz, *Mazungumzo: Dialogen tussen Afrikaanse en westerse filosofieën.* Amsterdam: Boom, 1995.

King, Ursula, *Women and Spirituality: Voices of protest and promise.* London: Macmillan, 1989.

Kivilu, Sabakinu, 'Le radio-trottoir dans l'exercice du pouvoir politique au Zaïre', in B. Jewsiewicki et H. Moniot (eds), *Dialoguer avec le léopard?,* Paris: L'Harmattan, 1988, pp. 179–93.

Knight, Stephen, *The Brotherhood: The secret world of the Freemasons.* London: Granada, 1984.

Kopytoff, Igor, *The African Frontier: The reproduction of traditional African societies.* Bloomington: Indiana University Press, 1987.

Kourouma, Ahmadou, *En attendant le vote des bêtes sauvages.* Paris: Edns. du Seuil, 1998.

———, 'Kourouma, griot à la dent dure', interview by Rachel Eklou Assogbavi, *L'Autre Afrique,* 60, 23 Sept. 1998, pp. 50–3.

———, 'Entretien avec Ahmadou Kourouma', interview by Comi Toulabor, *Politique africaine,* 75 (1999), pp. 178–83.

Kouvouama, Abel, 'Imaginaire religieux et logiques symboliques dans le champ politique', *Rupture*, nouvelle série, 1, Paris: Karthala, 1999, pp. 76–92.

Kreijen, Gerard, 'The transformation of sovereignty and African independence: no shortcuts to statehood', in Kreijen et al. (eds), *State, Sovereignty and International Governance*, Oxford University Press, 2002, pp. 45–107.

Krige, E. Jensen, and J. D. Krige, *The Realm of a Rain-Queen: A study of the pattern of Lovedu society*. London: Cambridge University Press for the International African Institute, 1943.

Kudadjie, Joshua N., *Moral Renewal in Ghana: Ideals, realities and possibilities*. Accra: Asempa Publishers, 1995.

Kulah, Arthur F., *Theological Education in Liberia: Problems and opportunities*. Lithonia, GA: SCP/Third World Literature Publishing House, 1994.

La Fontaine, Jean S., *Speak of the Devil: Tales of satanic abuse in contemporary England*. Cambridge University Press, 1998.

Lal, Deepak, *Unintended Consequences: The impact of factor endowments, culture and politics on long-run economic performance*. Cambridge, MA: MIT Press, 1998.

———, 'Asia and Western dominance: retrospect and prospect', *IIAS Newsletter* (International Institute of Asian Studies, Leiden), 24 (2001), p. 3.

Lan, David, *Guns and Rain: Guerrillas and spirit mediums in Zimbabwe*. London: James Currey, 1985.

Larbi, E. Kingsley, *Pentecostalism: The eddies of Ghanaian Christianity*. Accra: Centre for Pentecostal and Charismatic Studies (CPCS), 2001.

Lasswell, Harold D., *Politics: Who gets what, when, how*. New York: Smith, 1936.

Le Billon, Philippe, 'The political economy of resource wars', in Jakkie Cilliers and Christian Dietrich (eds), *Angola's War Economy: The role of oil and diamonds*, Pretoria: Institute for Security Studies, 2000, pp. 21–42.

Lefebvre, Georges, *La grande peur de 1789*. Paris: Armand Colin, 1970.

Levack, Brian P., *The Witch-Hunt in Early Modern Europe*. 2nd edn, London: Longman, 1995.

Lewis, I. M., *Ecstatic Religion: A study of shamanism and spirit possession*. London: Routledge, 1989 (first published 1971).

———, *Religion in Context: Cults and charisma*. Cambridge University Press, 1986.

Lex, Barbara, 'The neurobiology of ritual trance', in E. G. d'Aquili, Ch. D. Laughlin and J. McManus (eds), *The Spectrum of Ritual: A biogenetic structural analysis*, New York: Columbia University Press, 1979, pp. 117–51.

Leys, Colin, *The Rise and Fall of Development Theory*. London: James Currey, 1996.

Lippmann, Walter, *Public Opinion*. London: Geo. Allen & Unwin, 1922.

Lonsdale, John, 'States and social processes in Africa: a historiographical survey', *African Studies Review*, 24, 2–3 (1981), pp. 139–225.

———, 'The moral economy of Mau Mau: wealth, poverty and civic virtue in Kikuyu political thought', in Bruce Berman and John Lonsdale, *Unhappy Valley:*

*Conflict in Kenya and Africa*, 2 vols, London: James Currey, 1992, II, pp. 315–504.

———, 'Ethnicité morale et tribalisme politique', *Politique africaine*, 69 (1996), pp. 98–115.

Loomba, Ania, *Colonialism/Postcolonialism*. London: Routledge, 1998.

'Loto, PMU, millionaire…qui gagne?', *L'Autre Afrique*, 38, 18–24 Feb. 1998, p. 13.

Ludwig, A. M., 'Altered states of consciousness', in R. Prince (ed), *Trance and Possession States*, Montreal: R. M. Buckle Memorial Society, 1968, pp. 69–95.

Luhrmann, T. M., *Of Two Minds: The growing disorder in American psychiatry*. New York: Knopf, 2000.

Lukes, Steven, 'On the social determination of truth', in Robin Horton and Ruth Finnegan (eds), *Modes of Thought: Essays on thinking in western and non-western societies*, London: Faber & Faber, 1973, pp. 230–48.

Luttwak, Edward, 'The missing dimension', in Douglas Johnston and Cynthia Sampson (eds), *Religion, the Missing Dimension of Statecraft*, New York: Oxford University Press, 1994, pp. 8–19.

MacGaffey, Wyatt, *Modern Kongo Prophets: Religion in a plural society*. Bloomington: Indiana University Press, 1983.

———, 'Preface to the English language edition', in Geschiere, *The Modernity of Witchcraft*, pp. vii–ix.

McNeill, William H., 'The changing shape of world history', in Philip Pomper, Richard H. Elphick and Richard T. Vann (eds), *World History: Ideologies, structures and identities*, Oxford: Blackwell, 1998, pp. 21–40.

Magesa, Laurenti, *African Religion: The moral traditions of an abundant life*. Maryknoll, NY: Orbis Books, 1997.

——— and Zablon Nthamburi (eds), *Democracy and Reconciliation: A challenge for African Christianity*. Nairobi: Acton Publishers, 1999.

Maier, Karl, *This House Has Fallen: Nigeria in crisis*. London: Allen Lane, 2001.

Maja-Pearce, Adewale, 'Onitsha home movies', *London Review of Books*, 23, 9 (10 May 2001), pp. 24–6.

Malaquais, Dominique, 'Arts de feyre au Cameroun', *Politique africaine*, 82 (2001), pp. 101–18.

———, *Architecture, pouvoir et dissidence au Cameroun*. Paris/Yaounde: Karthala/UCAC, 2002.

Malkki, Liisa H., *Purity and Exile: Violence, memory, and national cosmology among Hutu refugees in Tanzania*. University of Chicago Press, 1995.

Mamdani, Mahmood, *Citizen and Subject: Contemporary Africa and the legacy of late colonialism*. Princeton University Press, 1996.

Mampouya, Joseph, *Une histoire de rat: contribution à la critique du messianisme politique au Congo Brazzaville*. Paris: Edns. Encre noire, 1999.

Marshall-Fratani, Ruth, 'Prospérité miraculeuse: les pasteurs pentecôtistes et l'argent de Dieu au Nigéria', *Politique africaine*, 82 (2001), pp. 24–44.

——— and Didier Péclard, 'La religion du sujet en Afrique', *Politique africaine*, 87 (2002), pp. 5–19.

Martin, David, *Pentecostalism: The world their parish*. Oxford: Blackwell, 2001.

Martin, Marie-Louise, *Kimbangu: An African prophet and his church*. Oxford: Basil Blackwell, 1975 (originally published in German as *Kirche ohne Weisse* in 1971).

Marx, Karl, and Friedrich Engels, 'Manifesto of the Communist Party', in Lewis S. Feuer (ed), *Marx and Engels: Basic writings on politics and philosophy*, New York: Fontana, 1969, pp. 43–82 (essay first published 1848).

Masquelier, Adeline, *Prayer Has Spoiled Everything: Possession, power and identity in an Islamic town of Niger*. Durham, NC: Duke University Press, 2001.

Matory, J. Lorand, 'Government by seduction: history and the tropes of "mounting" in Oyo-Yoruba religion', in J. and J. Comaroff, *Modernity and Its Malcontents*, pp. 58–85.

Mbembe, Achille, 'An essay on the political imagination in wartime', *CODESRIA Bulletin*, 2–4 (2000), pp. 6–21.

———, 'A propos des écritures africaines de soi', *Politique africaine*, 77 (2000), pp. 16–43.

———, 'At the edge of the world: boundaries, territoriality and sovereignty in Africa', *Public Culture*, 12, 1 (2000), pp. 259–84.

———, *On the Postcolony*. Berkeley: University of California Press, 2001.

Mbiti, John S., *African Religions and Philosophy*. Second revised and enlarged edn, Oxford: Heinemann, 1990 (first published 1969).

Metogo, Éloi Messi, *Dieu peut-il mourir en Afrique? Essai sur l'indifférence religieuse et l'incroyance en Afrique noire*. Paris/Yaounde: Karthala/UCAC, 1997.

Meyer, Birgit, 'Commodities and the power of prayer: pentecostalist attitudes towards consumption in contemporary Ghana', *Development and Change*, 29, 4 (1998), pp. 751–66.

———, *Translating the Devil: Religion and modernity among the Ewe in Ghana*. Edinburgh University Press, 1999.

Miller, Joseph C., *Way of Death: Merchant capitalism and the Angolan slave trade, 1730–1830*. Madison, WI: University of Wisconsin Press, 1988.

Minear, Larry, Colin Scott and Thomas Weiss, *The News Media, Civil War, and Humanitarian Action*. Boulder, CO: Lynne Rienner, 1996.

M'Nteba, Metena 'Les Conférences Nationales africaines et la figure politique de l'évêque-président', *Zaïre-Afrique*, 276 (1993), pp. 361–72.

Moeller, Susan D., *Compassion Fatigue: How the media sell disease, famine, war and death*. New York and London: Routledge, 1999.

Moran, Mary, 'Warriors or soldiers? Masculinity and ritual transvestism in the Liberian civil war', in Constance R. Sutton (ed), *Feminism, Nationalism and Militarism*, Arlington, VA: Association for Feminist Anthropology/American Anthropological Association, 1995, pp. 73–88.

Morehouse, David, *Psychic Warrior*. London: Penguin, 1997.

Morin, Edgar, *La rumeur d'Orléans*. Paris: Edns. du Seuil, 1969.

Morris, H. F., and James S. Read, *Indirect Rule and the Search for Justice: Essays in East African legal history*. Oxford University Press, 1972.

Moyo, Ambrose, 'Religion in Africa', in April A. Gordon and Donald L. Gordon (eds), *Understanding Contemporary Africa*, 3rd edn, Boulder, CO: Lynne Rienner, 2001, pp. 299–329.

Moyroud, Céline, and John Katunga, 'Coltan exploitation in the eastern Democratic Republic of Congo', in Jeremy Lind and Kathryn Sturman (eds), *Scarcity and Surfeit: The ecology of Africa's conflicts*, Pretoria: Institute for Security Studies, 2002, pp. 159–85.

Mudimbe, V. Y., *The Invention of Africa: Gnosis, philosophy, and the order of knowledge*. Bloomington, IN: Indiana University Press, 1988.

Mugambi, J. N. K., and A. Nasimiyu-Wasike (eds), *Moral and Ethical Issues in African Christianity: Exploratory essays in moral theology*. 2nd edn, Nairobi: Acton Publishers, 1999.

Myers, Mary, 'Community radio and development: issues and examples from francophone West Africa', in Richard Fardon and Graham Furniss (eds), *African Broadcast Cultures: Radio in transition*, Oxford: James Currey, 2000, pp. 90–101.

Nagbe, K. Moses, 'Liberia: a land of the magic God', *Daily Observer* [Monrovia], 10, 76 (12 June 1990).

Nandy, Ashis, *The Intimate Enemy: Loss and recovery of self under colonialism*. New Delhi: Oxford University Press 1988 (first published 1983).

Niehaus, Isak, 'Witches of the Transvaal Lowveld and their familiars: conceptions of duality, power and desire', *Cahiers d'études africaines*, 138–9, XXXV (1995), pp. 513–40.

———, 'Witchcraft in the new South Africa', *African Legal Studies*, II (2001), pp. 116–48.

——— with Eliazaar Mohlala and Kally Shokane, *Witchcraft, Power and Politics: Exploring the occult in the South African Lowveld*. London: Pluto Press, 2001.

'Nigeria: beware false profits', *Africa Confidential*, 43, 14 (12 July 2002), pp. 1–3.

Nkemnkia, Martin Nkafu, *African Vitalogy: A step forward in African thinking*. Nairobi: Paulines Publications, 1999.

Nkwoka, A. O., 'Acts 19[18–19]: the Ephesian Cultists and the Nigerian campus secret cults: a study of the spiritual and social side of cultism', *African Journal of Biblical Studies*, XV, 1 (2000), pp. 148–63.

Nlandu-Tsasa, Cornelis, *La rumeur au Zaïre de Mobutu: radio-trottoir à Kinshasa*. Paris: L'Harmattan, 1997.

Nwankwo, Agwuncha Arthur, *Nigeria: The stolen billions*. Enugu: Fourth Dimension, 1999.

O'Brien Wicker, Kathleen, 'Mami Water in African religion and spirituality', in Olupona, *African Spirituality*, pp. 198–222.

Obiechina, Emmanuel, *Literature for the Masses: An analytical study of popular pamphleteering in Nigeria*. Enugu: Nwamife Books, 1971.

Observatoire géopolitique des drogues, *Les drogues en Afrique subsaharienne*. Paris: Karthala, 1998.

Oduyoye, Modupe, 'Potent speech', in E. A. Ade Adegbola (ed), *Traditional Religion in West Africa*, Ibadan: Daystar Press, 1983, pp. 203–32.

Offiong, Daniel A., *Witchcraft, Sorcery, Magic and Social Order among the Ibibio of Nigeria*. Enugu: Fourth Dimension, 1991.

Ojo, Matthews, 'Deeper Life Christian Ministry: a case study of the charismatic movements in western Nigeria', *Journal of Religion in Africa*, 18 (1988), pp. 141–62.

———, 'The contextual significance of the charismatic movements in independent Nigeria', *Africa*, 58 (1987), pp. 175–92.

Okon, Ekpenyong E., 'The association of bloodmen (in old Calabar): a reinterpretation', *Africana Marburgensia*, 21, 2 (1988), pp. 51–62.

Okri, Ben, *The Famished Road*. London: Jonathan Cape, 1991.

Olukoju, Ayodeji, 'Christianity and the development of the Nigerian state', in Akinjide Osuntokun and Ayodeji Olukoju (eds), *Nigerian Peoples and Cultures*, Ibadan: Davidson Press, 1997, pp. 136–56.

Olupona, Jacob K. (ed), *African Traditional Religions in Contemporary Society*. New York: Paragon House, 1991.

——— (ed), *African Spirituality: Forms, meanings and expressions*. New York: Crossroad Publishing, 2000.

——— 'Introduction', in idem, *African Spirituality*, pp. xv–xxxvi.

Omenyo, Cephas Narh, *Pentecost outside Pentecostalism: A study of the development of Charismatic Renewal in the mainline churches in Ghana*. Zoetermeer: Boekencentrum, 2002.

Oomen, Barbara, *Chiefs in South Africa*. Oxford: James Currey (forthcoming).

Orwell, George, 'The lion and the unicorn: socialism and the English genius', in Sonia Orwell and Ian Angus (eds), *The Collected Essays, Journalism and Letters of George Orwell*, 4 vols, Harmondsworth: Penguin, 1970, II, pp. 74–134.

Ostien, Philip, 'Ten good things about the implementation of shari'a in some states of northern Nigeria', *Swedish Missiological Themes*, 90, 2 (2002), pp. 163–74.

Otayek, René (ed), *Le radicalisme islamique au sud du Sahara: Da'wa, arabisation et critique de l'Occident*. Paris: Karthala, 1993.

Palmer, David, 'Falun Gong: la tentation du politique', *Critique internationale*, 11 (2001), pp. 36–43.

Péan, Pierre, *Affaires africaines*. Paris: Fayard, 1983.

Petros, Yohannes, 'A survey of political parties in Ethiopia', *Northeast African Studies*, 43, 2–3 (1991), pp. 141–64.

Platvoet, Jan G., 'To define or not to define: the problem of the definition of religion', in Jan G. Platvoet and Arie L. Molendijk (eds), *The Pragmatics of Defining Religion: Contexts, concepts and contests*, Leiden: E. J. Brill, 1999, pp. 245–65.

———, 'Contexts, concepts and contents: towards a pragmatics of defining religion', in idem, *The Pragmatics of Defining Religion*, pp. 463–516.

Pobee, John S., *Kwame Nkrumah and the Church in Ghana, 1949–1966*. Accra: Asempa Publishers, 1988.

Polanyi, Karl, *The Great Transformation*. New York: Octagon Books, 1975 (first published 1944).

Popper, Karl, *The Poverty of Historicism*. London and New York: Ark Paperbacks, 1986 (first published 1957).

Raison-Jourde, Françoise, *Bible et pouvoir à Madagascar*. Paris: Karthala, 1991.

Ranganathan, M. A., *The Political Philosophy of President Kaunda of Zambia*. Edinburgh: Holmes McDougall, 1985.

———, Interview with Shikha Trivedy, *Illustrated Weekly of India*, 23 August 1987.

Ranger, T. O., 'African Traditional Religion', in Stewart Sutherland and Peter Clarke (eds), *The Study of Religion, Traditional and New Religion*, London: Routledge, 1991, pp. 106–14.

Raombana (ed. Simon Ayache), *Histoires*. Vol. I, Fianarantsoa: Ambozontany, 1980.

Rathbone, Richard, *Murder and Politics in Colonial Ghana*. New Haven, CT: Yale University Press, 1993.

Rattray, R. S., *Ashanti*. Oxford University Press, 1923.

Regan, Donald T., *For the Record: From Wall Street to Washington*. New York: Harcourt Brace Jovanovich, 1988.

Rice, Alan, '"Who's eating whom?" The discourse of cannibalism in the literature of the Black Atlantic from Equiano's Travels to Toni Morrison's Beloved', *Research in African Literatures*, 29, 4 (1998), pp. 107–19.

Richardson, J., *A New Malagasy-English Dictionary*. Farnborough: Gregg International, 1967 (first published 1885).

Riggs, Fred W., 'Indigenous concepts: a problem for social and information science', *International Social Science Journal*, 114 (1987), pp. 607–17.

Rimmer, Douglas, 'Learning about economic development from Africa', *African Affairs*, 102, 408 (2003), pp. 469–91.

Roberts, Andrew, *A History of Zambia*. London: Heinemann, 1981.

Rowlands, Michael, 'Accumulation and the cultural politics of identity in the Grassfields', in Peter Geschiere and Piet Konings (eds), *Itinéraires d'accumulation au Cameroun*, Paris: Karthala, 1993, pp. 71–97.

Sahlins, Marshall, *Culture in Practice: Selected essays*. New York: Zone Books, 2000.

Sarbin, Theodore R., 'Believed-in imaginings: a narrative approach', in De Rivera and Sarbin, *Believed-In Imaginings*, pp. 15–30.

Sassou N'Guesso, Denis, *Le manguier, le fleuve et la souris*. Paris: J.-C. Lattès, 1997.

Saul, John Ralston, *The Unconscious Civilization*. New York: The Free Press, 1997.

Schaffer, Frederick C., *Democracy in Translation: Understanding politics in an unfamiliar culture*. Ithaca, NY: Cornell University Press, 1998.

Schatzberg, Michael G., *Political Legitimacy in Middle Africa: Father, family, food*. Bloomington, IN: Indiana University Press, 2001.

Schoffeleers, J. M. (ed), *Guardians of the Land: Essays on central African territorial cults*. Gwelo: Mambo Press, 1978.

———, 'Ritual healing and political acquiescence: the case of the Zionist churches in southern Africa', *Africa*, 61, 1 (1991), pp. 1–25.

———, 'The AIDS pandemic, the prophet Billy Chisupe, and the democratization process in Malawi', *Journal of Religion in Africa*, XXXIX, 4 (1999), pp. 406–41.

Schumpeter, Joseph, *A History of Economic Analysis*. London: Routledge, 1986 (first published 1954).

Senghor, Léopold Sédar, 'Eléments constructifs d'une civilisation d'inspiration négro-africaine', *Présence Africaine*, 24–5 (1959), pp. 249–79.

Serfontein, J. H. P., *Brotherhood of Power: An exposé of the secret Afrikaner Broederbond*. London: Rex Collings, 1979.

Shaw, Rosalind, 'The production of witchcraft/witchcraft as production: memory, modernity, and the slave trade in Sierra Leone', *American Ethnologist*, 24, 4 (1997), pp. 856–76.

———, *Memories of the Slave Trade: Ritual and the historical imagination in Sierra Leone*. University of Chicago Press, 2002.

Shepperson, George, and Thomas Price, *Independent African: John Chilembe and the origins, setting and significance of the Nyasaland native rising of 1915*. Edinburgh University Press, 1958.

Shoemaker, Robert B., 'The decline of public insult in London, 1660–1800', *Past and Present*, 169 (2000), pp. 97–131.

Shorter, Aylward, and Edwin Onyancha, *Secularism in Africa. A Case Study: Nairobi City*. Nairobi: Paulines Publications, 1997.

Shubin, Vladimir, *ANC: A view from Moscow*. Bellville: Mayibuye Books, 1999.

Simmel, Georg, *The Philosophy of Money*. Second enlarged edn, London: Routledge, 1990 (first published in German 1900, revised 1907).

——— (trans. and ed Kurt H. Wolff), *The Sociology of Georg Simmel*. New York: The Free Press, 1964.

Smith, Adam (ed Kathryn Sutherland), *The Wealth of Nations: A selected edition*. Oxford University Press, 1993 (first published 1776).

Soyinka, Kayode, *Diplomatic Baggage. MOSSAD and Nigeria: The Dikko story*. Lagos: Newswatch Books, 1994.

Stadler, Jonathan, 'Witches and witch-hunters: witchcraft, generational relations and the life cycle in a Lowveld village', *African Studies*, 55, 1 (1996), pp. 87–110.

Strandsbjerg, Camilla, 'Kérékou, God and the ancestors: religion and the conception of political power in Benin', *African Affairs*, 99, 396 (2000), pp. 395–414.

Tall, Emmanuelle Kadya, 'De la démocratie et des cultes voduns au Bénin', *Cahiers d'études africaines*, 137, XXXV, 1 (1995), pp. 195–208.

Tamuno, Tekena, and Robin Horton, 'The changing position of secret societies and cults in modern Nigeria', *African Notes*, 5, 2 (1969), pp. 36–62.

Taussig, Michael, *The Devil and Commodity Fetishism in South America*. Chapel Hill. University of North Carolina Press, 1980.

Tawney, R. H., *Religion and the Rise of Capitalism: A historical study*. Harmondsworth: Penguin, 1975 (first published 1926).

Tempels, Placide (trans. A. Rubben), *La philosophie bantoue*. Elisabethville: Lovania, 1945. The original Dutch text was later published as *Bantoe-filosofie*, Antwerp: De Sikkel, 1946. An English translation was published by Présence africaine, Paris, in 1959.

Ter Haar, Gerrie, *Spirit of Africa: The healing ministry of Archbishop Milingo of Zambia*. London: Hurst & Co., 1992.

———, 'African Independent Churches: the ideological implications of continuity and change', in Anton Houtepen (ed), *The Living Tradition: Towards an ecumenical hermeneutics of the Christian tradition*, Zoetermeer: Meinema, 1995, pp. 159–170.

———, *Halfway to Paradise: African Christians in Europe*. Cardiff Academic Press, 1998.

———, *World Religions and Community Religions: Where does Africa fit in?* University of Copenhagen, occasional paper, 2000.

———, *Rats, Cockroaches and People Like Us: Views of humanity and human rights*. The Hague: Institute of Social Studies, inaugural address, 2000.

———, 'Religious fundamentalism and social change: a comparative inquiry', in Ter Haar and Busuttil, *The Freedom to do God's Will*, pp. 1–24.

———, 'A wondrous God: miracles in contemporary Africa', *African Affairs*, 102, 408 (2003), pp. 409–28.

——— (ed), *Imagining Evil: Witchcraft beliefs and accusations in contemporary Africa*. Trenton, NJ: Africa World Press (forthcoming).

——— and James J. Busuttil (eds), *The Freedom to do God's Will: Religious fundamentalism and social change*. London: Routledge, 2003.

——— and Jan Platvoet, 'Bezetenheid en christendom', *Nederlands Theologisch Tijdschrift*, 43, 3 (1989), pp. 176–91.

Terray, Emmanuel, 'Le pouvoir, le sang et la mort dans le royaume asante au XIXe siècle', *Cahiers d'études africaines*, XXXIV, 4 (1994), pp. 549–61.

Tetteh, M. N., *Anatomy of Rumour Mongering in Ghana*. Accra: Ghana Publicity Ltd, 1976.

Tive, Charles, *419 Scam: Exploits of the Nigerian con man*. Lagos: Chicha Favours, 2001.

Tokpa, Henrique F., 'Cuttington University College during the Liberian Civil War: an administrator's experience', *Liberian Studies Journal*, XVI, 1 (1991), pp. 79–94.

Tonda, Joseph, 'La guerre dans le "Camp Nord" au Congo-Brazzaville: ethnicité et ethos de la consommation/consumation', *Politique africaine*, 72 (1998), pp. 50–67.

———, 'Capital sorcier et travail de Dieu', *Politique africaine*, 79 (2000), pp. 48–65.

———, 'Economie des miracles et dynamiques de "subjectivation/civilisation" en Afrique centrale', *Politique africaine*, 87 (2002), pp. 20–44.

Tonkin, Elizabeth, 'Investigating oral tradition', *Journal of African History*, 27, 2 (1986), pp. 203–13.

Toulabor, Comi M., *Le Togo sous Eyadéma*. Paris: Karthala, 1986.

———, 'Bellissima basilica yamoussoukroensis: l'entéléchie du "miracle ivoirien"', *L'Année africaine* (1990–1), Talence: Centre d'étude d'Afrique noire, 1991, pp. 191–213.

———, 'Sacrifices humains et politique: quelques exemples contemporains en Afrique', in Piet Konings, Wim van Binsbergen and Gerti Hesseling (eds), *Trajectoires de libération en Afrique contemporaine*, Paris: Karthala, 2000, pp. 207–21.

Touré, Abdou, and Yacouba Konaté, *Sacrifices dans la ville: le citadin chez le divin en Côte d'Ivoire*. Abidjan: Douga, 1990.

Truell, Peter, and Larry Gurwin, *False Profits: The inside story of BCCI, the world's most corrupt financial empire*. Boston: Houghton Mifflin, 1992.

Tuquoi, Jean-Pierre, 'L'affaire des faux dinars de Bahreïn', *Le Monde*, 23 June 1999, p. 16.

Turner, Edith, with William Blodgett, Singleton Kahona, and Fideli Benwa, *Experiencing Ritual: A new interpretation of African healing*. Philadelphia: University of Pennsylvania Press, 1992.

Turner, V. W., *The Ritual Process: Structure and anti-structure*. Harmondsworth: Penguin, 1969.

Tutuola, Amos, *My Life in the Bush of Ghosts*. London: Faber & Faber, 1954.

Tylor, E. B., *Religion in Primitive Culture*. New York: Harper Torchbooks, 1958 (first published 1871 with the title *Primitive Culture*).

UNESCO, *Rapport mondial sur la culture, 2000*. Paris: UNESCO, 2000.

United Nations, *UN Statistical Yearbook*. 45th edn, New York, 2001.

United States Senate, *The BCCI Affair: A report to the Committee on Foreign Relations, United States Senate, by Senator John Kerry and Senator Hank Brown*. Washington, DC: US Government Printing Office, 1993.

———, *Private Banking and Money Laundering: A case study of opportunities and vulnerabilities*. Hearings before the Permanent Subcommittee on Investigations, 9–10 November 1999, Washington, DC: US Government Printing Office, 2000.

Van Beek, W. E. A., 'A model of escalation of witchcraft accusations', in Ter Haar, *Imagining Evil*.

Van Gennep, Arnold, *The Rites of Passage*. University of Chicago Press, 1975 (first published in French 1908).

Wacquant, Loïc, 'From slavery to mass incarceration: rethinking the "race question" in the US', *New Left Review*, second series, 13 (2000), pp. 41–60.

Walls, Andrew, 'Foreword', in Bediako, *Christianity in Africa*.

Wamue, Grace Nyatugah, 'Revisiting our indigenous shrines through *Mungiki*', *African Affairs*, 100, 400 (2001), pp. 453–67.

Weber, Max, *The Sociology of Religion*. Boston: Beacon Press, 1964 (first published in German 1922).

———— (ed Max Rheinstein), *Max Weber on Law in Economy and Society*. Cambridge, MA: Harvard University Press, 1954.

————, *The Protestant Ethic and the Spirit of Capitalism*. London: Routledge, 1992 (first published in German 1904–5).

Weller, Robert P., 'Living at the edge: religion, capitalism, and the end of the nation-state in Taiwan', in J. and J. Comaroff, *Millennial Capitalism*, pp. 215–39.

Welsh, Frank, *Dangerous Deceits: Julian Askin and the Tollgate scandal*. London: HarperCollins, 1999.

Werbner, Richard, 'Introduction: multiple identities, plural arenas', in Richard Werbner and Terence Ranger (eds), *Postcolonial Identities in Africa*, London: Zed Books, 1996, pp. 1–25.

White, Luise, 'The traffic in heads: bodies, borders, and the articulation of regional histories', *Journal of Southern African Studies*, 23, 2 (1997), pp. 325–82.

————, *Speaking with Vampires: Rumor and history in colonial Africa*. Berkeley, CA: University of California Press, 2000.

Whitehead, Neil, and Sylvia Vidal (eds), *In Darkness and Secrecy: The anthropology of assault sorcery and witchcraft in Amazonia*. Durham, NC: Duke University Press, 2003.

Wilks, Ivor, 'Space, time and "human sacrifice"', in *Forests of Gold: Essays on the Akan and the Kingdom of Asante*, Athens: Ohio University Press, 1993, pp. 215–40.

Williams, T. David, *Malawi: The politics of despair*. Ithaca, NY: Cornell University Press, 1978.

Winnicott, D. W., 'Transitional objects and transitional phenomena', in *Collected Papers: Through paediatrics to psycho-analysis*, London: Tavistock, 1958, pp. 229–42 (paper first published 1951).

Wiredu, Kwasi, 'Custom and morality: a comparative analysis of some African and Western conceptions of morals', in Albert G. Mosley (ed), *African Philosophy: Selected readings*, Englewood Cliffs, NJ: Prentice-Hall Inc., 1995, pp. 389–406.

———— 'Modes of thought in African philosophy', in John Middleton (ed-in-chief), *Encyclopedia of Africa South of the Sahara*, 4 vols, New York: Charles Scribner's Son, 1997, III, p. 171.

'Witchcraft Violence and the Law,' special issue of *African Legal Studies*, II (2001).

Wolf, Eric, *Europe and the People without History*. Berkeley, CA: University of California Press, 1982.

World Bank, *African Development Indicators 2003*. Washington, DC: World Bank, 2003.

Yamba, C. Bawa, 'Cosmologies in turmoil: witchfinding and AIDS in Chiawa, Zambia', *Africa*, 67, 2 (1997), pp. 200–23.

Yang, Anand A., 'A conversation of rumours: the language of popular *mentalités* in late nineteenth-century colonial India', *Journal of Social History*, 20 (1986–7), pp. 485–505.

Yankah, Kwesi, *Free Speech in Traditional Society: The cultural foundations of communication in contemporary Ghana*. Accra: Ghana University Press, inaugural address, 1998.

Yengo, Patrice, 'Guerre des légitimités et démocide convenu: la restauration autoritaire au Congo-B', *Ruptures*, 'Les Congos dans la tourmente', nouvelle série, 2, Paris: Karthala, 2000, pp. 77–116.

Young, Crawford, 'The end of the post-colonial state in Africa? Reflections on changing African political dynamics', *African Affairs*, 103, 410 (2004), pp. 23–49.

Zeleza, Paul Tiyambe, 'Fictions of the postcolonial: a review article', *CODESRIA Bulletin*, 2 (1997), pp. 15–19.

## UNPUBLISHED THESES AND PAPERS

Centre for Law and Research International (CLARION), 'The anatomy of corruption: legal, political and socio-economic perspectives', Clarion research monograph no. 7, Nairobi, 1994.

Dovlo, Elom, 'Religion and the politics of Fourth Republican elections in Ghana', Department for the Study of Religions, University of Ghana, Legon.

Ebigbo, Peter, 'Child trafficking in Nigeria: the state of the art', International Labour Organisation, Geneva, 2000.

Nandi, Jack, 'The Jerusalem Church of Christ: a historical and theological analysis', MA thesis, Department of Religion, University of Nairobi, 1993.

Ojo, Matthews, 'The growth of campus Christianity and charismatic movements in western Nigeria', PhD thesis, University of London, 1986.

Rip, Arie, 'Indigenous knowledge and Western science—in practice', paper presented at a conference on Demarcation Socialized, Cardiff, 2000.

Terre des Hommes, 'Handel in Nigeriaanse meisjes naar Nederland', The Hague, 1999.

Thomas-Queh, James, 'La politique de contrôle social dans un pays en voie de développement: analyse des lois, des institutions judiciaires et de l'application de la justice pénale au Liberia', thèse de 3e cycle, Sorbonne-II, Paris, 1985.

Udelhoven, Bernhard, 'Missionary curses on the Luapula', paper for project on 'Memory and Reconciliation: The history of the Catholic Church in Zambia, 1895–1995', Lusaka, 2002.

Vegter, Ineke, 'Waar olifanten vechten, groeit het gras niet: apartheid en de Zion Christian Church', MA thesis, Free University of Amsterdam, 1988.

## RELIGIOUS TRACTS AND PAMPHLETS PUBLISHED IN AFRICA

Abadamloora, Lucas, *Types of Mystical Experiences and their Practical Aspects with Certain Allusions to the African Context*. Ghana: no place or publisher given, 1986.

Abékan, Norbert, *Mon combat contre le diable*. Abidjan: CEDA, 1996.

Abosi, Kalu, *Born Twice: From demonism to Christianity*. 2 vols, Ikoyi, Lagos: Franco-Bon publishing, 1995.

Adom-Frimpong, Mrs, *alias* Akosua Oforiwaa, *From Witchcraft and Fetishism to Christ*. No publisher or place given, 1993.

Damuah, Osofo Okomfo, *Miracle at the Shrine: Religious and revolutionary miracle in Ghana*. Accra, no publisher given, no date [1994].

Dua-Agyeman, Kwaku, *Covenant Curses and Cure*. Kumasi: no publisher given, 1994.

———, *Doorway to Demonic Bondage*. Kumasi: no publisher given, 1994.

Eni, Emmanuel, *Delivered from the Powers of Darkness*. Ibadan: Scripture Union, 1987.

Eto, Victoria, *Exposition on Water Spirits*. Warri, Nigeria: Shallom Christian Mission International, 1983.

Hassim, Bruno, *Les plus étonnantes révélations du monde des esprits malins*. Brazzaville: Ferlo, 1994.

Hove, M. M., *Confessions of a Wizard*. Gweru: Mambo Press, 1985.

Kaniaki, D. D., and Evangelist Mukendi, *Snatched from Satan's Claws: An amazing deliverance by Christ*. Nairobi: Enkei Media Services, 1994.

Mbunwe-Samba, Patrick, *Witchcraft, Magic and Divination: A personal testimony*. Bamenda: private publication, 1996.

Mbuy, Tatah H., *Handling Witchcraft-Related Illness*. No place, date or publisher given [Bamenda, Cameroon].

Milingo, Emmanuel, *Plunging into Darkness*. Broadford, VA: Scripture Keys Ministries Australia, 1993 (original paper published in Zambia, 2 June 1978).

Mmasi, Alois Samia, *Satanic Tortures*. Dar Es Salaam: DUP, 1998.

Moreau, A. Scott, *The World of the Spirits: A biblical study in the African context*. Nairobi: Evangel Publishing House, 1990.

Okeke, S. N. I., *Satanic Ministers: The ministries of Lucifer*. Isolo, Lagos: Emabal Company, 1991.

Onyinah, Opoku, *Ancestral Curses*. Accra: Pentecost Press, 1994.

Pianim, Ernest, *Ghana in Prophecy*. Kumasi: no publisher given, 1995.

Uzorma, Iyke Nathan, *Occult Grand Master Now in Christ*. Benin City: private publication, 1994.

## NEWS MEDIA

The following is a list of newspapers, media and magazines quoted in footnotes. The most important individual articles have been listed in the main section of the bibliography under the name of the author or, where anonymous, under the first letter of the title.

*Africa Confidential* (London)

*Algemeen Dagblad* (Rotterdam)

*L'Autre Afrique* (Paris)

BBC World Service radio

*Cameroon Tribune*

*Daily Observer* (Monrovia)

*Guardian* (London)

*Guardian Weekly* (London)

*Le Monde* (Paris)

*New York Times*

*Observer* (London)

*Le Soir* (Brussels)

South African Broadcasting Corporation 'Special Assignment', documentary film broadcast, 7 May 2002.

*This Day* (Lagos)

*Trouw* (Amsterdam)

*de Volkskrant* (Amsterdam)

*Washington Post*

*Weekly Mail and Guardian* (Johannesburg)

*West Africa* (London)

## INTERNET PUBLICATIONS

Akosah-Sarpong, Kofi, 'Voodoo rule in Africa', part 5, *Expo Times*, http://www.expotimes.net/issue000913/renaissance.htm

Furedi, Frank, 'History has not yet begun', *Spiked Politics* (15 May 2002), http://www.spiked-online.com/Articles/00000006D8EE.htm

'Nigeria—the 419 Coalition Website', http://home.rica.net/alphae/419coal/scamstat.htm

Olukoya, Sam, 'Nigeria grapples with e-mail scams', BBC news, 23 April 2002: http://news.bbc.co.uk/hi/english/world/africa/newsid_1944000/ 1944801.stm

Smillie, Ian, Lansana Gberie and Ralph Hazleton, 'The Heart of the Matter: Sierra Leone, diamonds and human security', Partnership Africa Canada, 2000: http://action.web.ca/home/pac/attach/Heart%20the%20Matter%20complete.rtf

Winners' Chapel website:http://www.winners-chapel.com

# INDEX